HAWAII'S MISSIONARY SAGA

D1557913

HAWAII'S MISSIONARY SAGA

Sacrifice and Godliness in Paradise

By LaRue W. Piercy

Aloha greeter and historian at Historic Mokuaikaua Church

The Oldest and First Founded Christian Church
in the State of Hawaii

MUTUAL PUBLISHING

Book Design
Michael Horton Design

Imagesetting
Femar Graphics

LCC 91-067617

First Printing August 1992
Second Printing November 1998
2 3 4 5 6 7 8 9

ISBN 0-935180-05-2

Mutual Publishing
1215 Center Street, Suite 210
Honolulu, Hawaii 96816
Ph: (808) 732-1709 / Fax: (808) 734-4094
email: mutual@lava.net
url: http://www.pete.com/mutual

Printed in Korea

DEDICATED TO

those amazing characters who,
with innovative genius and devoted good will,
consecrated their lives to establishing
in the hearts of Hawaiians
the virtues of American freedom and democracy
and the high moral aims of belief in God,
and spirit of fairness, helpfulness and enterprise.

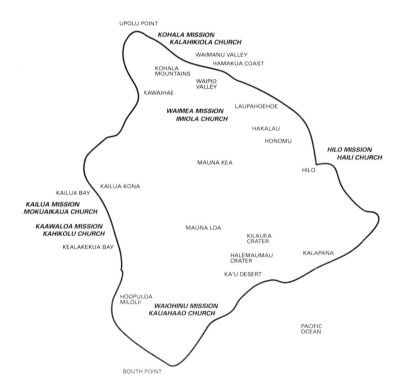

CONTENTS

LIST OF ILLUSTRATIONS

PREFACE

"A truly devoted missionary is among the happiest of mortals."
—Samuel Chenery Damon, seamen's missionary in Honolulu, 1842-1884.

A complete saga of the Sandwich Islands Mission would depict the lives and work of 169 people who felt the glow of endeavor and spirit of helpfulness to desert their comfortable homes and to endure an almost six months' wearisome voyage across two vast oceans to bring man's lore and God's love to the natives on those faraway Pacific isles.

Tales of these brave men and women have been told and retold in parts though not in one great story. Here I have aimed to create a connected account of this ambitious undertaking, beginning on Hawaii Island where 28 missionaries, with the stalwart aid of their wives, labored to create six great missions — Kailua, Kaawaloa (later Kealakekua), Hilo, Waimea, Kohala, and Waiohinu.

This saga offers the stories of a variety of unusual characters: the rather miraculous life of Obookiah; the adventures of four other Hawaiians in America and back home; the particular makeup and experiences of the pioneer party; the very helpful Chief Kuakini who so exasperated the men of God; Kapiolani's brave struggles for Christianity; and the varied lives of the great mission leaders.

The Big Island story presents the contrasting lives of 28 couples coping according to their strengths with the extra-challenging conditions there including its severe hazards and hardships, its greater extremes of climate, and its mountainous barriers. A devoted and enduring six men — Asa Thurston, David Lyman, Titus Coan, Lorenzo Lyons, Elias Bond, and John Paris stand out as heroes who struggled on through the rest of their lifetimes devoting from 47 to 55 years each to such strenuous endeavors, a total of 304 years of service on Hawaii. Dr. Charles Wetmore, in Hilo, also lived out his final 49 years of life on the island. Artemus Bishop worked valiantly on Hawaii 12 years, then added 37 more on Oahu. Dr. Dwight Baldwin added 50 more years at Lahaina to his five years in the cold and wet at Waimea on Hawaii. Such were the supermen in body and mind.

These outstanding leaders managed to provide education in new types of schools, fresh goals in life and ways to attain them, and a spiritual force to give the people a sense of values. Doing so, they had to plod wearily on foot over rough, shoe-slashing lava, climbing up and down deep chasms with precipitous walls, crossing raging torrents on this great island — the largest, most rugged and hazardous of all. At high altitudes they got soaked in chilling cold storms. Others wilted in the humid shoreline heat. At times some contended with other severe physical forces -- hurricanes, earth-quakes, tidal waves and volcanic eruptions.

But these superior men stuck it out as wholesome, broad–minded, spirited and inspiring persons, demonstrating their understanding of, compassion for, and helpfulness to these people they learned to love. And the people gladly helped them and grew to love them .

Especially taxing was the building of churches involving the hauling of materials to construct a worthy edifice that would deteriorate in bad weather or fall to some mighty wind, spiteful incendiary, or crushing earthquake. In all their varied and difficult endeavors, these special men displayed a range of practical abilities — developing agriculture, regulating business affairs, serving as doctors, and organizing and maintaining churches and schools throughout their mission. Thus these hardy, generous people toiled and sweated and suffered to the last days of their lives.

Here you may judge these 19th century adventurers by their lives — policies, efforts, foibles, failures, strong points and successes — retold from their own statements and the opinions of others. They did have their faults ingrained by their times and their upbringing, but they varied individually according to their personalities, characters, attitudes, energies and experiences.

I put together this compendium of missionary lives in Hawaii a few years ago after the pleasant success with my *Hawaii — Truth Stronger Than Fiction*, containing "entertaining true tales of missionary life and historic characters fictionized by Michener." As I serve as aloha greeter at historic Mokuaikaua Church, Kailua-Kona, this book was inspired by questions visitors asked about the novelist's historic accuracy in portraying his missionary characters. So I researched Michener's sources and offered in contrast, or sometimes in agreement, the true facts and the stories of the real people who became oddly different characters at the hand of the novelist.

Now here is my new book, a jigsaw puzzle put together from many sources in my personal library acquired during 30 years of collecting out-of-print volumes and new Hawaiiana and South Sea literature.

INTRODUCTION: LATTER DAY PILGRIMS

Revered are the Pilgrims of 1620 who braved a terrifying voyage across the stormy Atlantic to find a fresh place with freedom to worship according to their consciences. Famous is the Plymouth Rock on which they stepped ashore in Massachusetts.

Hawaii has its own less well-known "Plymouth Rock," said to lie under the pier at Kailua-Kona, where the Islands' first missionaries stepped ashore two centuries after their forebears had reached the rock-bound coast of New England. These newcomers to Hawaii arrived determined to establish their Puritan faith in the hearts of people whom they considered bereft of the benefits of holy leadership.

What they accomplished was far more than a religious reformation. They provided a written language, revelations of the modern world, the establishing of educational systems, higher standards of living, hope and pride and a better life. The sturdiest of these men sacrificed the rest of their lives, toiling in compassionate ways to help individually whoever was in their circle of endeavor.

On the Big Island they met their severest tests. Of the 28 men sent to the island of Hawaii, seven lived out their lifetimes in debilitating conditions and strenuous services to the people they came to help and learned to love. Six founded the great missions of this island. Their stories are of lives of devotion, self-sacrifice, and supreme efforts to overcome the most difficult conditions.

They came to fulfill the aspirations of the Hawaiian youth, whom they knew as Henry Obookiah, whose unexpected death had deprived him of personally returning to Hawaii to minister to the spiritual needs of his people.

So here begins the strange story of why the first missionaries came to Hawaii, followed by tales of heroic valor amid the extreme hardships of Big Island existence.

1

THE FATEFUL
LIFE OF
HENRY OBOOKIAH

Henry Obookiah — Source: Hawaii State Archives

T his Hawaiian boy led a life of strange destiny. Born in the district of Ka'u, in the southern part of the island of Hawaii, he was named Opukahaia, meaning "split belly," to connect his undated birth to some event at the same time. When he was about ten, his family, fleeing from enemy warriors, sought refuge on Mauna Loa but were captured and his parents killed. Opukahaia tried to escape carrying his baby brother on his back, but a warrior hurled his spear, killing the young child, and Opukahaia was captured and taken to his captor's home. Finally, an uncle, chief *kahuna* at Hikiau Heiau at Napoopoo, Kealakekua Bay, arranged for the boy's release and put him into rigorous training to become a *kahuna* or priest.

Hikiau Heiau, largest shrine of its kind in the Hawaiian Islands, was dedicated to Lono, the much-revered god of fertility and agriculture and of the *makahiki*, the end of harvest and the time for tax collecting. At Hikiau Captain James Cook received high homage and great adoration from chiefs and thousands of natives who believed he was the returning god Lono when he sailed into Kealakekua Bay, January 17, 1779, with his two ships, the *Discovery* and the *Resolution*. And it was here that Cook read the English burial service for one of his men, William Whatman, who died January 28— probably the first Christian funeral service performed in Hawaii.

Invited to go to America

But Opukahaia was not destined to become another *kahuna*. In 1808, an American trading ship, the *Triumph*, with Captain Caleb Brintnall of New Haven, Conn., in command, sailed into Kealakekua Bay. With natural curiosity, Opukahaia swam out to the ship. The eager youth, having dreamed of sailing away to faraway lands, was pleased when Captain Brintnall invited him to go with him to America as a cabin boy along with another Hawaiian boy named Thomas Hopu. Opukahaia was glad to go as the captain "was very agreeable, and his kindness much delighted my heart, as if I was his own son."

Today a plaque at Napoopoo near the *heiau* commemorates Opukahaia's life there from 1797 to 1808 and that "his zeal for Christ and love for his people inspired the first American Board Mission to Hawaii in 1820."

So off sailed Opukahaia (now called Henry Obookiah) to the Seal Islands in northwest America, then back to Hawaii, on to Canton, China, to sell the sealskins and load up with tea, cinnamon, nankeens, and silk and then to New York and finally to New Haven.

In New Haven, Obookiah, eager to learn English, met a Yale

student, Edwin D. Dwight, who spent several months teaching him to read and write and also became his best friend. An oft-repeated story tells of Dwight finding this poor Hawaiian boy "weeping on the threshold of one of the [Yale] buildings, because there was no one to instruct him." Edwin later arranged for Obookiah to live with his father, Timothy Dwight, president of Yale College, while Edwin tutored him. The Dwights' emphasis on religious forms and spirit impressed Obookiah, but he admitted that, though he heard much about God, he "believed but little." As a student, he seemed at first to be rather dull, but Edwin soon discovered he had keen observation, a sly sense of humor, and the ability to imitate familiar characters.

Samuel J. Mills Jr.

A greater opportunity opened for Obookiah on meeting Samuel J. Mills Jr. one evening at Edwin's room. Mills, just graduated from Williams College, was eagerly interested in promoting a national missionary movement. At Williams, he and four like-minded friends prayed in nearby woods at afternoon sessions. One afternoon, a heavy thunderstorm drove them into the protection of a haystack. There they vowed to devote their lives to foreign mission endeavors. The Haystack Monument still marks the place where this historic group formed its ambitious missionary plans. Within two years, Mills and James Richards had organized The Brethren, a secret society pledged to missionary work. Richards would later go as a missionary to Ceylon in 1815, and his younger brother William would arrive with the second company to Hawaii in 1823 and become an important missionary leader.

In 1810, Obookiah went to live with the Mills family on their farm at Torringford continuing his studies and learning farm work. Mills marveled at how easily Obookiah had become expert with sickle and scythe by merely watching others. Obookiah advanced rapidly in his knowledge and use of English. He also found himself meeting many visiting ministers but avoided their company and talk about God, feeling he "was just as happy as ... those who do know about God much more than I do."

Meanwhile, at Andover Theological Seminary, Mills and his companions sought support from the Congregational Church's governing body which then formed the American Board of Commissioners for Foreign Missions (ABCFM) to take up the challenge, sending its first missionaries to Ceylon and India in 1812.

Early in 1811, Obookiah joined Samuel Jr. at Andover, where many willing students instructed him. "Here," he acknowledges, "my wicked heart began to see a little about the divine things." Mills then

3

arranged for him to enter Bradford Academy. As Obookiah's school life there lacked religious incentive, he drifted away from his new pious inclinations while playing with carefree schoolfellows and joining them in "talking many foolish subjects." At the close of school, he fled back to Andover. That spring, his guilty feelings overcame him; he felt himself an outcast from the Almighty Jehovah, "an undone and hell-deserving sinner."

In 1812, Obookiah lived at the home of the pastor or of one of the deacons of the Hollis, N.H., Church. Suffering a siege or fever for five weeks, he reconciled himself to "leave this world of sin and go to a better ," but, in spite of a renewed "hope in religion" after he recovered, he found that at times "my mind and my heart of wickedness would often turn back to this world." So he seesawed from worldliness to strengthening faith, finding "much comfort and happiness in my secret prayer and in serious conversation with others."

In the summer of 1814 he went to live with the minister at Goshen Conn., studying geography and mathematics and also starting to put his native language into written form.

First Hawaiian Christian

All this time Obookiah struggled to suppress his "own wicked heart" and to let his strong religious feelings dominate his life. The Mills family helped him win acceptance as a member of the church at Torringford on April 9, 1815, becoming the first Hawaiian Christian.

He returned to Goshen, now under the direction of the ABCFM, to prepare as a missionary to his "poor countrymen," whom Henry saw as living without any Bible and so "without knowledge of the true God." He felt afflicted "for the loss of their souls" and prayed the Lord to "pluck them from the everlasting burning." He concluded, "May the Lord Jesus dwell in my heart and prepare me to go and spend the remaining part of my life with them."

In October 1815 Obookiah transferred again, this time to a minister at Canaan, where he wrote the story of his life and recorded entries in his diary which revealed the ups and downs of his struggle to submerge his soul in religious beliefs.

The Board in late 1816 had him assist one of their agents on a tour of the section near Amherst, Mass., to attract funds for a proposed Foreign Mission School, which Mills had induced the ABCFM to establish to train foreign boys as missionaries to their homelands. Obookiah's appearance and his humble talks had such a profound influence on audiences that the appeals aroused great interest in the cause and produced surprisingly liberal contributions. People who had deplored the idea of trying to save ignorant savages changed their minds after seeing a manly, intelligent, deserving, dark skinned human.

Foreign Mission School

The Foreign Mission School found a home at Cornwall, Conn., in May 1817, providing education and religious training for Obookiah, Hopu, five other Hawaiian boys, one Bengalese, one Hindu, one Indian, and two Anglo-Americans. There Henry was eagerly preparing himself to share his new-found faith and knowledge with his unenlightened countrymen in Hawaii. He practiced translating Genesis from the Bible, part of it from Hebrew, which he had learned by himself, finding that it resembled his

Foreign Mission School — Source: The Mission Houses Library Collections of the Hawaiian Mission Children's Society

native language more than English did.

Mills's plan for evangelizing Hawaii and the earnest efforts of so many others in aiding Obookiah in his religious endeavors seemed about to bear fruit. They believed the Lord had shown the way and they had collaborated by developing Obookiah as a capable missionary. But "God took to himself Obookiah." Stricken by typhus fever, Henry Obookiah departed his life peacefully, February 17, 1818, at age 26, as recorded on his long flat gravestone in the cemetery at Cornwall. Among his parting words were "God will do right — he knows what is best." His native friends gathered about his bedside, and to them he offered "Aloha oe" — my love to you.

Neither did his ardent sponsor become a foreign missionary. Samuel Mills, determined promoter of the missionary cause, performed his role as organizer. He got the Presbyterians to form the United Foreign Missionary Society, which later combined with the American Board. His advice prompted the development of the American Bible Society. He also helped found the American Colonization Society to help freed slaves return to Africa, a project that later developed into the country of Liberia.

On the return voyage from a trip to Africa where he had gone to seek the right place for such a colony, he died at age 31. His achievements assured him a high place of honor in the field of human welfare endeavors. Heaven had to be the final meeting place for these two faithful servants of the Lord.

2

THOSE EAGER
VOLUNTEERS

Mills and Obookiah had paved the way to greater missionary endeavor. Many who had seen this capable Hawaiian lad and heard his humble pleas for help to the lost souls of his countrymen felt deeply his loss and the need to take up the cross and carry on in his stead. Religion was too integral a part of the lives of these descendants of the Puritans to allow them to let Obookiah's precious goals go unfulfilled.

Edwin Dwight intensified this strong feeling by publishing in 1818, just a few months after Obookiah's death, the small book *Memoirs of Henry Obookiah*, followed by a second printing the next year. The Hawaiian boy's tragic story touched the hearts of many and aroused determined souls to volunteer for service to the Lord in his behalf. Obookiah's strange life, his honest devotion, intense sincerity of purpose, and strong faith in God stirred the spirits of Christian people to sacrifice themselves for the sake of the Jesus Christ he had come to love and to worship.

Hiram Bingham

From Andover Seminary graduating Hiram Bingham joined in this "ardor ... for evangelizing the Hawaiians" and offered his life and talents for the Sandwich Islands Mission being organized by the ABCFM. Hiram, a graduate of Middlebury College, would go as an ordained minister leading the mission. A farm lad, born at Bennington, Vt., October 30, 1789, he had seemed destined to carry on in his father's footsteps, but religious influences decided him to seek more education and "watch the dealings of providence." Having to earn his way, he taught school during winter months until he finally had enough funds to enter college when he was 22. There he worked his way through the divinity course aiming to become a minister.

7

Asa Thurston

Bingham's classmate at Andover, Asa Thurston, a graduate of Yale, also agreed to join the mission as the only other ordained minister. Born at Fitchburg, Mass., October 12, 1787, he was two years older than Bingham. He too had decided late on a religious career having been induced to turn to the Lord from his youthful carefree ways following his family's tragic deaths.

Living a life devoted to the strictures of religion, Asa was far from his early merry life in Fitchburg. His was a happy, loving family, so expressive in song that they were well-known as the "gay singing Thurstons." Asa's father Thomas, a singing teacher who had wed one of his charming, sweet-voiced pupils at Concord, Mass., directed the church choir in Fitchburg for 30 years. As a youth, Asa showed prowess in sports, grace on the dance floor, and enjoyed a reputation as the "gayest of the gay" and the life of the party. Religion was no pressing matter to him despite warnings from his sister and friends that he should forsake his "beloved sinful companions and repent, turning to God and holiness."

Then typhoid fever struck and, in spite of his fine physique, Asa succumbed quickly to the epidemic. His mother nursed him back to health, but then fell prey to the disease and died. His devoted sister and older brother Thomas both became fatal victims of the fever. Overcome by the swift and tragic losses, Asa readily accepted his dying brother's plea that he carry on in his place as a minister of the gospel.

Samuel Whitney

Samuel Whitney of Branford, Conn., an apprentice shoemaker and also educated at Yale, became inspired by a call of the Lord and pledged himself to the missionary cause. Feeling his physical aptitudes outweighed his "mental exertion," he offered himself as an assistant and instructor. The Board accepted him as teacher and mechanic. He was 26 years old then, born April 28, 1793.

Samuel Ruggles

Samuel Ruggles, in rather dire circumstances and unable to go on to complete his higher education, had already found a place under the Board's supervision as a teacher at the Foreign Mission School where he knew Obookiah personally. He held the position of teacher and catechist. He was 24, born at Brookfield, Conn., March 9, 1795.

Daniel Chamberlain

Daniel Chamberlain of Brookfield, Mass., devoted himself, his wife and five children, and the proceeds from the sale of his well-managed farm to the missionary cause sacrificing everything he owned to pass on to the simple people of Hawaii his talents of energetic farming that they might forsake their indolent ways and convert their islands into rich farmlands. He had served as a captain in the War of 1812. In preparation for his missionary work, Daniel and his sons, Dexter and Nathan, studied at the Foreign Mission School in Cornwall, where they gained understanding of the life and language of the Hawaiians from the Hawaiian boys who would accompany them.

Thomas Holman

Samuel Ruggles had suggested to his older sister Lucia, teaching at Cooperstown, N. Y., that he get her an appointment as teacher for the mission. Though the idea did not appeal to her at first, her fiance, Dr. Thomas Holman beginning his medical career at Cooperstown, saw the financial advantage of joining this expedition. Such an arrangement would ensure them a safe basis for their marriage. So Holman, who had studied at Cherry Valley Medical School, applied, was accepted, and also took training at the Foreign Mission School that summer of 1819. Thomas had been born at New Haven, November 26, 1793.

Elisha Loomis

At Canandaigua, N.Y., a printer's apprentice, Elisha Loomis, read the *Memoirs of Henry Obookiah* and responded so emotionally that he begged his employer to release him from the remaining months of his 5-year apprenticeship if he was accepted by the Board for the mission. Two months later he was in training at Cornwall, his application still under consideration. From the Hawaiian boys he eagerly gained valuable lessons. Elisha was the youngest, just 19, born at Rushville, N.Y., December 11, 1799.

Thus these seven volunteers prepared to undertake an arduous journey to a strange land faraway to devote their lives to instilling in heathen savages (as they considered them) the holy spirit of Christianity.

The Men Must Woo Some Women Too

An all-male party of missionaries was not what the ABCFM had in mind. Perhaps tales of human behavior in the South Seas made these religious leaders wary. They recognized that men devoting their energies to learning how to exist in a strange environment and leading people to a better life would need female help to maintain their households and set a family example. Thus the Board insisted that each man find a wife before departure.

Nancy Wells Ruggles

Samuel Ruggles was the first to hold his wedding — at the home of his bride, Nancy Wells, in East Windsor, Conn., on September 22, 1819. Her ready acceptance may have been partly due to the fact that she was already 28 years old (the oldest of the brides-to-be.)

Lucia Ruggles Holman

Lucia Ruggles, Samuel's older sister, was probably even happier to marry her long-time admirer and suitor, Dr. Thomas Holman. She was almost 26, and Thomas just two months younger . They had grown up together at Brookfield, Conn. Their wedding on September 26 was the second one of the Missionary Party.

Maria Theresa Sartwell Loomis

Next day young Elisha Loomis took for his wife Maria Theresa Sartwell at Utica, N.Y. Theirs had been a most fortuitous meeting, one of those that seemed marvelously arranged by destiny at the hands of God. Elisha, finally approved by the Board, was hastening to his home at Rushville, N.Y. Not one to desecrate the Sabbath by traveling on that holy day, he stopped off Saturday at Utica to visit a printing plant and to rest the next day. Employed at the plant was Maria, a former teacher seeking "to engage in a Mission." Such a find, Elisha felt, was indeed "a particular interposition of Divine Providence," as Maria was experienced not only in printing but also "skilled in the household arts," especially linen weaving.

Mercy Partridge Whitney

Finding a suitable partner proved a problem for some. Friends proved a great help in some cases. Samuel Whitney enjoyed such help in meeting Mercy Partridge of Pittsfield, Mass. Impressed with stern religious convictions and impelled by eager determination that Obookiah's aims not become a lost cause, she consented to Samuel's marriage proposal. Whitney had assured the Board that Mercy was one "whose piety and missionary qualifications have been highly recommended." They were the fourth couple to perform their nuptials — on October 4, 1819.

Sybil Moseley Bingham

Hiram Bingham, after his early acceptance by the Board, had a few months before the mission was to depart. He felt confident of his future, having already won the love of a minister's daughter named Sarah. Busy with his own preparations, he let the marriage business ride along three months before he sought final acceptance. Alas, daughter and parents refused to be separated by thousands of miles and the prospect of Sarah living in an uncivilized land perhaps meeting some dreadful fate. Friends suggested other prospects, but Hiram felt he had no time now to go forth seeking a suitable partner. Strong in his religious principles, he put his faith in the Lord.

At Canandaigua, N.Y., another soul besides that of Elisha Loomis was profoundly stirred by Obookiah's powerful example and the urgent need to carry on his noble endeavors. Her impulse was to go to honor those who had so generously responded to the missionary call. She and her minister arrived at Goshen late just before the special ordination ceremonies of Bingham and Thurston.

For such an unusual event, the small town was crowded. When these travelers applied for accommodations at the parsonage, the one to receive them was weary Hiram Bingham made more uncomfortable by a sore throat. He dutifully led these respected guests to a room at the deacon's home.

How marvelously this all worked out. Hiram found that Sybil Moseley was one of the pious, missionary-inclined girls his friends had advised him to visit. No doubt their meeting was heaven-sent. Sybil was eager to join in the mission, and she was just the answer to Hiram's prayers. Twelve days later they united in marriage at Hartford, Conn., on October 11.

11

Lucy Goodale Thurston

Asa Thurston felt even more satisfied with his prospects of marriage. Socially active in his youth at Fitchburg, he was already engaged to a girl happy to go to faraway Hawaii. But her mother refused to let her heed the call of love and God. To give up both handsome Asa and a grand opportunity to serve the Lord broke the girl's heart. She fell ill and died. The tragedy was too much for her mother who died of grief shortly after.

Now friends came to Asa's aid. At Andover, one of his classmates recalled that, on a visit to Deacon Abner Goodale at Marlboro (now Hudson), Mass., the deacon had mentioned that his daughter Lucy was fitted for missionary work. As another Andover student, William Goodell, was related to Lucy Goodale (the spelling of names did not matter then), they asked him to urge her to consider "engaging in the missionary enterprise" and to grant a personal interview with Asa. To complete such arrangements, William went to visit his cousin Lucy.

William put such feeling into his appeal that it made Lucy tremble and left her with "an almost bursting heart" and unable to eat or sleep. His final proposition was to ask whether she would become "connected with a missionary now an entire stranger, attach herself to this little band of pilgrims, and visit the far distant land of Obookiah." The subject became "utterly overwhelming" to her mind. At that time she was alone, teaching at a country school six miles from home. As William informed her family "that the waters were troubled," two sisters came to comfort her but left the momentous decision up to her. She wavered between this great need for service and her own love of friends and home.

"The poor heathen possess immortal natures, and are perishing," she anguished. "Who will give them the Bible, and tell them of a Savior? Great as must be the sacrifices, trials, hardships, and dangers of such an undertaking, I said, 'If God will grant His grace, and afford an acceptable opportunity, Lucy and all that is hers, shall be given to the noble enterprise of carrying light to the poor benighted countrymen of Obookiah.'" With that declaration, she could then "contemplate the subject with a tranquil mind and unmoved feelings."

On September 23, exactly just a month before the final date of departure, Lucy had returned home, "with composure and serenity, buoyed by a noble purpose," receiving from her close family "their full sympathy and approbation." Now William and Asa arrived for this "strictly private family interview... There were my two brothers and their wives, all belonging to the house. There, too, was Uncle Wm. Goodell, cousin William's own father...," Lucy long after recalled. After "free family sociality, singing, and evening worship, ... the family dispersed, leaving two of similar aspirations, introduced at sunset as strangers, to separate at midnight interested friends." By next morning they were "pledging themselves to each other as close companions in the race of life, consecrating themselves and their all to a life work among the heathen."

They had just time, three Sabbaths, for publication of the banns. They set Tuesday, October 12, as their wedding day. From Marlboro they would "proceed directly to Boston" for their departure, then only 11 days away. Now Asa had to leave at once to join Bingham at Goshen for his ordination.

┌─────────┐
│   │
│ **3**   │
│   │
└─────────┘

THAT LONG,
HARD JOURNEY
TO OWHYHEE

"**N**ever did so small a ship bring so great a cargo."—"*Shipwrecks in Paradise*," by Jim Gibbs

Five days after their marriage at Marlboro, the Thurstons joined the missionary party at Park Street Church in Boston on October 17, 1819, to become "organized into a distinct Missionary Church, to be transplanted to the Pagan Islands of the Pacific," as Lucy phrased it. They received instructions, detailed over 15 printed pages, from first secretary of the American Board, Dr. Worcester. He warned that anyone not entirely committed "to Christ for the high and holy service of missionary work" should "stop where you are," and promised they should glory in "whatever of earthly privations, or labors, or sufferings await you." He summed up with, "You are to aim at nothing short of covering those Islands with fruitful fields, pleasant dwellings, schools, and churches." They should convert Owhyhee to the New England of the Pacific.

Next day, Asa Thurston offered the parting address. "The Church is opening her eyes on the miseries of a world lying in wickedness," he declared. "We have felt that the Savior was speaking to us, and our bosoms have panted for the privilege of engaging in the blessed work of evangelizing the heathen."

So on April 23, 1819, they set forth aboard the brig *Thaddeus*, on an arduous sea voyage 18,000 miles and almost six months long. It would be 17 months before their families and friends would get word that they had survived this ordeal by sea.

Once again religion was driving Puritans over rough ocean expanses. Just two centuries after the *Mayflower* reached Plymouth, the *Thaddeus* was plowing its way to a far more distant land. The *Mayflower* struggled

14

through terrible conditions for 65 days with a load of 102 passengers and all their luggage. The *Thaddeus* carried only 23 plus a crew of 20. About five feet shorter than the equal 90-foot-long *Mayflower*, it outweighed the earlier vessel by 241 equal tons to 120.

However, the *Thaddeus'* departure was not without a delay. When the *Thaddeus* became becalmed 10 miles out to sea, Lucia Holman reported in her diary that this was willed by "a kind providence" as "it was ascertained that our soft bread and crackers and all the ardent spirits were left behind." It took that night and the next day for a boat to return to the dock to retrieve the missing items.

MODEL OF THE BRIG THADDEUS *Built by sailors of the Pacific Fleet Command at Pearl Harbor, Oahu and presented to the Hawaiian Evangelical Association in Honolulu in 1934. It has been on display at Mokuaikaua Church since 1975 by permission of the trustees of the Hawaii Conference Foundation.* Source: author

Braving the Buffets of the Deep

While the four Hawaiian boys rejoiced in their native element, "the horrors of seasickness" assailed the American landlubbers. Lucia Holman observed, "Sorrow and despondency were depicted on every countenance, while scarcely a look of love or complacency was discernable [sic] one towards the other. To multiply our sorrows we were visited with unfavorable winds, high seas, and heavy gales, the first three weeks of our voyage." Talk of the homes and friends they had left behind formed their only consolation during the first five weeks.

Lucy Thurston described the awful seasickness more vividly. They lay, at first, nauseated, in their six-foot-square bunkroom piled high with "chests, trunks, bundles, bags," so that with "such confined air, it might well be compared to a dungeon." Later they managed to crawl up the stairs to fresh air. There they found the deck covered with "a boat, hogsheads, barrels, tubs, cables… a dog, cats, hens, ducks, pigs, and men, women, and children." It was a pitiful scene as "all [were] under the horrors of seasickness, some thrown on their mattresses, others seated in clusters, hanging one upon the other, while here and there individuals leaned on the railing, or supported themselves by hanging upon a rope."

Conditions eased some as they sailed on. After supping at first on deck, "sipping broth or picking bones" from a large container, "this rude manner" gave way to "a well regulated table." Lucy began to feel "contented and happy" when she found "our little room" freed from the excess storage so that they could join in "family devotions in the cabin morning and evening" and a religious service Sunday forenoons with another on deck "when the weather allows."

Homesick as she may have felt, she still persevered bravely, declaring, "No trial or privation which I have experienced, or now anticipate, has ever caused me to cast a lingering look back to my native shores. If I may best contribute to the happiness and usefulness of one of Christ's own ministers, of assisting in giving civilization, the Bible, and letters, to one of the tribes of men in utter darkness — it is enough that I bid farewell to everything my heart so late held dear in life, and subject myself to all the trials, privations and hardships of a missionary life."

But worse hardships were yet to come. By January 27, 1820, the *Thaddeus* pushed on into the Strait of Le Maire. Two days later Lucy reported that a strong wind had driven the ship 50 or 60 miles back, and she lay prostrate on her couch. By February 1, Lucia Holman had to roll herself in her blanket and lie in her berth to keep warm, as the ship was "within 8 days sail of the regions of perpetual ice."

Five days later Lucia recorded: "February 6, Sabbath, Lat. 59 —
off the Straits of Magellan, west of Tierra del Fuego. Last night, the winds
began to blow and the seas to roll, as we had never before witnessed; so that
the two conflicting powers seemed to agitate the ocean to its very foundations. Our vessel labored excessively, the seas constantly breaking over
threatened every moment to overpower her. I think I never so much realized
the weakness of man, and the power of the Almighty."

Two weeks later Lucia was peacefully writing, "It is delightful
sailing in the Pacific." She could also rejoice at enjoying perfect health and
anticipating arrival at Owhyee.

Appalling Sights, Fears, and Good Tidings

As the island of Hawaii came in sight, great excitement stirred
among the *Thaddeus's* weary travelers. As the ship cruised along the shores
of Kohala on the north shore of the island of Hawaii, native canoes pushed
out to greet the newcomers. Hiram Bingham, his mind filled with his initial
thoughts of these people as pagans, heathens, idolaters, savages, lewd and
loathsome beings, sadly looked upon this "appearance of destitution,
degradation, and barbarism, among the chattering, and almost naked
savages" and called the scene "appalling."

At the first opportunity Captain Blanchard sent one of his officers,
James Hunnewell, ashore on the western coast of Kohala with Thomas
Hopu and John Honolii, two of the four Hawaiian boys from the Foreign
Mission School, to find out what the affairs of the kingdom might be. After
three hours of anxious waiting by those aboard ship, the boat returned and
Hunnewell excitedly burst out with the astonishing news: "Kamehameha is
dead; — his son Liholiho is king; — the kapus are abolished; — the images
are burned; — the temples are destroyed. There has been war. Now there
is peace." The missionaries felt that the Lord had truly prepared the way
for them.

Though Kamehameha had died more than five months before the
missionaries sailed, they had no way of knowing this. The overthrow of the
religious kapu system had been arranged by the two dowager queens:
Kaahumanu and Keopuolani. Kaahumanu had claimed the dying
Kamehameha had made her joint ruler with Liholiho, Kamehameha II.
As a woman, she was precluded from eating with men and from joining the
male chiefs in state deliberations. As such limitations would interfere with
her powers as a ruler, she and Liholiho's mother, Keopuolani, convinced
the young king to break the kapu by eating with them at a banquet.
Emboldened by this act and without any ill effects from his Hawaiian gods,

17

King Kamehameha The Great, Queen Kaahumanu, Kamehameha II and Kalanimoku — Source: Hawaii State Archives

King Kamehameha II boldly sent word that the native religious structure was abolished and that wooden images should be burned and *heiau* destroyed.

Strong opposition developed. Issues could not be resolved. Battle lines were drawn. The defeat of Chief Kekuaokalani at Kamoo, between Napoopoo and Honaunau, finally brought peace in December, more than three months before the missionaries' arrival.

Amazingly, the priesthood had also agreed to the overthrow of the kapu system. Hewahewa, a high priest, declared, "I knew the wooden images of deities, carved by our own hands, could not supply our wants, but worshipped them because it was a custom of our fathers. ...My thought has always been, there is one only great God, dwelling in the heavens." So he welcomed the missionaries as "brother priests." A descendant of the priest Paao from Tahiti, he is said to have predicted the coming of a new god. Later, at Waimea on Oahu, he became a Christian.

Getting Acquainted with Royalty

At the port of Kawaihae, Hopu was sent ashore to invite the highest chiefs to visit the mission company aboard the *Thaddeus*. Having visited other foreign ships, the chiefs were eager to meet the newcomers. The first visitor, prime minister Kalanimoku, impressed Lucy Thurston as having "the dignity of a man of culture." She glowed over his friendly handshake, "that first warm appreciating clasp" from such a special "specimen of heathen humanity." As commander of the army, he had led the way to victory for the king in the recent civil war. Britishers and others called him "Billy Pitt," after the famous prime minister William Pitt. Seven months earlier, he had received Catholic baptism by Captain Freycinet on his ship *L'Uranie*.

Two of Kamehameha's five dowager queens, Kalakua and Namahana, also came aboard, their bodies "of giant mould" covered, as Hopu had diplomatically requested, with the native *pa'u*. Lucy learned it "consisted of ten thicknesses of bark cloth [tapa] three or four yards long, and one yard wide, wrapped several times round the middle, and confined by tucking it in on one side. The two queens wore loose dresses over these. Trammeled with clothes and seated on chairs, the queens were "out of their element," Lucy noted. "They divested themselves of their outer dresses. Then the one stretched herself at full length upon a bench, and the other sat down upon the deck. Mattresses were then brought for them to recline in their own way."

The two plump widows of Kamehameha sailed with the missionary party to Kailua. "Kalakua," Bingham relates, "shrewdly aiming to see what the white women could do for her temporal benefit, asked them to make a gown for her in fashion like their own."

Lucy explains the proceedings: "Monday morning, April 3d, the first sewing circle was formed that the sun ever looked down upon in this Hawaiian realm. Kalakua, queen dowager,was directress. She requested all the seven white ladies to take seats with them on mats, on the deck of the *Thaddeus*. Mrs. Holman and Mrs. Ruggles were executive officers, to ply the scissors and prepare the work. ...The four native women of distinction were furnished with calico patchwork to sew, —a new employment for them. The dress was made in the fashion of 1819. The length of the skirt accorded with Brigham Young's rule to Mormon damsels, —have it come down to the tops of your shoes. But in the queen's case, where the shoes were wanting, the bare feet cropped out very prominently."

At Kailua, the dressmaking achievement was received "by hundreds with a shout" as Kalakua stepped out in her "newly-made white dress ...with a lace cap, having on a wreath of roses, and a lace handkerchief, in the corner of which was a most elegant sprig of various colors ...presents we had brought her from some American friends." Thus the *Thaddeus* reached Kailua, then home of the Hawaiian king, on April 4, 1820, 164 days out of Boston. Bingham observed the "large heathen village of thatched huts, though in a dry and sterile spot, ornamented with cocoanut and *Kou* trees." Inland lay numerous trees and plantations on the slopes of Mt. Hualalai,which had erupted 19 years earlier (the last volcanic activity there to date).

An excited throng welcomed the strangers, "shouting, ... swimming, floating on surf-boards, sailing in canoes, sitting, lounging, standing, running like sheep, dancing, or laboring on shore." Bingham saw them not as beautiful, carefree, sportive people. His religion-dominated view still considered them in terms of "degradation, ignorance, pollution and destitution."

Amid the crowd on the beach, one man stood out prominently. Governor Kuakini greeted the missionaries with some English words and invited them to his home. After a brief visit there and at John Young's, they "eagerly sought the king, at his dingy, unfurnished, thatched habitation." Welcomed by the royal smile and "*Aloha*," the mission party stated their purpose of "teaching the nation Christianity, literature and arts."

4

GETTING
THE MISSION
STARTED

Let us Serve the Lord in Hawaii

These "ambassadors of the King of Heaven" were eager to get to Honolulu and start their tremendous tasks. But they had to learn the meaning of "Hawaiian time." The king felt no hurried interest in their aims. With five wives, why welcome a religion that opposed polygamy? Bingham and his party knew they had to act cautiously and diplomatically. Gifts to the king came first—an elegant Bible that looked impressive even though the king had no use for it and some optical instrument sent by the Board. Other Bibles were presented to the dowager queens.

To foster friendly relationships, the missionaries invited the royalty aboard the *Thaddeus*. Dignified Bingham questioned the king's style, noting it was "according to the taste of the time." His majesty wore the native *malo* or girdle, a green silken scarf over his shoulders but nothing formal such as "coat, vest, and linen." His neck was naked except for a string of large beads and his head was adorned with a feather wreath. Here he was meeting "the first company of white women he ever saw" "destitute of hat, gloves, shoes, stockings, and pants" —a certainly uncivilized appearance in the eyes of proper New England missionaries. On deck after dinner, the mission family entertained with hymns of praise as Prince George Kaumualii played the bass viol.

However, friendly visits to the king failed to obtain permission to start the work of the Lord at Honolulu. They offered to leave some of their party in Kailua so the others could go on. Liholiho was suspicious. "White men all prefer Oahu," he pointedly remarked. "I think the Americans would like to have that island."

Instead he offered quarters for the mission company at Kailua. One look at the rude native affair and the missionaries could not imagine how they could be "reasonably comfortable" in such a hovel—a "barn-like, thatched structure, without floor, ceiling, partition, windows or furniture." They put off Captain Blanchard, who was fretting to get away, and excused themselves to the king by assuring him they could not disembark on the Sabbath as "Jehovah has a tabu" then. Realizing the Lord was trying their spirit, patience, and faith, they resorted to imploring Him with prayers.

Another try for agreement was held up because Liholiho was awaiting the return of his joint ruler, Kaahumanu, who was off fishing. The Lord was on their side and soon Kaahumanu and high chief Keeaumoku, her brother, returned. All next day they sought a favorable arrangement with the chiefs, until "a band of rude musicians" started an outdoor entertainment with dancers of the "heathen hula" absorbing the attention of chiefs and commoners while the missionaries waited fretfully. John Young, knowing the ways of the land, further dampened their spirits by advising them they would be lucky if they got approval of their aims in six months.

They decided to pare down their request and the following day begged that they be allowed to stay at least a year. As that seemed fair enough to Liholiho, he granted them permission to go to different islands and have "grassy huts" supplied them, adding his royal request that a physician, a preacher, and two of the Hawaiian boys remain with him in Kailua.

Bingham was pleased with his diplomatic success. Dr. and Lucia Holman would stay. The company took a vote and the unpleasant fate of remaining in this unattractive native village fell to the Thurstons, truly a hardy pair, as time would prove. Now the others could be on their way. And the work of the Lord could begin.

Life in Honolulu — The Bingham Era

The rest of the eager mission family sailed off to settle the main station at Honolulu under the eloquent leadership of Hiram Bingham. Since 1787, Honolulu had become a convenient stop for ships from Britain, France, Russia, and New England loaded with furs from North America to sell in China. By 1810 enterprising New England vessels were also eagerly loading up with the much-prized Hawaiian sandalwood.

Among those who set up business in Honolulu from about 1790 on were an odd variety of both good and bad. Good men like John Young, Isaac Davis, and Francisco de Paula Marin, a man of great versatility, served as important advisors to King Kamehameha. The crippled Archibald Campbell, who stayed with King Kamehameha in 1809, reported about 60 white men there, mostly British and American, who "pay little attention either to the education or to the religious instruction of their children" born to the native women whom they took as wives.

Some of the sailors released from their ships or who had deserted formed the bulk of the city's growing population serving as "carpenters, joiners, masons, blacksmiths, and bricklayers," some of them "sober and industrious." But many remained as idle, dissolute drunks, often sitting for days drinking a keg of liquor. Some were escaped convicts from New South Wales. Seeing such a great need for missionaries, Campbell "was often much surprised" that none had come yet.

Hiram and Sybil Bingham —
Source: HMCS Library

In 1819, the very year the missionaries had set sail for Owhyhee, a great new trade, oil from sperm whales in the Pacific, sent more and more ships to the Pacific. Within two years as many as 60 whaling ships crowded into Honolulu harbor for supplies. When the first missionary party landed, Honolulu was a motley town, a haven for many undesirables, producing a class of uncared-for half-breed Hawaiians. Bad as some of Honolulu's residents were, they were overshadowed each spring and fall by whaling sailors who swarmed through the dusty or muddy streets to indulge in drunkenness and debauchery.

Infectious diseases new to this distant land were cutting down the native population. Captain Cook's aim to deny shore leave for any disease carrier and his threats to punish severely any who molested women failed because of the welcoming generosity of these Pacific island women, who, he noted, "visited us with no other view than to make a surrender of their persons." And, of course, the men so passionately sought such feminine favors that some Polynesian men believed them to be deprived males who had come from lands inhabited only by men.

These were some of the problems that would complicate the mission's religious efforts in the years ahead. Personal problems such as poor health would also play a role in determining each missionary's fate. The Chamberlains with their six children, one born in Hawaii, were the first to give up, leaving in 1823. Health troubles and farming discouragements were contributing factors, but the major factor was the need to take their children back for proper American schooling.

Elisha Loomis, after serving as teacher and printer, had to leave for health reasons in 1827. He printed three of the gospels in Rochester, N.Y., served two years as missionary to the Ojibway Indians at Mackinac Island, Mich., and then, back home in Rushville, he opened a select school in 1832. He died in 1836. His wife Maria lived another 26 years.

Samuel Ruggles and Samuel Whitney, dispatched on the *Thaddeus* to return young Prince George to his father, king of Kauai, established the mission at Waimea. Health problems so afflicted them that Ruggles returned to America in 1834; Whitney struggled on in poor health until 1845, dying at age 52. His wife Mercy survived him in Hawaii for 27 more years, passing away at age 77.

Hiram Bingham proudly guided the Honolulu mission for 21 years, astutely winning over many leading chiefs to Christianity. The high-born queen Keopuolani became the first native chief accepted as one of the strictly limited favored members of the sacred Christian church of Hawaii. This was not until 1823 and then only because she was suffering her last earthly struggles. Death brought her the additional honor of receiving "the first Christian funeral of a high chief that had ever taken place in the islands." But it was the chief ruler, Queen Kaahumanu, whose conversion in 1826 gave Bingham the political leverage he needed.

Such power and his forthright denunciations of those with less strict morals naturally bred opposition and conflict among the less religiously inclined citizens. Even some of the brethren felt that Bingham stirred up unnecessary antagonism to the Mission.

Bingham climaxed his career in Hawaii with the design and building of the present great Kawaiahao Church after having served in four previous native buildings. He regretfully had to leave Hawaii in 1841 because of his wife Sybil's ill health. His hope of returning never became fulfilled.

The Binghams' son, Hiram II, graduated from Yale and Andover Theological Seminary and returned with his wife to Honolulu in 1847. They then devoted their missionary career to the Gilbert Islands, living there from 1857 to 1865 and making repeated visits afterwards as they mastered the language, translated the Bible and prepared a dictionary and many other books. Their son Hiram III, also a Yale graduate, acquired more liberal views of religion, married a rich Tiffany heiress, and enjoyed the high life. Later he became an explorer, winning lasting fame as the discoverer of Machu Picchu, an ancient Inca fortress village in Peru.

Queen Kaahumanu listens to a sermon by Hiram Bingham at Waimea, Oahu (1826) — Source: Hawaii State Archives

5

THREE CHRISTIAN
NATIVES AND THE
THE PRINCE

Thomas Hopu, William Kanui, Honolii and George Prince Tamoree
— Source: HMCS Library

Along with the missionaries, four Hawaiian youths educated at the Foreign Mission School had come on the *Thaddeus:* Thomas Hopu, William Kanui, John Honolii, and George Tamoree, prince from Kauai. They had led adventurous lives in America and were destined for various successes and failures as they returned to their native land. Obookiah and Hopu were just two of many from Hawaii who sought adventures abroad. Chief Kaiana of Kauai was taken in 1787 by a British captain to Canton, China, where he met a Hawaiian woman, probably the first feminine foreign traveler from the islands, who had been hired as a maid for a captain's wife. Historian James Jarves found that the king of Kauai had as interpreter "a middle-aged native, [who] had dined with General Washington in New York, who gave him clothes and treated him with kindness as a native of the islands where Cook was killed." The four Hawaiian boys served as seafarers while Obookiah kept to his studious ways.

Thomas Hopu

Hopu's life story in America was written by the Rev. Joseph Harvey, pastor of the church at Goshen, Conn., who tuned it to his own deeply religious interpretations before he sent it on to Andover Theological Seminary on August 29, 1822.

Hopu "learned to write, and to spell some easy words" and acquired some religious training. Then his "wicked disposition seemed inclined rather to rove the sea," where he had a tumultuous life. He made 12 voyages, and, during the War of 1812, "was taken four times by the British" and imprisoned for several months on St. Kitts in the West Indies. That winter he returned on an American ship and next spring "went out to sea again, in a small vessel, about 30 tons." Shipwrecked about 400 miles from the West Indies, he rescued crew members from drowning by helping them get out of their clothes in the water. Then he swam back to the wreck, tied a swamped boat to the mast, bailed it out and got the swimming crew aboard it. Next day he made a sail from the captain's "frock," and navigated by sun and stars six days to the West Indies. With a former sea captain friend, he sailed back New to England, but the British seized this ship, took Hopu and the captain back to Bermuda and relieved them of everything except the clothes they were wearing. Later they were freed and returned to Nantucket.

Hopu settled down with a Grangor family at Whitestown, N. Y., for about nine months serving as a servant and a coachman. He lived with various families, until September 1815, when he joined Obookiah who was studying at Goshen. There the Rev. Mr. Harvey claimed Hopu suffered torments over his lack of religious faith and his past sins as he spent time with the Rev. Mr. Mills at Torringford. Then at Canaan "the fears of hell" caused him "awful distress" in an intense struggle to gain Christian peace and forgiveness of sins while attending the school of Mr. Prentice, who fervently searched the poor fellow's soul.

Hopu and Obookiah stayed together in school at Litchfield Farms from late 1816 until April 1817, when they started their training at the Foreign Mission School in Cornwall. Of the four Hawaiian boys who came with the pioneer party, Hopu was best prepared to serve, for he had proved a good scholar, even in theology. At the mission's departure from Boston, he offered an eloquent speech in English. After Obookiah's death in February 1818, Hopu and the other boys remained in training at the school until the mission left for Hawaii in October 1819.

Hopu and Kanui were chosen to remain with the Thurstons and Holmans at Kailua to serve as interpreters and aides to the king. Lucy was amused to watch the two boys the first morning all dressed up in their Boston finery marching proudly to visit the chiefs. Hopu was happily reunited with his father, who moved his family to Kailua, where Hopu lovingly cared for him, teaching him to know Jesus and praying with him faithfully. He also served the king's household and aided Asa by translating his teachings and preachings.

Later, at Lahaina with the king, Hopu met and fell in love with an 18-year-old girl. He took her to Honolulu to live with and learn from Lucy Thurston. Hopu declared that since the Almighty has "excited in my heart such yearnings for her, I think it is his will that I marry her." Lucy named her Delia and delighted in the girl's adaptability to private domestic life, as she proved to be "amiable, piously disposed, with a warm heart, ever open to receive instruction." Delia was thus prepared to be led by Hopu "to the hymeneal altar" in a public church ceremony attended by the king, high chiefs and foreigners, the first Christian wedding service in the islands. Hopu appeared in his black suit, with Delia in "fashionable white dress," her crowning glory "a trimmed straw bonnet."

After helping Bingham in Honolulu for some time, Hopu settled in Kailua where he kept busy teaching, holding Sabbath meetings for the governor, assisting in translating the Bible, and caring for his father who died after four years at the age of 80. His funeral service was the first missionary one to be held in Hawaii.

Throughout those early missionary annals in Hawaii, Hopu appears here and there performing his duties: forcibly delivering a sermon; spreading cheer, comfort and aid to those suffering from dysentery; commanding the schooner *Young Thaddeus* as the wild, reckless hand of George Tamoree crashed it on the rocks of Kauai; teaching, translating, and serving in hard labor. Devoted as Hopu was to his Christian associates and his work with them, he later fell from grace when he had to admit having slipped back into the native pitfall of adultery.

Chester Lyman, a sometime Yale professor, visiting the islands in 1846 - 1847, found Hopu working in a store in Honolulu. He reports he was "over 50 & an interesting man. ... He has been a consistent and useful man since he returned, & is now one of the Deacons of the Kailua Church where he resides."

William Kanui

William Kanui arrived in Boston about 1809 at the age of 12. He worked for a time as a servant, known by the English rendition of his name, William Tenooe. During the War of 1812 he found adventures aboard privateering vessels. At length he went to New Haven to learn the trade of a barber, where Yale students urged him to a better future, took care of his debts, and gave him lessons until he joined Obookiah and Hopu at Goshen.

Back in Hawaii, Kanui proved less amenable to missionary discipline and demands. At Kailua with Hopu, he "in a few short months violated his vows by excess drinking, was excluded from Christian fellowship, but still performed some service for the chiefs for a time, then became a wanderer for many years," Bingham recorded. Kanui took off to California, made a small fortune in the gold fields, lost it in a bank failure, ran a restaurant, and then made his way as bootblack and junk dealer. He even taught a Bible class and had some contact with other Hawaiians who were serving as missionaries to the Indians.

After an absence of 20 years, he was accepted back in the church in Hawaii. He lived another 24 years, and was buried next to Kawaiahao Church in Honolulu.

John Honolii

John Honolii had shipped from Hawaii as a sailor to take the place of one who had died. After arriving in Boston in 1815, he found admiring and interested friends who offered to help him acquire an education. The ship company agreed to release him and generously added $100 toward his expenses. When he later joined the others at the Foreign Mission School, he became a valuable Hawaiian language instructor because, having come at a later age, he still had good command of his native tongue. He also won praise for his "considerable vigor and intellect" and his "discreet and stately deportment."

Honolii proved an important assistant at Kailua, Honolulu, and briefly at Kauai, during those early days while the missionaries were still acquiring their later expertness in the Hawaiian tongue and faithful to his Christian training, he "walked irreproachably with his church," as missionary Titus Coan recorded. Honolii died in February 1838.

Prince George Tamoree

Perhaps the earliest of the boys to leave his native land was the son of Kaumualii, king of Kauai, a friendly, intelligent and enterprising ruler. Trustfully, the king had sent the young boy off with a ship's captain to get an education in America. This may have been for the boy's protection as, being born of a commoner mother, he was not considered favorably by the high-ranking queen. Later, when he was aboard the *Thaddeus*, Lucy Thurston considered him an "illegitimate son" sent away by his father "to save him from falling a victim to the malice and jealousy of his wife." Of course that was Lucy's religious-minded interpretation as the Hawaiians never considered children to be "illegitimate."

Though the captain had been provided with some means for taking care of his seven-year-old charge he left the lad in the lurch and, as the boy later wrote his father, the captain "be-came intemperate & exposed with the property you sent with him...and I have to shirk for myself." He had gained a fair feeling for English expression if not the exact words.

As Hawaiian names are puzzling to the uninitiated, Kaumualii became Tamoree in English and was dubbed George. His first four years were spent with Captain Rowan at Worcester, Mass., then four more years with a Captain Samuel Cotton, a "school keeper." After that, he spent time at Fitchburg, acquiring some ability as a carpenter.

Restless, Tamoree left for Boston to look for passage home but finally enlisted in the U.S. Navy in 1815 as George Prince. He served first on the *Enterprise* and then on the *Guerriere* under Stephen Decatur in the Mediterranean, who was sent to put a final stop to the harassment of the Barbary Pirates. Discharged in 1816, George was next reported "living with the Pusser of the Navy" at Charlestown, Mass. He too was later discovered and invited to join the others at the Foreign Mission School.

Though the young prince performed creditably in navigation and astronomy at the school his religious attitude failed to meet the strict standards of the ABCFM. They had observed too much of his demanding ways and his head unbowed before God to count him as a promising proponent of the work of salvation. But, since his father was king of Kauai, it seemed advantageous to pay for George's passage home to his royal parent and to win favor there.

From Honolulu, Captain Blanchard on the *Thaddeus* delivered George to his long-bereft father on Kauai. On leaving the mission family, young George shed tears, "though," Bingham adds, "we had no evidence that his heart was interested in religion." The king rejoiced at this long-awaited reunion and warmly embraced the two missionaries, Ruggles and Whitney, even offering them special privileges that, quite unlike other white men, "they did not covet," such being quite contrary to their religious moral standards. The king generously awarded the captain free supplies for his ship and added "sandal-wood, valued at $1,000."

The happy father lavished on his repatriated son princely powers, chests of rich clothes, the stone fort, and overlordship of the fertile valley of Wahiawa. All this proved to be too much for the long-deprived lad and led to his undoing. He later withdrew to his valley and reverted to native ways with his bride from Honolulu, Betty Davis, whose father had served along with John Young for Kamehameha the Great, the two of them holding high positions in the kingdom.

The favored prince, known locally as Humehume, met his downfall four years after his return. Revolting with other dissident chiefs after the death of his father, he and his forces were quickly defeated, his wife and infant daughter captured, and he was chased down and found in the mountains, naked, foodless and drunk. Taken to Honolulu, he succumbed to a fever two years later, the victim of despair, hatred and rum. He spurned spiritual aid for his soul, clinging to indifference and antipathy till his death.

6

HARDSHIPS OF MISSIONARY LIFE IN KAILUA FOR THE HOLMANS AND THURSTONS

As the *Thaddeus* sailed off to Honolulu that evening of April 12, 1820, the Holmans and Thurstons found themselves left behind by their dear associates in this "noisy, filthy heathen village" that so disturbed the soul of Brother Bingham. He expressed sympathy for these poor souls "left to the toils and privations and privileges of foreign missionaries, on a barbarous, heathen island, where no Christian family or civilized female could be found." Having avoided such a fate, he took a look at the missionaries' crude dwelling and remembered it as "a frail hut, 3 1/2 feet high ... without flooring, ceiling, windows, or furniture, invested with vermin." Kailua lay on a sun-drenched lava field shaded by merely a few coconut and kou trees. The Holmans and Thurstons felt rather depressed and forsaken after a rather brusk but sad leave-taking that concluded the long day laboriously spent putting ashore their goods.

Sad and weary, they crawled into their inhospitable lodgings, which Lucy generously classified as "an abode of the most uncouth and humble character" and stretched out on mattresses atop their trunks and boxes. There they found the horde of fleas "a secret enemy" that rendered the night almost sleepless. Relieved that such a night was over, they welcomed the next day as they set in with vigor to clear out their piles of luggage and clean up the accumulated dirt and the hostile inhabitants. The only ones pleased to remain here were Hopu and Kanui.

A most serious drawback for these prim Puritans was the lack of fresh water. They had to depend on natives to bring it down in calabashes from pools in caves some miles away. Unlike the carefree Hawaiians, the prudish New Englanders had to bathe themselves in fresh water privately, instead of splashing about in the unlimited supply of sea water beyond the nearby shore. Lucy tried at first to rely on native help in laundering her tropical dresses but gave up after one came back with five holes resulting from pounding it on sharp lava rock.

During the first three weeks curious natives crowded around the missionary house from dawn to dusk, 30 or 40, and sometimes 80, peering in unabashedly. The necessary outdoor cooking always attracted a throng of gaping watchers. When Lucy tried to find comfort from the burning heat of the sun by sitting under a shade tree, she could count 70 companions in five minutes staring at this rare specimen—a white woman! Crowds followed the two women about, peering under their bonnets and feeling their strange clothes. The natives decided they had "hats with a spout," and called the missionaries "Long Necks."

To these missionaries, the Big Island was certainly no paradise of the Pacific in those rugged days. Only brave, determined, devoted souls could put up with such situations: overpowering mountains—nearby Hualalai at 8,271 feet high; Mauna Kea, 13,796 feet; and Mauna Loa, almost as high, stretching 60 miles long and 30 miles wide, the most massive mountain in the world looming 10,000 cubic miles across the whole island, greater than all the seven others combined. Such was the imposing island terrain with up and down climbs, rough lava surface, and severe weather conditions, making communication with other parts most difficult. Some men would falter, but more stalwart ones would hang on tenaciously to their stations in spite of the extremely difficult conditions and would devote their long vigorous lives to the physical and spiritual welfare of their people.

Fitting Into Native Life

The Holmans and Thurstons found that life in the native hut improved as royalty began to understand their needs and supplied better furniture. Queen Kamamalu sent over two Chinese bedsteads. And the king gave them a Chinese round table to replace the large chest first used as a dining table.

Then, on April 29, came the great feast to commemorate the death of King Kamehameha I, preceded by two days of noise from yelping dogs destined for the festive board. Queen Kamamalu's attire attracted Lucy's interest the most, as she watched with amazement the well-developed queen roll her ample form with 70 thicknesses of yard-wide *pa'u*.

Asa held church services and reading classes for the royalty, who felt they must be the first to learn in order to maintain their superiority over the common people. In a native hut Asa preached to the first Christian congregation in the Sandwich Islands. Liholiho, instead of applying himself to learning, decided to let two of his favorites do it for him and sent them to study with Asa. One of them, John Papa Ii, later played important roles in the Hawaiian government.

33

The king and his royal family, and a large retinue of 70, came to call on the missionaries providing their own regal repast which all heartily enjoyed, though their hosts refrained from partaking of baked dog.

What a surprise one evening to hear a cultivated voice call in, "Good evening, Mr. Thurston." An American vessel was visiting Kailua. Deeds of kindness from these mariners prompted Lucy to hail them as "the links that connect us to the father-land." But her admiration sank as she saw "a whole sisterhood" of 15 to 20 girls and women taken aboard to spend the night and return with their prizes of foreign cloth.

Two months after their arrival, the missionaries found a new home when the king, having a compound built for himself and his household, gave his former "palace" to the missionaries. No common hut, this one boasted two doors, the one 2 1/2 feet high and the main portal at the side rising 3 1/2 feet.

Those Not So Holy Holmans

Even such self-sacrificing Puritans as the Thurstons from hardy New England found life in Kailua hard to endure. But the Holmans soon showed they were not of the same persevering ilk. From the first, doubts began to shadow the views of Lucia Holman. Even before they landed at Kailua, she felt disheartened at the sight and noise-making of the naked savages, almost wishing she were peacefully back home.

The Holmans were just basically of a different upbringing from the other missionaries in their company. Unlike the others, their marriage had not been one of emergency but of love and opportunity. Their inducement to missionary labors was the financial provision that solved their problems. They were bound not by an eager adventure in saving heathen souls but by their personal longing for love and life. While culturally religious, they were not impelled by the strong feelings of obligation and self-sacrifice that bound the others together and to the mission. Dr. Francis J. Halford explains their situation in his *9 Doctors and God*: "Faithful churchgoers though they were, they did not subscribe to the frigid prudishness then prevalent in New England and considered essential to the soul's salvation."

In Boston, the Holmans got off to a bad start with their companions. Halford pictures the missionary women going to the *Thaddeus* in the harbor, stumbling into the barge without male support because of their Puritan prudery that would not "permit strong arms to ease the way; that is, for none save one, Lucia Ruggles Holman, who came aboard held high and safe in the arms of her 6-foot doctor husband. From that moment on, she was suspected of being no better than she should be."

This unrestrained familiarity between the Holmans caused the others to look askance at them. Affection was a private matter not for open display. Aboard the *Thaddeus*, disputes arose over the dispensing of wines and liquors for medicinal needs, and a misunderstanding as to personal rights and agreements.

Thomas and Lucia Holman
— Source: HMCS Library

Dissension! Who Was To Blame?

Thomas Holman's independent, practical attitude and his love for Lucia led to prolonged provocations. Also, Lucia was not as hardy and determined a type as were the other women pledged to their husbands and to their ideals of endeavor. She was somewhat spoiled, and Thomas's devotion to her reinforced this.

The Holmans, trapped into staying at caloric Kailua by the king's undeniable request, within three days registered dissatisfaction with their situation. Lucia was full of complaints. She felt overwhelmed at the prospect of a lifetime "upon these barren rocks and among this heathen people,whose manners and habits are so rude and disgusting." She had begged her husband not to agree to stay, but he was reluctant to offend the sovereign. She felt despair that, after their long voyage, they had six months of washing to do; and she deplored the very lack of water that left her without tea or soup if she used the precious liquid to wash herself. Lucia declared to Lucy Thurston (according to Lucy's record) that "she never would be willing to exercise that degree of self-denial which was called for by a situation among this people." The lack of water and the diet of "heathenish" tasting foods proved too much for Lucia, as did also the stern and hard-driving ways of the Thurstons.

Dr. Holman! Where Art Thou?

The Holmans were determined to leave for Maui without the consent of the missionary authorities. Asa showed his opinion of their companions deserting Kailua by writing for replacement aid and requesting help of a different caliber: people with souls, "crucified to the world, ... their hearts fixed on the glory of God in the salvation of the heathen, ... [ready] to sacrifice [and] cheerfully and constantly labor...." The Holmans were not the kind to devote their lives to such stringent demands.

The unapproved move by the Holmans to Maui from their assigned post brought on more conflicts, accusations, and denials. But after less than a month at their new Lahaina Eden, the doctor was called to Honolulu to save the life of a critically ill ship's captain. The Holmans received a chilly reception from Bingham, as he had already taken steps to suspend the doctor "from the privileges of the church." Dr. Holman passionately denied Bingham's charges against him.And nothing but bitterness existed between these two men with quite opposing views. Recriminations continued to fly back and forth between the Holmans and Bingham, supported by some of the mission family.

Sinful as Thomas was considered by some, he was needed for bringing new life into the world. In October he sailed to Kauai to assist "Sister Whitney whose time was nigh." The Whitneys eagerly received this one and only available doctor, as did Nancy Ruggles, who needed his aid two months later. Happy to get away from the Bingham hierarchy in Honolulu, the Holmans stayed on at Kauai until after the birth of their own daughter, Lucia Kamamalu, on March 2, 1821. Then the call came to rejoin the royal court now removed to Honolulu. They were joyfully received by the king and queen and continued to serve wherever needed.

Many seemed to profit by and appreciate the doctor's ministrations, except the mission leader, who kept on sending back biting accusations to Boston. The doctor had provided beneficial care to the company during the long voyage. He enjoyed good success at Kailua in treating one of the queens, as well as other members of the royal household, winning the complete confidence of the king. On Kauai his services as physician kept him busy and in the good graces of the king there. Back in Honolulu his good work was also in constant demand. Dr. Halford praises Holman's medical record as "exceptionally brilliant," considering the standards of those times and the slender resources. Perhaps it was partly the doctor's professional success and the favors he received that really discomfited the company's religious leader so much.

Holiness or Health?

All this wrangling over who did wrong struck Halford as a senseless "hodgepodge of inconsistencies"—the mission company worrying about their health and then "hounding their only physician and his wife out of the Mission and out of the Islands as well."

The division between the Holmans and the doctrinal-motivated Bingham and others of the mission who sided with him was one of fundamental differences. They had started out with different goals and aspirations and never learned to reconcile their views. The Holmans represented many more in New England who did not go off on missions, being basically concerned with enjoying what they could in life rather than seeking to live among savages to try to save their souls. The missionaries stood firm in a strong faith that looked down upon those who did not conform. No matter how much they avowedly needed the doctor, their duty to God seemed more dear to them than their health needs and putting up with any who failed to follow in their footsteps in the ways of the Lord.

At last, as the antagonisms grew too bitter and prolonged, the Holmans decided it was best for Thomas to leave his practice and return home. They sailed that October 1821 on a ship to Boston by way of China. Thus Lucia became the first American woman to sail around the world. Thomas died less than five years later. Lucia remarried and lived to age 93, the last of the pioneer company to die.

7

THOSE INDOMITABLE THURSTONS

Asa and Lucy Thurston — Source: HMCS Library

Fitting Into Native Life

With no way to latch the doors, the Thurstons after the Holmans left, saw the only protection for their goods was to have one of them home all the time. Samuel Whitney was sent by the mission to invite the now-isolated Thurstons to join those in Honolulu. After a long conference, Asa declared he preferred to remain, and Lucy steadfastly determined to abide by his decision. The Thurstons felt it was their main responsibility at that time to teach and Christianize those in authority. Admiringly, Whitney asserted, "I believe you were made to be missionaries."

Life alone presented problems for Lucy. Being by herself one day, she was alarmed by a dozen drunk natives making frantic gestures towards the house from beyond the yard's fence. Frightened by "the fiery glances of their wild eyes," she shut herself inside and for an almost interminable hour peeked out through a crevice to see whether they would just besiege or invade her dwelling. What a relief when Asa's return sent the offenders on their way and Lucy enjoyed her safety and peace once more.

Another day an intoxicated old pagan priest gave Lucy her greatest scare. He marched right in, tossed off his girdle and showed he meant business. Still awed by the priesthood, the young prince, whom Lucy was teaching, and his attendants all fled. The naked intruder chased her around the room for some time, then flung himself onto the bed, rolled around with pleasure, then took up his pursuit again. They raced out one door and in the other repeatedly, until Lucy, almost cornered, resorted to a big stick and gave the fellow a sound rap across his arm. Enraged, her pursuer started throwing clubs at her. She ran out through the crowd that had gathered and headed for the palace, happily meeting Asa coming back as soon as he had heard the news from Hopu.

Overcome by such an experience, Lucy fell trembling as the tears came to relieve her tensions. The queens came with many others and joined their tears with hers, rubbed noses and assured her of their great love for her. When she compiled her memories later, she was pleased to add that the pagan priest eventually became a Christian and that this was the only known case of a Hawaiian insulting a missionary lady.

As all agreed the home must be protected lest the priest in his anger return to set the thatch-work afire, their two devoted pupils representing the king spent the next two weeks sleeping there with their weapons by their pillows. Asa restrained the king from putting the priest to death for his evil acts.

Two Sad Sea Trips — Honolulu and Back

Relief for the Thurstons came after seven months in Kailua. The king then decided to move to Honolulu and that the missionaries should too. As the king's ship was overcrowded, the Thurstons stayed, expecting to leave a few days later. With all their belongings carefully packed, they waited day after day until at last, three weeks later, they got aboard a ship for Maui.

The Thurstons were the first of the missionaries to have to endure such a trip across the waters. Though the *Thaddeus* seemed crowded, conditions aboard it could not compare with the awfulness of inter-island sea traffic, as numerous missionary accounts attest. Sereno Bishop later summed up the tribulations of transportation across the turbulent channels in his *Reminiscences of Old Hawaii*. The small coastal vessels, he wrote, "were usually in very filthy condition, swarming with cockroaches and reeking of bilge water," the decks crowded with natives with their calabashes and dogs. The narrow cabins were "intolerable for stench." All this and the often protracted trip, caused by calms and adverse winds, aggravated the accompanying seasickness.

Asa took Lucy through the heavy crowd on deck to the cabin, but oppressive heat and sickness forced her out of that "pesthole," as Artemas Bishop later termed it. In spite of every spot above being covered with humanity and its belongings, Asa managed to make space for her atop the companion way. She looked about at the massive throng on deck—475 men, women, children, babies, in all sorts of positions squeezed together along with hundreds of calabashes providing poi, fish, water and other provisions for the journey besides plenty of dogs with a few nests of puppies.

The natives treated Lucy with kindness, presenting her with fruit, vegetables and fresh meat. They inquired about her family and talked about how smarter the people in America must be. They fingered her clothes and minutely examined her hands, fingers, and nails. "They were all good, very good," Lucy declared. This was one of the less tormenting such trips she was to take.

Stuck again after they reached Maui, the Thurstons had to wait another four weeks to get the royal release for them to continue to Honolulu. This trip was more elegant — aboard the famous luxury ship *Cleopatra's Barge*, which the king had extravagantly purchased for about $ 80,000 worth of sandalwood. Hiram Bingham welcomed them on shore at their arrival in Honolulu, and the two weary travelers from Kailua were happy to join the missionary family.

Life in Honolulu

It was a heavy loss Lucy had to face at the end of this long-delayed journey. Having had no chance to wash her clothes for two months before they left Kailua and deprived of the opportunity of getting them from the ship at Maui,where fine streams flowed, she finally retrieved them at Honolulu, soaking wet and mostly ruined. Such a wardrobe was impossible to replace.

Almost three years of relative comfort and contentment blessed the Thurstons' lives as they remained safely in Honolulu. Lucy was the last of the six new wives to be a mother, giving birth twice in this period. Persis Goodale arrived September 28, 1821, and then Lucy Goodale on April 25, 1823. After the first birth, a tubercular condition Lucy had suffered in Marlboro during the death of her mother struck her down again, causing general concern that the mission family would lose her "by a quick consumption." But Lucy's hardy spirit prevailed, although this latent condition would trouble her more in the future.

Two days after daughter Lucy's birth, came the second contingent of missionaries to Honolulu. Mother Lucy was delighted to welcome her hometown friend Elizabeth Edwards, with her husband Artemas Bishop. With seven newcomers added to their ranks, the mission could expand their activities. William Richards would establish the Lahaina mission on Maui, aided by Charles Stewart until 1825, when his wife Harriet's illness would force him to return home. Richards would continue at Lahaina until 1838, when he would resign from the mission to aid the king spiritually and politically. Levi Chamberlain would ably conduct the business affairs of the mission until his death in 1849. Abraham Blatchely would serve as physician, much in demand from isle to isle, until his own health gave out and he returned to the United States in 1827.

The Thurstons were to return to Kailua, and Bishop, John Goodrich, and James Ely would also help expand stations on Hawaii. But first they must explore this land. Along with William Ellis, an English missionary from Tahiti, they visited the island's districts to decide where missions should be set up. Ellis remained to help the mission for 18 months and wrote a book on his observations in Hawaii.

More Suffering for Lucy

Lucy Thurston's last record of their stay in Honolulu was of being knocked to the ground by an over playful horseman. Aiming only to give her a scare, he guided his steed so close that the sudden proximity, plus trying to manage her bonnet and shawl in the blowing tradewinds, was too much and she fell. In bed suffering from her injuries, she felt strong indignation that such reckless acts could go uncontrolled in this savage country. Nor did the perpetrator of her afflictions receive any forgiveness by presenting Lucy with a shawl. She declared that she, "the wife of a man of holy calling was trifled with" and awarded the same sort of gift as had lured "many of the down-trodden women of the land into sin."

After that bad experience, Lucy had to return to Kailua late in 1823, again undergoing the disgusting conditions of a sea voyage. On board, she did accept without protest a bowl of tea inspite of seeing the high chief's servant cleaning the bowl with his girdle, dumping in the sugar with his hand, "and crumbling in the sea bread with his teeth." In the cabin she was almost overcome by odorous tobacco fumes and the stench of "nauseating messes of fish laid open." She was startled by swarms of cockroaches taking improper liberties with her person. And the suffocating heat and constant clamor of "songs and chit-chat" in the crowded room made it almost unbearable to Lucy, valiantly trying to care for her two babies.

From the deck above, with men, women, children, dogs and puppies massed together, sounds of tumult kept rousing Lucy from her much-needed sleep "in the gloom of midnight" and causing her "apprehensions that the vessel was floundering," because she considered the white captain's capabilities "on a level with the lowest sailor." She had to suffer through "four dreadful nights" before they reached Lahaina. Lucy arrived there almost exhausted and very grateful for a week's "haven of rest" with mission companions.

Then came the uncomfortable means of reboarding the vessel, each of the Thurston parents hanging onto a child as they sat on a board seat across the top of the canoe with their feet soaking wet. Aboard the ship again, Lucy found herself and her babies back in the same awful conditions, though just for one more night, arriving at Kailua Bay next afternoon. There John Young took care of them, providing a pleasant meal in comfortable conditions. After a peaceful night in "undisturbed repose," they found themselves back in a native abode, now with two babies and Hopu and Honolii serving as helpers. Again they provided "a spectacle for the rude throng" from morning to night.

The distressing voyage and all Lucy's trials in getting settled again in such conditions had brought back her pulmonary difficulties. But it was the situation of discomfort for her small children that bothered her the most.

Exploring the Island

The four exploring missionaries left Honolulu, June 24, 1823, and returned September 3. They first studied the Kona district, until Ellis joined them about three weeks later. Then they set out, July 18, traveling, talking with natives and learning the characteristics of this expansive island. They aimed "to investigate the religious and moral condition of the people, communicate to them the knowledge of Christ, unfold the benevolent objects of the mission, inquire whether they were willing to receive Christian teachers, and select the most eligible places for missionary stations." Also, they collected detailed information on the geography of the island and the "system of idolatry, the traditions, manners, and customs" of the people.

Most heartening after their long, hard journey was the sight of the first church being built by order of Governor Kuakini at Kailua. Using stones from an old temple built by King Umi in the 16th century, the workers formed a solid foundation for a native building 60 feet long, 30 wide, with walls 10 feet high, a door at each end, four windows on each side, and room for 600 to 1000 natives crowding on mats on the floor as was their custom.

8

THURSTONS — KEEP THE CHILDREN'S MINDS PURE

As Lucy was regaining her strength, she became alarmed that this native environment was dangerous to her children's virtue, noting that Persis was "picking up language and receiving permanent impressions." The only remedy was to keep the young children inside their rude habitation and forbid Persis from having any communication with the natives. To Lucy this was essential, even though she realized the cottage would thus become a dungeon for the child. So she concentrated on diverting her child's attention from such prevalent dangers.

What caused Lucy the most concern was the amoral attitude towards sex among the natives. Sarah Lyman at Hilo a decade later more explicitly detailed the facts. "Little boys and girls have as much intercourse as they please. Children are as wise as their parents. Things which are kept private from children at home [among us] are common talk among children here." Such dangers horrified Lucy and dominated her policies in her children's childhood years. She must save them from such contamination.

The other missionaries, so intent on their duties towards saving the heathen, agreed that their only way of protecting their beloved little ones from the evil infections about them was as Lucy put it, "children in childhood must be sent to America or be ruined." And so children were sent away to the spiritual safety of the homeland, heart-breaking as the partings were for both parents and the young ones.

But not Lucy. She declared she would "make better provision for them." Through "dark, sleepless, suffering midnight hours," her determined mind evolved a definite plan for their missionary home with three distinct departments, one exclusively for children, one for her native household help, and one for visiting natives. She would keep her children under her personal supervision, teaching them until they were ready for higher education.

44

Lucy's dream house became a reality two years later, when the Thurstons set about establishing their home on five arid acres of land about a third of a mile from the shore at Kailua. With fortress-like protection, they surrounded that area with a stone wall three feet wide and six feet tall and inside built a large thatched house with three apartments. Asa had his study table and chair and held his classes in a 25-square-foot reception room for natives, barred from advancing farther except by invitation. Beyond lay an equally large room for Lucy's classes and also for dining and the sphere for household helpers, who lived in their own house in a backyard. From this room, a hall led to a door, the sole opening to a three-acre yard in which stood the family house with sitting room and bedrooms.

Specially invited native friends might join Lucy in her sitting room, but then the children must exit through the back bedroom, the only means of reaching a safely walled-in yard, where the children could play out of earshot of the Hawaiian language. Guarding that portal, Lucy rejoiced at having her children safe from any inkling of native influence. The Thurstons called their domain Laniakea, "the broad heavens," taking the name of the large cave with two openings in their kitchen yard.

In this home they carefully instructed their children to develop their knowledge and their character. Lucy, an experienced school teacher, saw that they became proficient in grammar, geography, history, arithmetic, philosophy and whatever else she felt of value. Asa happily took up the Thurston role as singing master and served his Latin instruction after every meal as a pleasant exercise for their minds.

Earlier Lucy had run into a problem with taking the children to church each Sunday. Though they took books in English to read while their father was preaching in Hawaiian, Persis began to feel the uselessness of such a situation and tearfully entreated her mother, "What do I go to church for?" Lucy understood. She changed the routine to a stay-at-home hour of religious instruction.

Their native thatched shelter gave way in 1834 to a New England wooden house, awarded them by the mission. This dwelling had been a gift from friends to Charles Stewart, a missionary on Maui, who had been forced to leave because of his wife's poor health. Now Lucy saw her precious children better provided for.

Lucy realized continued restraint and dissociation from everything Hawaiian could thwart her children's development if continued too far. So, when the girls became 12 and 13, Lucy felt they had been rescued from the times "when thick darkness was still brooding over this polluted land." Now, with the girls' "Christian habits and principles" so well established, she allowed them to read and listen to Hawaiian and even gave each a class of little girls to teach. "But," she warned, "the restriction of non-intercourse among the natives is not removed."

45

The results of this partial freedom greatly pleased Lucy as she looked back over five years of her daughters' service as teachers. She saw they had "exerted a powerful influence over the native mind." But never were they allowed to become more intimate than as teachers — never as associates. Lucy in the 20th year of the mission was proud that she and Asa "stood alone in thus making the experiment of retaining children on heathen ground." More than 40 other missionary children had been shipped off in heart-breaking leave-takings to be educated in civilized America.

Hardships May Seem Fun When You're Young

Toilsome travel over mountainous Hawaii wore out some, but such harsh conditions failed to dampen the hardy, youthful spirit of adventuresome, 16-year-old Lucy Thurston during a long island excursion with her family in March 1839. The story appeared in the record of her life as revealed in her journal and published as *The Missionary's Daughter* after her death in 1841.

The family packed their clothes in two large calabashes and set off to visit the mission stations and gaze on the wonders of the volcano before mother Lucy and the five children were to depart for America about a year later. For three-year-old Thomas and eight-year-old Mary, a crib hanging from a pole carried by two of the ten natives took care of their transportation. Two chairs, carried in like manner, gave Lucy, Persis and their mother a chance to rest occasionally when the traveling got rough. Young Asa, 12 years old, must have had to step along with the other walkers.

They climbed, after their start on Wednesday morning, August 7, five miles up the side of Hualalai to get to the route to Kiholo, 20 miles north of Kailua. Down poured the rain. The young ones in the crib were covered, but the others tramped along for 15 more miles with wet feet and clothes only partly protected by shawls and umbrellas, mother and the two older girls taking turns in riding the chairs.

They stopped for lunch in a clearing among some tall *kukui* trees, kindled a fire, spread their provisions on large leaves and, sitting on some big rocks, appeased their hearty appetites. Starting on at three o'clock, they crossed a broad expanse of lava and arrived at Kiholo about nine o'clock, "weary and hungry." They awakened one of the sleeping villagers who showed them to a new house and gave them a mat to spread on the sand floor. There they supped, said their prayers, laid down and, fatigued, "slept as soundly as though we had reposed upon feathers."

In the morning, Asa preached to the people, thus carrying his holy message "to those who seldom hear instruction." Moving on, they found smooth walking over another lava flow several miles in extent. As the

46

burning sun beat down upon them, they rested a short time in the shade of a lava tube cave, then pushed on across this dreary region till, "exhausted with fatigue and heat," they found comfort on a beautiful grass-plot in a coconut grove and enjoyed a refreshing drink of coconut water from nuts that natives brought down from the trees.

Reaching Kawaihae about sunset, they rejoiced at finding civilized accommodations — the luxury of beds in the stone house of their friends Puna and his wife. Next morning they traveled by canoe supplied by Puna, 15 miles to Kohala, where Asa had another chance to speak to an attentive audience. Now they had to push ahead uphill, the wind driving the rain into their faces, as they pressed on ten miles inland to the mission houses. They reached there about six o'clock, "thoroughly drenched." "This would be a pleasant station," Lucy comments, "were it not for the frequent rains and high winds." Next day, Sunday, Asa preached to large audiences. As this was a new station, Lucy noted that the native people were as yet "more rude and uncivilized than at Kailua."

Now, on Monday, they could ride in turns on a horse provided by Isaac Bliss, the missionary then at Kohala. The bright spots of the 30-mile trip to Waimea were dining in a grove of trees, sighting Venus at noonday and then observing the occultation of the star. As night overtook them, they still had to pick their way "over steep hills, rough stones, and decayed trees" until they reached the road to the house of missionary Lorenzo Lyons at Waimea. The natives had to carry them over streams that crossed their path. By the time they had struggled through to Lyons' home by 10 o'clock, "extremely tired and faint," they were revived somewhat by their hearty reception, a warm supper and a good night's slumber.

After a day of much-needed rest, they set out on the long trek to Hilo. Walking through the uninhabited region on the north side of Mauna Kea was very pleasant. Lucy admired the "singular and beautiful appearance" of old *koa* trees with branches covered with white moss. At night they camped by a large fallen tree, built a big fire, spread their mat on the ground, and slept comfortably in spite of the cold. They felt less comfortable in the morning when they found their clothes "considerably damp with the dew."

Now on the eastern side of Mauna Kea at a height of several thousand feet, Lucy looked out at the ocean, appearing "like a high mountain above the clouds" below. Walking at that elevation, they suffered from fatigue more easily. In the distance they caught sight of herds of wild cattle and came across carcasses stripped of their hides by the hunters. At sundown as they reached "the edge of the woodland, which extends 16 miles towards the seacoast," Lucy reveled in the beauty about her. It was "enchanting" — behind her, "the heights of Mauna Kea, ... beautifully sprinkled with clumps of trees." Looking down ahead of her, she gazed upon the upper surface of "fleecy clouds, resting gracefully on the tops of trees," beyond that, "the 'illimitable sea,'" and to her right, "the blue peaks of Mauna Loa ... in the distance." It all gave her "emotions of sublimity."

They spent that night in a small, damp cave with water dripping from the roof. The men kept a fire burning. In the morning the guide and horses returned to Waimea, and the family entered the woods to make what they considered an eight-mile hike to reach the other side by noon. In high spirits, they laughed merrily at each other's mishaps as they tried to push along "through mud and water, over slippery bogs and stumps, till we could scarcely see the road before us." When one of the men who was sent ahead found some higher ground, they felt their way along to this place, still wet but solid enough to keep them from sinking. There they sat, "cold and weary, clothes saturated with water and well beplastered with mud."

They desperately wanted a fire, but all wood was soaked. "By taking one of the poles belonging to the crib, splitting it, and rubbing two pieces together for some time, the natives lighted the lamp, but despaired of being able to kindle a fire." But that did not satisfy the strong-willed matron. "Mother," her daughter admiringly noted, "used all her eloquence to encourage them, and they collected some green wood, cut it into small pieces, and in the course of three hours, a comfortable fire was built." They all joined in gathering ferns to spread on the ground as padding for their mat, changed their wet clothes, and retired supperless, fearing they were lost and their provisions would not hold out.

Next morning they "breakfasted on dry fish and sour poi, without any water to moisten our lips." Now the road grew worse and worse. So, about noon, it was with "inexpressible joy" that they met a white man coming to their assistance. He had heard of their predicament from a native they had sent ahead the night before. Both good and bad news he announced: it would be only two miles to the good road, but those were the worst miles yet. Next came "a messenger from Mrs. Coan with food and notes of welcome." By nine o'clock that evening they were forgetting their fatigue in the pleasant missionary home but "were very lame for several days."

After a week at the Hilo mission, they started on horseback on a two-day trip to the volcano. The second night they spent in "a little hut at the edge of the crater," from which they beheld several times during the night the fearful sight of raging fires and trembled at the "unearthly sounds."

Down into the crater they descended next morning, "sometimes passing within a few inches of a frightful chasm." As they walked across the floor of the crater, the "brittle shining crust ... often broke" under their weight. A large lava lake "boiled and foamed with great fury." When it kept spouting up higher and higher, they "quitted the place in great haste."

"During the night," Lucy continues, "the action was more violent than before. We saw fine eruptions, in which the redhot stones were thrown to the height of 50 or 60 feet. A new lake broke out and burned brightly during the night. We realized more than when in the crater, that we had been exposed to imminent danger, yet no life has ever been lost there."

With feet blistering, "probably the effects of walking in the hot volcano," they made their way next day 20 miles to Kapapala. The following night they spent at Punaluu, where Asa preached again and married a couple. On Saturday, they stopped three times to meet with the people. At Waiohinu, Asa held services on the Sabbath in a grove of *kukui* trees. "The people here greatly need a teacher," Lucy noted. "They are seldom privileged with hearing the gospel. This is an eligible place for a missionary station." John Paris was to establish that station two years later.

It took them until four o'clock Monday to descend a 300-foot-high precipice to reach the shore to continue on by canoe. They did not get away until noon next day, "as the people were required to work for the king." Then this family of seven with six natives set off in a single canoe, with their baggage and other men in a smaller one. The rough sea developed into high swells that threatened to capsize the canoes. Fearing they would be upset, they stopped at a small cove to remove their bonnets, shawls and shoes. The waves dashed so high that they once filled the canoe about a third. But soon they reached smooth water, put up the sail, and made rapid progress to arrive at a small village by dark. Taking off before daylight next morning, they reached Kaawaloa about two o'clock to enjoy "a pleasant season of social intercourse" with the missionaries Cochran Forbes and Mark Ives and their wives. Next day they were back home after an absence of four weeks.

They had spent 12 days forcing themselves over rugged terrain, often in miserable conditions of heat or rain, to cover from 15 to 30 miles a day. They had traveled by canoe about three full days to complete a tour of more than 300 miles. All this was the natural part of serving in the missionary ranks on the Big Island. They were staunch servants of the Lord and wasted little pity on themselves for all that they endured.

Two Trips Back to America

By 1840 the three older children, Persis almost 19, Lucy 17, and Asa 13, were ready for the advanced schooling their parents had been preparing them for. So off their mother sailed with all four children to New York, another six-month voyage in a bobbing sailing ship.

To young Lucy, long pressured into religious thought and devotion to the Lord, the trip proved a revelation of people in the world beyond her sphere. She found fresh attitudes and enjoyments which she did not know just how to take. She confessed in her journal, "I am ashamed of myself many times a day for giving way to so much laughter, but there are so many witty remarks made, that it is almost impossible to refrain from it. I have heard more jokes, hyperbolical expressions and comical remarks on board, than I did during seventeen years of my residence at the Sandwich Islands."

She felt guilty indulging in such merriment instead of dedicating her thoughts to the Lord. "I feel that I have parted far from God and my duty since being on board," she repented later. For she felt the ship was not the proper place for pious persons, "not favorable to growth in grace ... no retired place for meditation and prayer, I feel I have dishonored my Savior." Such had been her life. And soon would come her final freedom from the restraints of missionary life. At a home in New York she became ill and entered her heavenly resting place.

Again in 1850 the strong-willed Lucy took her last two children, Mary 19 and Thomas 14, aboard ship and on to her beloved homeland so they too might complete the education for which she had laid the foundation. This brave woman thus made five long voyages across the two oceans.

Kailua Church

The simple thatched church Governor Kuakini had erected in 1823 was a great glory to God in "the benevolent mind" of Asa Thurston when he returned to Kailua from Honolulu. "There may the mighty God vouchsafe his presence," he wrote to the Board, "and repenting sinners give joy to angels." Until the building was completed December 10, Asa conducted Sabbath services in the king's yard shaded by *kou* trees.

Asa beheld the vast opportunities before him. For he had traveled this "long-neglected island" and beheld "the miseries of the people ... sunk in all the pollution of sin, and groping their way through life in all the darkness of nature."Now he could guide the souls to heaven, bringing them inestimable happiness if saved from the misery they must endure if they remained lost. By July 1825, Asa could be proud that some 60 of his flock had "declared their resolution to forsake their heathen habits and enter on the service of the Lord." Weekly meetings brought in more applicants with "a good degree of proficiency in Christian knowledge, but also marks of hopeful piety."

As Asa's church soon became "too strait" to hold the throng of worshipers, Asa's eager followers set about in February 1826 constructing a grand new church edifice. Thousands of willing workers cut and dragged down timber and in a few weeks had erected and thatched an immense structure nearly eight times the size of the first church, providing space for a congregation of 4,800. "This new and magnificent temple had ... its large roof, sides, and ends, thatched, and its corners ornamented, and made an imposing appearance in the dingy village." The proud missionaries reported it to be "the largest and most elegant native building ever erected" in Hawaii. James Ely, from his station at Kaawaloa, preached the dedication sermon before a full house on September 27, a great missionary triumph, "a day of jubilee and rejoicing" never before experienced by these people. Pupils and teachers from 40 schools joined in the crowd of about 5,000 attending. The missionaries held their annual meeting and made several resolutions, including one to make known their religious requirements and restrictions no matter whether they might be opposed "to the former customs and present practice of the people."

It was March 9, 1828, that the first sure rewards of the mission's soul-saving efforts were baptized and received into the fellowship of the church — two men and four women. This public acclaim of the virtues of these few inspired many more in the congregation "to seek the Lord and ...

Kailua Church, Kailua-Kona, 1826-1835. Rendering by Ted-Bee — **Source: Author**

become hopefully new creatures." This resulted in twelve more men and eight women being propounded in August but cautiously not admitted to the church until November. Among the "persons of distinction ... was a chief of the first rank," Keoua, wife of Governor Kuakini. But not the governor himself. He was to become more of a perplexing problem.

Mokuaikaua Church

Aboard the crowded schooner from Kailua in December 1835, the missionaries on their way to the general meeting in Honolulu, beheld great flames ascending from the town. Three weeks later when they returned, they learned it was their precious church destroyed by an incendiary. A man who witnessed the disaster claimed he had never seen such mourning among the natives since the death of Kamehameha.

Mokuaikaua Church — Source: Author

Eager workers set about at once to build a permanent edifice. Women collected lava rocks. Men dived for coral, broke it up on hot fires and prepared the mortar. Large crews of workers climbed Hualalai to find and fell huge *ohia* trees, hew them into shape with adzes and apply herculean efforts to drag them down to Kailua. Within the year, construction was nearly complete. Lucy Thurston was pleased. "The belfrey, spire and vane, give quite an American look to our village," she wrote.

The great stone walls rose a solid 27 feet high with 50-foot *ohi'a* beams supporting the *koa* shingled roof, all complete in 13 months, the cornerstone laid January 1, 1836, and the building completed by January 31, 1837, and dedicated four days later. Thirteen-year-old daughter Lucy Thurston recorded, "The pillars which support it are painted to resemble marble; which last cost about $500. Most of the people sit on settees and chairs of their own construction,which look very well." The total cost of construction was between $2,000 and $3,000.

This introduction of benches instead of floor mats for some of the congregation somewhat restricted the number of people who could crowd into the church. By 1838 Artemas Bishop wrote that they now had about 4,000 on Sunday morning. So they built outside a lanai 165 feet long and 72 wide where most of the crowd could sit on the ground.

Francis Allyn Olmsted, a Yale alumnus and son of a professor, on a whaling expedition, visited Kailua in 1840 and in his *Incidents of a Whaling Voyage* reports that he visited the church with Dr. Andrews and declares it was "one of the best native places of worship on the island. It is built of dark grey compact lava, with a modest little cupola rising above its shingled roof, in which there is a bell to summon the people to worship on proper occasions. A row of glass windows above and below, gives to the building an appearance which would not be discreditable to many of our beautiful villages in New England. A congregation of two or three thousand assemble here for worship and, in addition to the benches in the body of the church, there are accommodations provided in a large gallery extending around on the sides of the building, and supported by slender columns painted blue. The pulpit is constructed of elegant *koa* wood, as also the panelling [sic] of the gallery."

Olmsted remarks then, "At the completion of this place of worship, I have been told, Governor Kuakini gave imperative commands that at the expiration of a month, no woman should be admitted inside the church who did not make her appearance in a neat gown, with a decent bonnet upon her head. His mandate was very generally complied with, as the fair sex have never been known to be dilatory in adopting the latest fashions."

Devotion Supreme

Asa toiled faithfully at Kailua for nearly 40 years, never leaving the islands, devoting himself whole-heartedly to the tasks before him. At home he diligently pursued the task of translating the Scriptures preparing 15 books of the Bible. His athletic abilities carried him along as he energetically moved about his mission territory. The strong force of his efforts to spread the love of God was brightened by his quiet humor so that he came to be remembered for his "Christian mirthfulness" which made him "agreeable in social life, and ... buoyant in spirit under all the trials of missionary labor." Added to this virtue was "his peculiarly rich and well trained voice," which produced "a feast of melody." Thus he was fondly remembered when his days were over.

It took strokes of paralysis to make Asa give up his service at Kailua in 1861. He and Lucy withdrew to Honolulu. Two years later they visited California in hope that the change of climate might improve him. After another five years in Honolulu, the end mercifully came to the suffering Asa on March 11, 1868, almost 48 years after he had arrived at the islands. With his great white beard he appeared like a biblical patriarch. In this long missionary life he had set an impressive record of service and attainments.

No less outstanding than Asa's strong character was the valiant spirit of Lucy Thurston. She struggled and suffered and overcame afflictions of the flesh and of the spirit. Three years after her early attack of consumption, following the birth of Persis, she found that "the hard struggles of pioneer life, its efforts and its privations, again prostrated me with pulmonary complaints. Nature triumphed and I was again free.

"Scarcely a year had elapsed, when we were visited by storms of fierce winds and deluging rains, uncommonly long and severe ... home was damp, cold, and bleak ... Disease took fast hold of my frame, and became obstinate. The very breath I drew daily fastened on my mind the impression I should soon die of consumption. Four years passed before I was restored to my vigor."

Then in June 1831, on the ship from Kailua to Honolulu in the brig's dark dungeon of a cabin, which reminded her of "the Black Hole of Calcutta," Lucy had to suffer through the birth of her daughter Mary, with the unprofessional aid of only her husband and Artemas Bishop.

From April 1850, it took her three months to recover from her "nearly fatal mistake of taking strychnine instead of quinine." After experiencing "multiple ills" for a fortnight, she had sought relief by use of a tonic but was confused by the label. In September this ever-resilient woman took her first long voyage to America with her children and returned the same way.

Tumor of the breast brought on another experience of Job's lot. Lucy sat for an hour and a half in a chair while a doctor cut out her entire breast, the glands beneath her arm, and sewed up and bandaged the foot-long bloody wound. After it was all over, the doctor took her hand and admiringly declared, "There is not one in a thousand who would have borne it as you have done."

Such was the superior strength and faith in the Lord of one of the first missionaries to Hawaii. The frailest of her family, who fully expected she was "sacrificing herself to early death" in that heathen land, Lucy kept active to her death, the last of the pioneer missionaries who remained in Hawaii. Lucy and Mercy Whitney, who lived to be 77, were the only pioneer missionary representatives left in Hawaii to join the mission's 50th anniversary celebration in 1870.

Lucy remained "a bright, active and lively old lady of 75 years, who drives herself to church Sundays in a one-horse chaise, and has her own opinions of passing events," as Charles Nordoff saw her in Honolulu in 1871. "How she has lived in the tropics for 50 years without losing an atom of the New England look puzzles you," he remarked, "but it shows you also the strength which these people brought with them, the tenacity with which they clung to their habits of dress and living and thought, the remorseless determination which they imported with their effects around Cape Horn." Nordhoff found it "a most touching sight to see, on a Sunday after church, Lucy, Dr. Judd's senior by many years but alert and vigorous, taking hold of his hand and tenderly helping him out of the church and to his carriage."

Thus she lived on to October 13, 1876, just 16 days short of her 81st birthday, her life span a month longer than that of her hardy husband. Considering all she had suffered over the years, she was a most remarkable woman.

Thurston Descendants

Persis Goodale Thurston was the first child born at Mission House in Honolulu, September 28, 1921. In 1841 her mother Lucy made a trip to the United States with her children. Her 18-year-old daughter Lucy Goodale Thurston died in New York. Persis, age 19, entered Mt. Holyoke Seminary and then taught there three years until she married Townsend Elijah Taylor at Brooklyn, N. Y., August 12, 1847. They came to Honolulu, June 28, 1848. Townsend preached at Lahaina to 1851, then at Honolulu Bethel a year before becoming pastor of Second Foreign Church (later Fort Street Church), until 1854. Poor health prompted him to move to California, where he died at Nordhoff, February 12, 1883. The Taylors had six children.

Asa Goodale Tyerman Thurston, born 1827, attended Williams College in Massachusetts and married Sarah Andrews, third child of seven of Lorrin and Mary Ann Andrews, who came with the 3rd company on March 20, 1828. Asa died in 1859, Sarah, in 1899.

Lorrin Andrews Thurston, son of Asa and Sarah, with a law degree from Columbia University, became a Honolulu attorney and held government positions starting in 1886. As minister of the interior, his interest in parks led to building the first road to the volcano, the first Volcano House, and the Kilauea Observatory. The Thurston lava tube bears his name. A leader in the revolution of 1893, he represented the Provisional Government in Washington, D.C., helping make arrangements for annexation in 1898, when he became a commissioner. From 1899 to 1915 he was active in plantation and railway developments, became publisher of the *Honolulu Advertiser* in 1900. His first wife was Margaret Clarissa Shipman, daughter of William and Jane Shipman, missionaries at Waiohinu, from 1855 to William's death in 1861.

Lorrin Potter Thurston was the son of Lorrin Andrews Thurston by his second wife, Harriet Potter, and successor to his father as publisher, until he retired in 1961 to his estate on Kailua Bay in Kona until his death, October 6, 1984, at age 84.

Thurston Twigg-Smith, great-great-grandson of missionary Asa Thurston, is the present *Honolulu Advertiser* publisher, son of Lorrin Potter Thurston's sister Margaret, who married William Twigg-Smith.

9

POWERFUL
ARTEMAS
BISHOP

Artemas and Delia Stone Bishop — Source: HMCS Library

Asa Thurston had insisted that his Kailua Mission absolutely needed Artemas Bishop, one of the three ordained ministers in the second company in 1823. Asa acted on behalf of Lucy determined on having her old-time New England friend, Artemas's wife Elizabeth Edwards, as her companion in Kailua. The Bishops, after a short time at Waimea, Kauai, joined the Thurstons at Kailua in 1824.

Artemas Bishop, graduate of Union College and Princeton Theological Seminary, was a vigorously active and hard-working fellow, similar to Asa Thurston in these respects, though more on the practical side and less religiously demanding. He was more outgoing and outspoken than others so that some sensitive ones felt he was "wholly wanting in common prudence."

The natives admired his physique and his commanding attitude, for he stood six feet three inches and weighed 250 lbs. They called him "Big Man." On travels they carried him across streams and afterwards rubbed his tired legs and shoulders and then heaped piles of food before him.

Bishop quickly acquired mastery of the language, as Thurston had, and helped carry forward the work of the mission. In fact, it was later reported that ambitious Artemas one Sunday overdid himself so much by preaching six sermons to some 2,500 people that he fell into a fever that laid him up for ten weeks before he could preach again.

Artemas visited the northern areas of the island on his tour of 1823 and again, in 1825, during an eight-day hike to Hilo. Next year he traveled there again to accompany Queen Regent Kaahumanu on her tour to impress on her people the duties of Christianity. Bishop reported that she warned them against "all their most abominable heathen practices, as well as their vices contracted by an intercourse with foreigners ..." In September 1828, Bishop once more visited Kohala, examined nearly 2,000 scholars and married 44 couples. Next day, "Examined 31 schools ... married 31 couples, and retired weary to rest, after having assisted Walawala in the cases of transgressors who had forsaken their wives."

On the Sabbath he held open-air services both morning and evening under a shady grove of breadfruit and *kukui* trees to about 4,000 people. On Monday, after marrying eight more couples, he headed back to Kailua, where he summed up his accomplishments on this eight-day tour to Waimea, Hamakua and Kohala: 111 schools examined, including 64 in Kohala, 134 couples married and preached 10 times.

Besides religious services in Kailua, these two ministers took weekly turns at preaching in villages six miles north or south along the coast, going by canoe or on foot, also superintending native teachers in local schools. Thus laboriously they built up health protection, morality and education.

First Tragic Death — Elizabeth Bishop

At Honolulu, Lucy had eagerly welcomed Elizabeth Bishop, her dear friend from back home. Then while the month-long discussions were going on, Elizabeth suffered agonies in giving birth to a dead baby. That ordeal over, and the Bishops later settled at Kailua, Lucy happily profited by the companionship and eager help Elizabeth offered. They "acted in concert .... to lift our female population, by meeting with them every Friday P.M." They taught the women to "lead in prayer" and "with great freedom, and seriousness too, express their religious convictions." They inspired them to feel a sense of shame in their "impurity of speech," by criticizing them for indecent talk in the presence of civilized persons such as themselves.

Elizabeth's rosy-hued and radiant appearance of health as she "exerted herself in the day school, in the Sabbath school, and in the female Friday Meeting" greatly pleased Lucy. On April 6, 1825, Elizabeth produced a daughter Jane, and then, on February 7, 1827, a son Sereno Edwards was born to her while at the Ely home at Kaawaloa.

Sereno was destined to become a missionary in Hawaii 26 years later after graduating from Amherst and Auburn Theological. He served as Seamen's Chaplain at Lahaina, 1853-1862, then, joining the ABCFM, spent three years at Hana, Maui, taught at Lahainaluna Seminary in 1865, and served as principal there from 1866 to 1877. After four years with the government survey department, he became an independent surveyor. He edited a monthly paper, *The Friend*, from 1887 to 1902, when he wrote his *Reminiscences of Old Hawaii*.

Soon after Sereno's birth, Elizabeth's health failed. She lay in her bed for more than half a year without finding relief from her internal suffering. In desperation, the family finally sailed to Honolulu in search of better medical assistance. Though a doctor diagnosed her case as dyspepsia, he failed to relieve her suffering during several more months there. Arriving back at Kailua, Elizabeth was welcomed by several native women aboard the vessel. "I shall soon die," she told them, "and my unfaithfulness to you makes me afraid to meet God in judgment." This perplexed the native women. "If after doing so much for us," they said, "she is afraid to meet God, how will it be for us?"

To provide more personal care for Elizabeth, the Bishops went to live with the Thurstons. By now the suffering girl was enduring such excruciating torture that even a spoonful of soup seemed to set her stomach afire and render her sleepless. She became extremely feeble, emaciated and distressingly nervous. The Thurstons moved to their other cottage to allow her quiet. But, within a week, Elizabeth and Artemas had their own cottage for her quiet abode. Devoted natives had quickly put up another thatched building as "their work of love" for their dear teachers.

Elizabeth's suffering grew even worse with "paroxysms of agony, and the frenzy of delirium." Finally, one midnight, the pain subsided. "Let me depart in peace," she murmured as she sank into everlasting rest. This was February 21, 1828, the first adult death in the Sandwich Islands Mission.

When it was necessary to remove her body 11 years after her burial, the mission family found in Elizabeth's spinal column a prominent curve. Two years later in America, Lucy talked with Mrs. Ephraim Spaulding, a returned missionary's wife, who, having suffered the same way, was convinced that Elizabeth also had been the victim of curvature of the spine.

Artemas Pushes On

Elizabeth's place in the Kailua Mission and in the Bishop family was taken by Delia Stone, member of the 3rd company, which arrived March 30, 1828. She was assigned to Kailua and Artemas married her on December 1 that year. She took care of the two children with true affection and efficiency, assisted Artemas with his children's school and supervised a school for women in arithmetic and Bible.

Though other missionaries strove to restrict the use of tobacco, Bishop felt no compunctions about having the natives raise their crops, produce 7,100 cigars and sell them at $10 a thousand to provide funds for building his house. In exchange, he supplied them with the books and slates they yearned for. He claimed this was the way to furnish the missionaries with good houses without putting extra strains on the meager financial resources of the mission. He pointed out that the Thurstons had lived there seven years and had a house that "leaks like a riddle." The Bishops had been living in two thatched cottages in the village.

In 1831 Artemas built a stone house with a cellar at the corner of Alii Drive and Hualalai Road. He used mostly *koa*, Hawaiian mahogany, then quite plentiful, with *koa* shingles for roofing, from which the family got its supply of rain water. The two-story house had three rooms on each floor, with lanais on the seaward side. The kitchen was equipped with a brick oven and an antiquated iron stove.

Asa and Artemas translated the scriptures, wrote hymns, prepared school textbooks, and provided medical aid. Artemas had a good supply of drugs on hand, including mercury for treating "the fearful syphilitic ulcers which disfigured so many of the people's limbs and faces." He was also adept at blood-letting according to his son Sereno.

In January 1832, the Bishop family went by canoe to Kawaihae to escort Dwight and Charlotte Baldwin with their 2-month-old son to their first post at Waimea, and help the Baldwins get started. For three months, Artemas did most of the preaching, while Delia took charge of school work, as the Baldwins acquired language skills.

The Bishops carried on the work of the Kailua Mission with the Thurstons for eight years after the death of Elizabeth. As Delia's health suffered from conditions in the heat of Kailua, they transferred to Ewa on Oahu in 1836 and developed that station for the next 20 years. Artemas still made monthly visits there later, while he was assisting at Kawaiahao Church and conducting theological classes at Honolulu. He died December 18, 1872, almost attaining age 77. Delia died April 13, 1875, about a month and a half before reaching age 75.

10

DOCTOR SETH ANDREWS SERVES NOBLY

Seth Andrews (1890) — Source: HMCS Library

Not since Dr. Thomas Holman's brief stay had the Kailua Mission been blessed with the presence of a doctor. The whole island rejoiced with the appointment of Dr. Seth Lathrop Andrews. He was granted the house that Artemas Bishop had built.

Both Seth and his wife Parnelly had rated high with Mrs. Amos Cooke, one of their companions with the 8th company that arrived at Honolulu, April 9, 1837, bringing 17 additional missionaries. She considered the amiable doctor "one of the pleasantest men that I am acquainted with, ... devoid of selfishness" in his willingness to perform "those numerous acts of kindness which serve to strengthen the bonds of affection which he silently throws around the hearts of all." His fine qualities were ably supplemented by those of his partner Parnelly Pierce, whom Mrs. Cooke judged to be "a superior woman" with "a remarkably sweet disposition, great prudence and penetration, full of sympathy, generosity, affection, and devotedness to the work of the Missions."

Home of Dr. Seth Andrews (1900) — source: Baker-Van Dyke
Collection

Seth Andrews, born at Putney, Vt., June 24, 1809, son of a Congregational minister, had a degree from Dartmouth College and had studied at Medical College, Fairfield, N. Y., then practiced at Pittsford, N. Y., where he married Parnelly Pierce less than five weeks before they sailed to take up missionary life in the Sandwich Islands. Little did he realize the strenuous demands of serving on the island of Hawaii, trying to minister to the needs of several far-flung missions.

Besides his medical duties, he was also to minister to the religious development of the natives. Thurston gave him the job of serving as superintendent over ten Sunday School classes learning on the "verse-a-day system." Calls of need for his medical service came to be considered by the mission as unhappy interruptions of his work as teacher and preacher. Seth loved children and enjoyed teaching them his special interests, botany, astronomy, and chemistry, and natural history.

Dr. Henry Lyman recalls in his *Hawaiian Yesterdays* several pleasant instances of Dr. Andrews' versatile knowledge and abilities. When young Henry in Hilo had failed in many frustrating attempts to make a workable rat trap, he reports, "Dr. Andrews came to the rescue and whittled out one that would work." With that sure-fire device the boys "massacred the foe until not one was left to lament the extinction of his tribe." When Henry and his friends engaged in war games, "the versatile Dr. Andrews" helped them add reality by showing them how to make explosive powder. And Parnelly also helped in the boyhood pleasures by supplying guidance in drawing "to sketch the beautiful landscape."

To take care of the health of the other overworked brethren, Seth had to journey long distances to Waimea, Kohala and Hilo. Elias Bond, rather isolated at Kohala, was most grateful for the good doctor's timely assistance. On March 6, 1843, he was greatly relieved that "Dr. Andrews was very unexpectedly and providentially with us, on his way from Hilo," when Mrs. Bond experienced the premature birth of a son that died within an hour. Among Bond's preserved letters were also medical directions from Dr. Andrews "for the sick baby or wife, whose distress passed the limits of the many medical books on the study shelves in Kohala."

Of less vital though quite serious concern to Elias Bond was his use of "Dr. Andrews' measure" for the tailor in Honolulu to cut out cloth for a sack coat for him. When the cloth arrived he found it "cut for a man not less corporal in development than our good Brother Bishop!"

Second Tragic Death — Parnelly Pierce Andrews

Seeing that the health of other missionaries on the island suffered from the climate and their exhausting efforts, Andrews wrote the Board pleading for assistance, asking them if they would let these self-sacrificing men and women "lie down in an early grave for lack of a few additional missionaries?"

Dr. Andrews was to realize well whereof he spoke. By 1846 the toilsome conditions of trying to take care of the health problems in the six widely scattered stations, and having to struggle over mountains, through deep valleys and across sometimes dangerous streams, gradually wore him out. His strength gave out and he succumbed to dysentery, which had already removed their daughter Lucy and the doctor's Hawaiian boy assistant. Seth lay confined to his bed for months as Parnelly did her best to take care of him.

Their eight-year-old son George Pierce did what he could to comfort his vainly struggling parents. Parnelly had lost her second child, Elizabeth, before she was a year old in 1842. Daughter Lucy had lived less than six months longer before she died in 1845. Then, during Parnelly's trials in nursing Seth back to health, she delivered their second son Charles Thurston. Such a siege of mental and physical cares became too great a load for Parnelly. She collapsed September 27, 1846, and died two days later.

Overcome by grief but longing to preserve some likeness of his beloved Parnelly, the poor doctor labored with shaky hands through the night trying to form a death mask of her in plaster of Paris. A missionary wife, finding him at dawn struggling with this task, tried to help, "but," she made note, "having no experience in the art, we did not succeed."

Prominent among the few tombstones in Mokuaikaua Church's front yard stands the tall white marker in Parnelly's memory, the only one there commemorating the valiant service of those early missionaries. On it is engraved, "PARNELLY P. wife of Dr. Seth L. Andrews died at Kailua September 29, 1846 Aged 39 y'rs assistant missionary of the ABCFM ten years 'I know that my Redeemer liveth.'"

Dr. Andrews, by then over the worst of his illness but still feeble, with his two sons found refuge in the Thurston home. Still suffering from grief for the loss of his devoted Parnelly, he took the boys to Lahainaluna in December but responded the next year to a call to return to Kailua. Then his young son Charles Thurston died at the age of 18 months on January 2, 1848.

Unable to revive his spirits in a place with such sad memories, he took his one remaining child George with him to America, arriving May 11, 1849. Recovering his health, he married again three years later, expecting to return to his mission work. As the ABCFM was then bringing to a close its support for work in Hawaii, Dr. Andrews settled at Romeo, Mich., where he remained active until his death, February 17, 1893, at the age of 83. A fine marble tombstone marks the graves of Seth and his wife in the Romeo cemetery. His surviving son George became a physician and returned later to Hawaii for his health.

11

GOVERNOR KUAKINI
AND GOD

Governor Kuakini — **Source: Hawai State Archives**

Kuakini, a man of high intelligence, played an important part not only as governor of the island of Hawaii from 1820 to 1845 and acting governor of Oahu from April 1831 to August 1833, but also as a valuable aid to the missionaries. As the younger brother of Queen Kaahumanu and of Keeaumoku, governor of Maui from 1820 to 1824, Kuakini ranked high. Given the name John Adams as a child, he preferred to be called by that name and so is referred to variously as Kuakini, Adams, John Adams or John Adams Kuakini.

Hiram Bingham first took note of this "tall, portly, gigantic figure of a native chieftain, in his prime" as he stood out prominently in the crowd when the missionaries landed at Kailua. Kuakini's huge proportions impressed all who wrote about him. Missionary Charles Stewart saw him as a man "so remarkably stout, as to be unequal to any exertion, and scarcely able to walk without difficulty." Reports placed his weight at between 400 and 500 pounds, making him have to turn sideways to enter the doorway of Mokuaikaua Church. Bradford Smith pictures him riding a "poor horse [that] sagged and nearly broke beneath him." But, as he was a great chief, "Men crouched and crawled in his presence."

Though Governor Kuakini generously contributed to the missionaries' successes, he often strayed from the straight and narrow path they expected him to follow. In his youth he had lived a rather checkered career being remembered as "a liquor-drinking, pleasure-loving chief —a patron of thieves —a stealer of wives."

Even in the more broad-minded sphere of Hawaiian society, cuckolding could sometimes prove dangerous as Kuakini found out to his own affliction. Discovered "associating in sin" with a man's wife, he ran off, jumped a wall and broke some bones in his foot. This physical "blemish ...changed a fine handsome person into an old man," historian John Ii regretted.

As Kuakini had already learned from foreigners at the court of King Kamehameha at Kailua, his keen mind was eager to grasp greater knowledge and examine new ideas. When the missionary press in Honolulu started turning out the marvels of printed communication in 1822, Kuakini grabbed the opportunity to become one of the first to master reading and writing.

Doubts About Religion

Though he learned from books, the governor was also a great student of people. He did not quietly accept doctrine; he had his doubts and questions. When William Ellis met him in 1823, he was impressed by Kuakini's sincere "desire after knowledge and improvement." He was then about 25, "tall, stout, well made, and remarkably handsome" and with "a great degree of native dignity."

At a later meeting, Adams showed his keen curiosity about these new religious ideas, "particularly respecting the resurrection of the body, the destruction of the heavens and the earth at the last day, and the final judgment." Then he wanted to know the location of heaven and hell, but Ellis had to admit no one had ever come back from either place. When told about the Bible, he inquired why if most people have read the Bible, do "such numbers of them swear, get intoxicated, and do so many things prohibited in that book?" He had observed other white men he had encountered.

Quite inquisitive about this new religion, he devised a scheme to test the powers of this new God at the funeral of his brother Keeaumoku, governor of Maui, in 1823. According to Hawaiian historian Kamakau, Adams slyly removed from the coffin the body of his brother before the funeral. He just wanted "to see whether the foreign God would know the difference."

When the Thurstons returned to Kailua in 1823, they found Governor Adams "a noble looking man" who had risen "higher in civilized habits than any other chief of his time; he [even] used coffee and tea daily on his own table, dressed uniformly in American costume, and was distinguished for a knowledge of the English language." And he was living in "a very pretty framed house with green window shades ... brought from America .... It made quite a distinguished appearance" as it "was placed in a capacious yard surrounded by a wall 10 feet in height, and about the same in width." Here indeed was civilized progress exemplified.

"Adams [was] shrewd as he was huge," Bradford Smith asserts. He craftily figured on maintaining his native prerogatives while also availing himself of whatever attractive advantages the missionaries offered, at the same time enjoying benefits from the church's worldly opponents. He set up price controls for goods and saw to it that the missionaries paid cash at set prices for whatever they bought from whalers. Nor did he allow them to offer goods in trade to buy goats in the country —just with cash at the price he had set.

Friend, Supporter and Uncertainty

Adams never became a total believer, the kind with "no cavilling or questioning the truth of our doctrines" and for whom "a 'thus saith the Lord' is a sufficient warrant of...faith." Such was certainly not John Adams Kuakini, high chief, clever politician, and seeker after the luxuries of life.

Just the same, Adams was a staunch supporter of missionary principles and enterprise that he favored. He provided for the building of three successive churches at Kailua. The Thurstons greatly appreciated such excellent help: "His influence was altogether on the side of civilization, order, and improvement," Lucy wrote. "He gave good laws, patronized schools, and for a time had both a reading and writing school in his own yard, under his own instruction. He read through his English Bible with care, and assisted in translating the Scriptures, asked a blessing at table, and attended public worship regularly." His Christian manners were certainly praiseworthy and his helpfulness admirable.

With all this in his favor, he must surely now be welcomed into their church in Christian comradeship. After all, other high chiefs had been granted church membership. Those missionaries looked not upon his deeds but into his heart. These men of God saw that "he had not yet himself come into the ranks of total abstinence from intoxicating liquor, nor of profession of faith and repentance."

So in spite of all his praiseworthy great works and his expressed devotion to the missionary cause, the stern followers of God's will denied him membership in their holy church. Not being able to show himself humble and contrite, a willing and devoted follower of Jesus Christ, he was deemed unworthy to be admitted to the ranks of the pure in heart.

With their strict standards of conduct, the missionaries turned him away even from the dedication of his own grand church in 1826. His forlorn situation is dramatically depicted by Albertine Loomis. She tells that "the chosen ones gathered together and closed the doors on him. He beat on the wooden panels ... and raged mightily..." Finally he got up and "stomped home.... All night long he read the English Bible and begged, "Teach me how I shall find a new heart and become one of God's people.""

This temporary contriteness and declaration of holy aims could not keep a man of his caliber passively submissive. Two years later another spiritually regretful scene occurred. Adams, having lived with a string of wives, finally decided to ask Bingham's blessing for holy matrimony to the woman that held his fancy at the time. When Hiram went to check up on the governor's former alliances, he found the chief had imbibed too deeply and refused to marry him in that condition. In drunken fury Adams drove the missionary out. Still chagrined at being left out of the chosen few of the high chiefs in the church, Kuakini used his wits and his learning to address a letter to the Board in Honolulu thanking them for a book and a portrait of J. Q. Adams and assuring them, "We have a large church, and its being filled every Sabbath is, I think, a good sign that the glorious light of the Gospel is doing great good for the removing of the clouds of heathenism from our once dark minds. I shall always love the missionaries and take care of them." He had acquired the proper missionary style of expression and was doubtlessly sincere in his respect and consideration for the teachers and preachers.

Even so, the guardians of the sanctity of their church were not fully satisfied. Bingham explained that "though for years he had been as favorable to Christianity and to our mission, as this letter shows him to be, and though his wife and some 20 others were reckoned as converts, yet he was not so reckoned by the missionaries, who, though they appreciated his kindness and cooperation, could give him no encouragement to think himself converted. They required something more than a readiness to read and hear the Word of God, to aid in building churches and in supporting schools, and to treat the foreign teachers with deference and kindness."

Ups and Downs of Salvation

By 1829, Adams was managing to behave so that even strait-laced Bingham could concede "indications that Adams, who had been instructed nearly ten years, had come, at length, to admit the high claims of the Word of God," even though previously "he had appeared ... to have his heart much interested in personal religion. It would seem difficult ," Bingham kept explaining, "if not beyond reasonable explanation, for a man of high rank, trained in heathenism and habitually exposed to the influence of artful enemies of truth, the drinking habits and sceptical slang of foreigners ... for a man... who daily took a little of the deleterious stimulus ... for a man of middle age, whose giant heart had been confirmed in the love of sin, ever to break away, and feel deeply and right on the subject of personal religion."

Yet, in spite of all this, Thurston and Bingham felt encouraged by Kuakini's "evidence of gracious change during the past year ... from being indifferent, has become our warm friend, and from a besotted sceptic has become moral and devout..." They were much impressed by his declaration after the Sabbath morning sermon, when he told his people, "I have resolved to serve the Lord, and seek for the salvation of my soul through Jesus Christ."

Bingham understood the governor's human frailty: "He read the Bible with more constancy.... But being free, he thought, like many Christians in the world, that a habitual or occasional glass, and a careful attention to wealth, was quite allowable and consistent with a Christian profession."

But at last, came Kuakini's day of glory. "On the 25th of October [1829] Gov. Adams, the only surviving brother of Kaahumanu, and 16 others were added to the church at Kailua." Adams had attained another political goal as leader of his people, if not a strictly spiritual one. As acting governor on Oahu the next year, he enforced new strict Christian laws to deter offenses by white men. "If you sell any more rum," he warned, "I will strip you of your property and tear down your houses."

Back home in Kailua in 1833, two years later, he started a business of weaving cotton grown on his own plantation. He had sent his young wife and others to Maui to learn from a missionary teacher there, Lydia Brown, how to work with the wheel and loom.

In 1836, the governor traveled to Kealakekua to greet Theodore-Adolphe Barrot, French diplomat on the sloop-of-war *Bonite*. He describes Kuakini as a man 6 feet 3 inches tall, dressed in a blue vest, grey pantaloons, shoes without stockings, and a straw hat. He spoke very good English. Though he had a reputation of being intelligent but quite avaricious, he generously supplied the ship with ample provisions, as usual from "the poor islanders." But he did get paid with iron bars and tools.

On board the *Bonite*, the governor and another chief even larger than himself demonstrated their insatiable appetites "in perfect keeping with their immense corpulency." Ignoring the temperance laws, they did full justice to the French wines, but later in the presence of Kapiolani and the missionary Forbes, Adams dutifully "scarcely dared to pour the least quantity of wine into his water," though at other times "he carefully avoided having any water put into his wine." Receiving these visitors at his home later, Kuakini offered the hot, thirsty Frenchmen nothing, until they requested water. Then he did order wine for them. But what amazed his foreign guests was the sight of the royal couple dining— Kuakini and his wife stretched out competing with ravenous messiness to empty large calabashes of baked pork, salted raw fish and poi. How different from the governor's restrained behavior aboard the *Bonite* properly using knives, forks, and spoons.

Always A Worldly Man

Kuakini kept his sights not so much on heaven as on his lifetime enjoyments on earth. By the next decade, he had slipped again. Titus Coan wrote he felt "overwhelmed" at the idea of Adams marrying again, concluding, "it is adultery of the most unblushing sort." His latest wife was a girl about 18 years of age from Hilo. Coan deplored the character of this man who "loved power and flattery, and, like Jehu, 'he took no heed to walk in the law of the Lord with all his heart.'" And he condemned his display of autocratic rule "when he swept around the island" with 20 or 30 men, women, and children as attendants, sometimes camping for a month in one spot and "consuming almost all the eatables within two or three miles."

With his love for wealth, Kuakini bucked Thurston's prohibition against raising tobacco. He ordered, "Listen to your teacher; do what I tell you. I tell you to plant tobacco." Coan had heard also that the governor sometimes hid a barrel of rum for his agents to sell at two dollars per bottle. He reports that Thurston had suspended Adams from the church for a long time, until he "fell ill and died" on December 9, 1844.

Kuakini led his own life, enjoying other religious friends in his latter days. Two Catholic priests came to Kona in 1840, and the governor put them up in Kaahumanu's "vacant and rambling old palace" near Mokuaikaua Church. They put up a small chapel with a large white cross. In public, Adams put on a cold front towards "the cursed *Palani* (Frenchmen)" to maintain his Protestant reputation and support. And Thurston, fearing to lose such an important ally, "was quick to reinstate the governor as a member in good standing."

The governor had such high respect for Father Heurtel that he addressed him in Hawaiian terms as his "beloved companion," "intimate friend," or "my good friend Ernest," providing food for the priest and granting him other favors. The governor came to admire the priest for his dauntless attitude. When Father Heurtel stalked into the governor's home and bluntly accused him of not observing agreements in the Franco-Hawaiian treaty, Kuakini angrily turned his back as he lay on his mat. The priest kept on threatening. "Exasperated, the governor shouted to the priest: `I can throw you out of here if I wish to!' Calmly, Father Heurtel came a step nearer, crossed his arms, and in a forceful voice said, 'Why don't you? I dare you!'... Kuakini turned toward his visitor, smiled, and they shook hands." Kuakini was especially grateful to this intrepid priest because, after the Protestant doctor told him he had but a short time to live, Father Heurtel got him out of bed and about within two days.

In the governor's last illness, Father Heurtel tried to convert Adams to the Catholic faith. Unsure of the divine truth, he responded," "They [Protestants] say their faith is the true one, and you say yours is; so we'll let it go at that." The leader of each faith held similar opinions of this chief they never succeeded in converting wholeheartedly. Coan, at Kuakini's death bed, heard him declare, "I am a great sinner, and I do not think the Lord will care for me or save me." At that Coan concluded, "There we leave him, thankful for all the good he did, and sorrowful that his light did not shine brighter." Father Heurtel summed up his impression of the great chief: "He had wronged us too much that I should praise him, and has done us too much good that I should speak evil of him."

12

KAPIOLANI SPREADS CHRISTIANITY

Of truer Christian character than Kuakini was Kapiolani, high chiefess of Kaawaloa on Kealakekua Bay. She, who had been "very intemperate, and for some time after hearing the Gospel lived with two husbands" (though she had given up a couple), finally endured the five years of training and then six months of strict missionary supervision and instruction to insure acceptance to the restricted Christian church. With seven other chiefs, she finally received the supreme recognition on December 5, 1825, and became a baptized Christian.

Kapiolani and her husband Naihe, king's orator, then became eager to provide a station on their lands at Kaawaloa, 16 miles south of Kailua on the north side of Kealakekua Bay "to lead her, her husband, and her people, in the paths of Christianity." They held Sabbath religious worship in several villages, "where some of them would lead in prayer, read, sing, and exhort, and tell of the great salvation." They also started schools. They often sent a boat to Kailua to bring a missionary to conduct services beneath a large *kou* tree near where Captain Cook had lost his life and where his monument now stands. They built a small church with "a neat pulpit, two rows of seats, three doors and 18 or 20 windows." Asa Thurston came down from Kailua, March 29, 1824, to preach the dedication sermon.

To demonstrate their readiness to take care of a mission family, the chiefs built a good house for their use and agreed to supply them with fresh food and carry water down for them from two or three miles away. So James Ely left Kailua in 1824 to take over this assignment.

Kapiolani Defies Pele

Just her local service to the Lord's cause was not enough for Kapiolani's missionary zeal. She felt urged to aid the struggling new Hilo Mission where Joseph Goodrich and Samuel Ruggles were "suffering privations" as they sought to subdue "superstitious reverence [for] the gods of the volcano, and other false deities." Setting out across the island, she trudged, much of the way with swollen feet, a hundred miles "by a rough, forbidding path."

Her mind was bent upon a greater conquest: she would defy the goddess Pele in her own realm at Kilauea. On December 22, 1824, she descended to a ledge in the crater and there proclaimed, "Jehovah is my God. He kindled these fires. I fear not Pele.... All the gods of Hawaii are vain. Great is the goodness of Jehovah in sending missionaries to turn us from these vanities to the living God and the way of righteousness." As a sign of her disdain for the goddess, she devoured some of the *ohelo* berries sacred to Pele, praised the Lord and offered prayers.

Bingham rejoiced at her power in saving her countrymen from "ignorance, superstition, sin, Satan and his legions." With her husband, she kept up her crusade against the powers of evil by making laws to curtail "murder, infanticide, theft, Sabbath desecration, drunkenness, and licentiousness."

James Ely Takes Up the Struggles

James Ely, a licensed preacher who came with the 2nd company in 1823, was sent to take over this new mission. He was ordained on June 4, 1825 at Honolulu. The next year, on September 27, he preached the dedication sermon at the grand new thatched building of the Kailua Church.

In early 1828, the Elys had trouble with sailors seeking native women. Coming ashore at Napoopoo, the men blamed the missionary for a *kapu* on feminine charms and threatened him. Notified by a messenger of this threatening situation across the bay, Naihe sent word that he alone had imposed the *kapu*. His men protected the Ely home, leaving the family to sleep in peace, ignorant of what was going on outside that night.

All was quiet then until, on March 18, a mob armed with clubs approached the Elys' guarded property and demanded to know why they could not have women aboard ship. After listening to their abusive language and threats, Ely told them the *kapu* was doubtlessly "occasioned by the word of God which the natives heard from us. They were much enraged,"

74

he wrote in a letter next day. "I endeavored to pour on cold water and, after they became cool, I invited them in and two of them dined with us. And when they left our house they appeared much ashamed of their conduct and expressed much respect for us."

James Ely — Source: HMCS Library

Health problems prompted the Elys to give up their mission work and sail for home on October 15, 1828, taking the Binghams' eight-year-old daughter Sophia with them to America. During his five years with the mission, James Ely translated the Gospel of John and five of Paul's Epistles.

Heat and Hard Work Take Their Toll

To succeed the Elys, Samuel and Nancy Ruggles came from Hilo, where they had been assisting Joseph and Martha Goodrich in establishing the mission there. This choice pleased Kapiolani, for *"Keiki,"* (Child), as Sam was fondly called by the natives, was a popular and hard-working servant of the Lord. In spite of bouts with ill health, he had previously aided Brother Samuel Whitney at the Waimea Mission on Kauai the first three years.

Nancy and Samuel Ruggles — Source: HMCS Library

A gathering of students at Kaawaloa from many schools on the island in 1831 much impressed Bingham and the chiefs when they met there to witness the demonstrations of learning. Bingham much admired the "long processions of scholars and teachers, coming in from different quarters, after dark, [that] moved in a single file with flaming torches of the candle-nut, and loud-sounding conches. Some ... came winding along around the head of Kealakekua Bay, high on the steep and craggy precipices, ... formed an immense column, still flourishing their fiery banners, and blowing their many shells of various keys, with as much spirit as if they expected the fortifications of darkness were to fall before them."

That year, Bingham explains, "an attempt was made for the permanent establishment of the Kaawaloa station at Kuapehu, ... about two miles inland, east of the bold and volcanic cliff at the head of the bay, ... 1500 feet above the sea." This location offered advantages of a cooler climate and fertile land, instead of the "dry and sterile shore" below, where the Ruggles family had suffered so much. Above, they enjoyed trees and native products — banana, sugar cane, taro, sweet potatoes, and melons. Naihe and Ruggles raised also "a variety of exotics — the grape, fig, guava, pomegranate, orange, coffee, cotton, and mulberry," though on a very small scale.

Naihe did not live very long to enjoy this more favorable climate. He died from apoplexy on December 29,1831. He had served for two years as acting governor of Hawaii while Kuakini was on Oahu. Before his death, he called in two of his confidential men to take care of his affairs and charged them, "Take care of the missionaries. Do for them as I have done." Lucy Thurston fondly remembered him as a man "of commanding stature, and distinguished for refinement and polish of mind and manners. ... As a magistrate he was as firm as he was affectionate and sympathetic."

Ruggles remained at Kaawaloa until 1832. The following year he translated the Catechism on Genesis while waiting for a ship to carry him back to the cooler climes of his homeland. In January 1834, he sailed to the United States with his wife and their two remaining children. Of their four other children, two had died and two had already been sent to New England. The change must have improved his health, for he lived at his home in Brookfield, Conn., and then at Fort Atkinson,Wis., until September 6, 1871, age 76. Nancy, almost four years older than her husband, died there on February 28, 1873.

Cochran Forbes Builds Up the Mission

A fresh, new missionary came to carry on the work of Samuel Ruggles. He was Cochran Forbes with the 5th company landing at Honolulu on May 17, 1832. They took over the new home prepared for the Ruggles family 1500 feet above the shoreline.

Barrot, the French diplomat whom Kuakini met at Kaawaloa in 1836, found the place a village of about 50 houses picturesquely situated among coconut and breadfruit trees. He and his companions visited Kapiolani, "about 50 years of age, of a colossal stature, 5 feet and 8 or 10 inches at least, very corpulent and very ugly," her excessive form gowned in European fashion — flowered English muslin, a blue silk sash, shoes, two tortoise shell combs in her hair and several silver rings on her fingers. She politely received them, offered them her hand, thus relieving Barrot from doubt as to whether the proper salutation was to rub noses with her. Real European chairs were brought for the men to sit. In rapt attention about them on the rocks with their chins supported by their hands lay the town's population. Their abbreviated dress consisted of odd pieces of clothes, a watchcoat without buttons, a shirt, pantaloons, or just the common *malo* or girdle, or some other tapa covering.

With her English sailor steward serving as interpreter, she quite ignored the Frenchmen's polite compliments, receiving them with only "a

Cochran Forbes — Source: HMCS Library

sort of grunt." Yet she appeared friendly, with "a singular expression of kindness and natural goodness," and a show of great pleasure when the French told her they would like to attend the divine worship next day.

For the ascent next day to the Forbes residence and the native church Kapiolani provided horses. The good, three-mile-long road up which they traveled had been built in just two years, due to the ardent cooperation of the people with the missionaries, who had decreed that every person, man or woman, convicted of adultery had to pay a fine of $15 or labor on the roads four months. Besides this road, a 25-mile road to Kailua was almost finished, "thanks to the amorous propensities of the Hawaiians," Barrot wrote, though doubling the actual distance.

At the church service, Kapiolani appeared in black satin dress and "wore upon her head a cloak of native fabric as glossy almost as satin." She appeared attentive and dignified, though "a pair of battered spectacles on her nose" gave her a "very singular" look.

At the Forbes home, the missionary with his wife Rebecca and their two lovely children welcomed the guests. Barrot noted a somewhat-neglected garden there, surrounded by a *ti* hedge. After the Forbes's short stay at Kaawaloa and another at Hana, Maui, they left the islands on October 29, 1839, because of ill health. The great achievement during Forbes's service at Kaawaloa was building the new stone church in 1839, with the help of Ives.

Toil and Trouble of Building a Stone Church

Kapiolani's original thatch church served for 14 years. Then, in 1839, Cochran Forbes and Mark Ives spent two years of intensive labor erecting a stone structure across the bay at Kepulu, where more people could easily reach it, a building 120 by 57 feet, twice the dimensions of the former.

Men carried large rocks on their shoulders to the building site. For lime, they dived 12 to 18 feet in the ocean, pried loose blocks of coral and heaved them into their canoes. Bingham estimated they had piles equal to 30 fathoms, or 7,776 cubic feet. A hot fire of hard *ohia* wood rendered the coral into lime. Men carried on their shoulders from the mountainside heavy logs to provide about 40 cords, or 5,120 cubic feet, of wood. To make the mortar, the women hauled the lime and supplies of sand and water in large calabashes on their shoulders a quarter mile-total loads equal to 2,000 barrels, or 350 wagonfuls, Bingham figured.

Dragging down timber from six to ten miles up the mountain required 40 to 60 men for each post or beam. Men toiled all day long to pull the heavy logs with ropes "over beds of lava, rocks, ravines, and rubbish, reaching the place of building about sunset."

Besides such strenuous labor, these devoted people contributed funds in money or produce, whatever they could spare, to pay the carpenters and masons for their skilled labor. Thus they erected "with a little foreign aid, amounting to two or three hundred dollars, ... a comfortable house of worship, valued at about $6,000," Bingham concluded.

Last Days of Kapiolani

Lucy Thurston visited Kapiolani's new house in Kealakekua in February 1839. "The air of civilized and cultivated life" there delighted Lucy. Several of the three rooms on each of the two floors "were carpeted with very fine mats, and curtained. Three high post bedsteads were hung with valances and musquito [sic] curtains. Three Chinese settees, handsomely trimmed, were placed one in each of the lower rooms ...with a writing desk, tables, chairs, looking glass." A waiter served tea in Chinese cups with saucers and silver tea spoons, soup on soup plates served with a silver ladle, "squash, potatoes, *kalo*, breadfruit, and radishes, on dining plates. Then there was the domestic altar, the Holy Book, the sacred hymns and reverential prayer."

Kapiolani had to undergo an operation for breast cancer on March 23, 1841. She steeled herself with prayer and sat through that half hour of agony without a murmur of distress. "It is painful," she admitted, "but I think of Christ who suffered on the cross for me and I am able to bear it."

The wounds healed well and all seemed favorable until she took a long walk in the heat of the sun six weeks later and felt pain in her side. Dr. Gerritt P. Judd, missionary physician who with the aid of two ships' doctors had performed the operation, relates: "The next day, April 29, she visited each of the missionaries at their houses, including those from other islands. Erysipelas now made its appearance, which after two or three days affected the brain by metastasis and she sunk away into palsy and death."

"In May 1841," Bingham sadly reports, "the nation lost one of its brightest ornaments, and the mission one of its finest fruits, by the death of Kapiolani.... For nearly 20 years, she had supported the mission, and for 15, had greatly adorned the Gospel, and endeared herself to the friends of improvement among the people of the nation. In her opposition to superstition, whether Hawaiian or Roman, and her support of the truth, she was kind, decided, dignified, and triumphant, while she exalted Christ and abased herself and made her adorning that of good works." Lucy Thurston referred to her as "second to no one in noble aspiration and acts."

For her great act of courage at the volcano, Kapiolani's fame spread. Alfred Lord Tennyson memorialized her great deed in verse, and later John Oxenham prepared a poem on the theme. In Hawaii this scene is recorded in art by Peter Hurd as one of the great events of history, and a painting of this event at the Church College of Hawaii illustrates the triumph of Christianity in Hawaii.

KAPIOLANI
by Tennyson

I

When from the terrors of nature a people have
    fashioned and worship a spirit of evil
Blest be the Voice of tha Teacher who calls to them,
    "Set yourselves free!"

II

Noble the Saxon who hurled at his idol a valorous
    weapon in olden England!
Great, and greater, and greatest of women, island
    heroine Kapiolani
Clomb the mountain, flung the berries and dared
    the Goddess, and freed the people
Of Hawai-ee!

III

A people believing that Peele the Goddess would
    wallow in fiery riot and revel
        On Kilauea,
Dance in a fountain of flame with her devils or
    shake with her thunders an shatter her island,
Rolling her anger
Thro' blasted valley and flowing forest in blood-red
    cataracts down to the sea!

IV

Long as the lava-light
    Glares from the lava-lake,
    Dazing the starlight;

Long as the silvery vapor in daylight,
    Over the mountain
Floats, will the glory of Kapiolani be mingled with
    either on Hawa-i-ee.

V

What said her Priesthood?
    "Woe to this island if ever a woman should
    handle or gather the berries of Peele!
Accursed were she!
And woe to this island if ever a woman should
    Climb to the dwelling of Peele the Goddess!
Accursed were she!"

VI

One from the sunrise
Dawned on His people and slowly before him
    Vanished shadow-like
    God and Goddesses,
None but the terrible Peele remaining as Kapiolani
    Ascended the mountain,
Baffled her priesthood,
    Broke the Taboo,
    Dipt to the crater,
Called on the Power adored by the Christian and
    crying, "I dare her, let Peele avenge herself!"
Into the flame-billows dashed the berries, and
    drove the demon from Hawa-i-ee.

The Mission Takes Its Toll

After a decade of heavy labor at Kaawaloa, Cochran and Rebecca, both 37 years old in 1842, felt "the encroachment of debility." Later he explained, "Everything hangs on the missionary. If he flags, all flag; he must sustain Sabbath" and day schools, train singers, lead devotions, teach and lead his deacons, "keep alive the spirit of benevolence, nay, create it" and "look after those who halt and are ready to fall. Our labors are necessarily incessant," he wearily regrets. But he kept on until 1845, when he transferred to Lahaina to serve as Seamen's Chaplain during two of those busiest years when up to 200 ships a year crowded the harbor.

Their first son Anderson Oliver Forbes returned to Hawaii and served at Kaluaaha Mission, then as pastor of Kaumakapili Church in Honolulu, then as teacher at Lahainaluna Seminary, then as pastor of First Foreign Church of Hilo, and finally as corresponding secretary of the Hawaiian Board.

After Cochran left, Mark Ives stuck it out until 1848, when ill health overcame him too and he returned to Connecticut.

In total five missionaries gave up the debilitating toil of the heat of Kaawaloa. Ely had lasted just four years. Ruggles held out for another four years. Forbes manfully held on for about 13 years. Van Duzee was good for about a year. Ives did well to survive about nine years at Kaawaloa. The Pogues, who came next, would be stationed there only about two years. This mission was falling apart.

John and Maria Pogue

John Fawcett Pogue came with the 11th Company in 1844 with Marie Kapule Whitney, daughter of Samuel and Mercy Whitney. Maria was the first missionary daughter born in Hawaii. Although Mercy opposed the union, John and Maria were married in 1848 and went to Kaawaloa, remaining there until 1850 and in mission work until 1877. John was the only one of the first six missionaries at Kaawaloa to serve out his career in Hawaii. Ill health and death caught up with him in 1877, when he was 62. The Kaawaloa station remained vacant until the coming of John Paris in 1852.

13

GOODRICH
STARTS
THE HILO MISSION

Joseph Goodrich was given the task of starting the station at distant Hilo with Samuel Ruggles to aid him. In January 1824, these two couples endured a nasty 10-day voyage to Hilo Bay. They found their "new missionary mansion" was large enough, 70 by 30 feet, a storage place for canoes, lumber and other supplies, no floor, partitions or windows.

A similar building, provided by Kaahumanu, served as their place of worship that Sunday. William Ellis, who had come with them, conducted the services, and found himself confronted not only by a large crowd but suddenly by a big, fat black hog with huge tusks. The natives, in an uproar and panic, pushed aside the missionaries to force their way out both doors, though not for fear of the tusks. This beast was sacred, being a pet of Kaahumanu and bearing her name. After the hog's keeper subdued the animal, the crowd dared to reenter and Ellis could resume his sermon .

The missionaries pitched right in to teach and convert these people. They got native teachers from other districts to come and help start training in schools. The Hawaiians erected a house for the missionaries and a church. When Kapiolani came to their aid in December, she saw they were "suffering privations," as "the local authorities... had not yet aspired after the blessings of civilization or Christianity." Ruggles, "for six months destitute of shoes," could not make the 30-mile trip to the volcano with Kapiolani and Goodrich, "who sometimes travelled barefoot." Kapiolani returned to the station to spend ten days convincing the people of the real values of education and reform. The Goodriches, after Ruggles left for Kaawaloa, struggled to take care of the Hawaiian population of 20,000.

Later in 1828, the Rev. Ephraim Clark came to Hilo for four months with a native teacher to train teachers. With the Clarks, the Goodriches made a two-day journey to the volcano, the two missionary wives being "the first foreign ladies to see the fires at Kilauea." Bingham with Kaahumanu and her company, visiting the windward islands "to encourage education, morals, and religion," reached Hilo in time for the dedication on October 15, 1830, of the large new church her brother Kuakini had had built. After the dedication sermon, the young (only 17 years old) king gave a very appropriate address and offered a prayer.

Goodbye, Mr. Goodrich

The missionary's activities at Hilo were causing the righteous-minded Bingham some concern. For he had heard that Brother Goodrich was indulging in other pursuits than education and religion by going fishing, bullock hunting, and engaging in mechanical work. Goodrich was indeed a good, capable, practical sort of fellow. The mission had already made good use of his special abilities by calling him back to Honolulu for two years in 1826-1828 to superintend the printing press and book bindery while the printer was away.

But Goodrich was also raising sugar cane, making in 1828 the first sugar and molasses produced there. The *Missionary Album* credits him with being an "agriculturist, keenly interested in teaching the people how to grow coffee and other food products necessary to life in the Islands." He also made scientific observations. But Bingham feared such preoccupations robbed the Lord of the mission's primary obligation — the saving of heathen souls.

The Goodriches returned to the United States in 1836 with their five surviving children, "to seek opportunities for the education of his children in the home-country," according to Henry Lyman.

Sheldon Dibble

While Goodrich was taking the place of the printer again in Honolulu in 1831-1832, he finished the printing of the *Hawaiian New Testament* and bound for Bingham the first copy in red morocco to present to the dying Kaahumanu. During this period, the Rev. Sheldon Dibble, who came with the 4th company in June 1831, took charge at Hilo until 1834. In November that year, the Dibbles removed to Lahainaluna, where his wife Maria died February 20, 1837. In poor health, Sheldon left for the United States in November with his daughter and a son born in 1835, married Antoinette Tomlinson, a relative of his wife, in 1839 and arrived back at Lahainaluna in 1840. Dibble became secretary of the Royal Historical Society, formed in 1841, and remained at Lahainaluna until his death, January 22, 1845, after suffering from severe bleeding of the lungs during his last six months.

84

His main contribution was his *History and General Views of the Sandwich Islands Mission*, published in 1843. This developed from a school project with his able students interviewing the people to collect original data on Hawaiian life, customs and history. But the bald fact of pagan life overwhelmed him so that he dared not specify such faults of virtue lest they be promulgated by his book. He denounced the native failings generally, summing up all that seemed repulsive to Puritan standards. These poor people, he regretted, "were sorely oppressed, wretchedly destitute, and exceedingly ignorant; stupid also to all that is lovely, grand and awful in the works of God; low, naked, filthy, vile, sensual; covered with every abomination, stained with blood and black with crime," and he deplored the "obscenity, frantic rage and... bleeding human sacrifices" of their idolatry.

Fortunately other missionaries, more sympathetic, dwelt on the more redemptive features of the native character. Deeble also devoted his scholarship to translating books of the Bible and a good number of text-books.

Jonathan Green

The Rev. Jonathan Smith Green also spent part of 1832 at the Hilo Mission. After arriving with the 3rd company in 1828, he had spent most of the year exploring along the coast of North America, then was stationed at Lahaina. From Hilo he went to Wailuku, Maui, founded the Girls' Seminary in 1836 and served as principal to 1842. Withdrawing from the American Board then, he became the independent pastor at Makawao, Maui, later went into raising wheat there, only to find it could not compete in price with American flour. One writer credits him with being "one of the few apostles with a prevailing sense of humor and a little latitude in his convictions." He died at Makawao, January 5, 1878.

14

THOSE INDUSTRIOUS
LYMANS

Sarah and David Layman with four of thier
seven living children (circa 1853) — Source:
HMCS Library

They Heed the Call — What a Voyage!

The Rev. David Belden Lyman and his eager and determined wife Sarah Joiner Lyman made the Hilo Mission the lasting success it became. David was the oldest of nine children in the farming Lyman family of New Hartford, Conn. His earnest religious parents destined him to the service of Almighty God and devoted their limited resources to his proper education at Williams College and Andover Theological Seminary. Heeding the call of the ABCFM for reenforcements in Hawaii, David volunteered in his senior year at Andover and was ordained in 1831. For his necessary female partner, he already had a promising prospect in the person of Sarah Joiner, of Royalton, Vt.

In September 1830, Sarah had ventured to Boston, where she met Henry Lyman at meetings of the ABCFM at Park Street Church. The ardent speeches there impressed Sarah with the terrible thought that "so large a portion of the earth is covered with moral darkness" that a dire need exists to carry the light of Christianity to these "benighted heathen." Henry, bent on his own noble mission plans, asked her if she did not consider it her "duty to go on a mission." Sarah spent a rainy day in serious meditation and prayed in her journal, "O that a way might be opened whereby I may labour for the good of souls."

A year later as a teacher, she found herself in the same quandary Lucy Goodale had once faced. David Lyman had asked her to be his helpmate on the mission. She made her decision. Two months later she tersely recorded, "November 2,1831. I was married, and on the morning of the 3rd I bade a final farewell to my father's house and started for Boston, where I spent two weeks in visiting my friends and making preparations for a long voyage."

Sarah's friend Henry Lyman (of another Lyman family) also accepted an ABCFM assignment and, with Samuel Munson, undertook a dangerous mission to Sumatra. Their early fate was to be devoured by cannibals.

At Boston the Lymans gathered with the other 17 members of this 5th company. Their ocean conveyance, the 350-ton whaleship *Averick*, was somewhat heavier than the 241-tons *Thaddeus*. But the 173 days before attaining their goal were no less frightful at times.

Between the Devil and the Deep Blue Sea

At the start the devil seemed to have lured them to destruction, the Board's fervent prayers for fair weather notwithstanding. The ship sailed to the outer harbor to anchor there until the last-minute stores

87

strewn about the deck could be put in order. But the lure of delightful Indian Summer weather prompted the captain to sail right on. All was well until night, when a gale started blowing and the waves swept across the deck clearing it of those provisions and supplies too lately deposited there. For two weeks the seas raged before crew and passengers had a chance to restore order and recover from a long siege of seasickness.

Sarah was ill with a billious fever that almost ended her missionary career. She lay in her berth for seven weeks until the ship reached Rio de Janeiro to replace its broken mast. "No tongue can tell how much I suffered during my seasickness and subsequent fever," she wrote in her journal.

She recovered during the stay at Rio while enjoying the hospitality of an Englishman at his villa near the city. Back aboard ship, she found her situation improved but still far from pleasant, as she noted how dirty the ship was and the mould covering her belongings. The crew were an unbelievably profane "wicked set of men." And, in the torrid confines of her cramped stateroom, she had to endure "quite intolerable" nights. Yet, in spite of all these miseries, she declared "we are contented and happy."

In early March, they again "encountered some severe gales of wind and squalls of rain and hail." Sarah spent "many a wearisome night" clinging to her mattresses so that the violent tossing of the ship would not throw her out of bed. As the sea became even rougher, Sarah gave way to "a feeling of terror" as she saw "the vessel tossing and plunging, the waves roaring and breaking angrily..."

As conditions improved, she felt "tolerably comfortable," baked some pumpkin pies and took daily walks on deck. One day's report ended with "Ate our last banana to-day [March 9, 1832] brought from Rio." Though the Lymans disliked this fruit, David brought a bunch so they could acquire a taste for it by sampling a banana each day. Sarah by now was pleased to minister to other sick ladies, to walk the deck 50 times twice a day, and to study Greek grammar. But a few days later, coming down with a fever, she rather unwillingly had Dr. Chapin bleed her and give her medicine. Though weakened, she was soon able to eat and walk the deck again.

After a favorable rounding of Cape Horn brought them into the Pacific, the cry of "Whale!" roused the crew to action several times, but without success. They sailed on during April, enjoying cool breezes and warm sun. On May 17, 1832, they at last reached Honolulu "after a long and tedious voyage."

Getting Started at Hilo

By arriving May 17, 1832, they were in time for the annual meeting, with about two months to get acquainted before they finally left Honolulu on July 5 for their first woes of inter-island sea voyaging a "tedious" passage to Lahaina with the deck, as usual, overcrowded with natives. They lay becalmed off Lanai from midnight that Thursday until late Sunday afternoon and did not get away until Wednesday noon. As violent winds rent the sails, the ship dared not proceed through the treacherous channel between Maui and Hawaii the next morning. So the captain turned south to Kawaihae Bay.

Lyman Home — **Source: Baker -Van Dyke Collection**

With the Goodriches and Greens, the Lymans spent the night and next day as guests of John Young reaching Hilo Monday evening, July 16. They stayed with the Greens until they left, August 15. It was two weeks before the rain stopped and they could enjoy the pleasant sunshine. Their son Henry later recorded that Hilo became "flooded by an annual rainfall of 150 inches," and "for long-continued, steady, straight-down, pouring rain, I have never seen the like in any place."

Sarah started a writing school for teachers. On September 5, representatives of 30 outlying schools met at the church in Hilo to be examined. Sarah's 100 pupils were nearly all adorned in black tapa gowns, straw hats that they had made, and flower leis.

The next week David went off with Dibble to dedicate a church and examine schools north of Hilo leaving Sarah alone for the first time in her native hut, disturbed by the wind howling, the surf roaring and the torrents of rain forcing a way through the thatch to soak the mats. When David got home next evening with Dibble, both were drenched, having had to swim across streams swelled by heavy rains. The same trip repeated in February 1833 was even worse. A raging storm caused flooding streams that David had to cross by rope.

Sarah's feelings fluctuated. At times she was homesick and the burden of missionary labor depressed her spirits. But again her determined spirit maintained "I am happy in my work," as she soon found the day passing swiftly away with her classes in language study, chemistry, map drawing, and in the afternoon, arithmetic. After 4:00 PM she was still working at school. In the evening, she went to singing school. On Sunday she "attended native service, the sabbath school, Bible class, and the English service."

Though, at first, they dwelt in "a small room in a native house with many of our goods in it," they enjoyed it with "tranquility and comfort." But what a thrill three months later to become "inmates of our own dwelling" in a native house, but "new and neatly finished," where they could spread their table for the first time since their marriage.

The cold of January 1833, down to 54 degrees, afflicted the Lymans, now accustomed to warmer climate. They wished for more heavy clothing and leather shoes.

Civilizing the Heathen

Deploring "the wretched condition of this people," native homes just "wretched hovels" full of vermin, the people living "more filthy than swine" and covered with sores, Sarah set forth to take care of the sick. For a woman with swollen eyes, she curdled some milk with alum and gave her salts and was happy to find the woman's eyes perfectly cured a few days later. Another time she was assisting in tying up the arteries on a man's ankle after a tumor had been removed. "The blind, the halt and the maimed are constantly calling for medical aid," she added.

Discouragement came as they saw some students forsaking them and giving themselves up again "to work iniquity." These deserters were reviving the forbidden hula, again tattooing their skin, and probably returning to the worship of idols. The one hope was that the chiefs were beginning to restrain them.

Native customs were shocking — their lack of dress and their unseemly habits. The women "think no more of going with their breasts exposed, than we do our hands, "she wrote her sister. Both men and women, like "dumb beasts" with no sense of shame, sat in the open "to do their duties, right before our eyes too." "One of the greatest evils" was having the whole family sleeping together, making the children "as wise as their parents," prompting "little boys and girls [to] have as much intercourse as they please." All this evil made Sarah "feel the importance of labouring to elevate them."

The problems of natives making intoxicating drink from potatoes, bananas and *ti* root and also "practicing some of the former foolish customs" were taken up by a large council. Their punishment was that each must "bring in a certain quantity of wood from the wilderness." Some of their students, they learned, met on the beach in the evening "to serve the devil, or in other words, to engage in some of their old customs." Even three of Sarah's "young girls of promise" were reported to have been involved."When will this people cease to do evil and learn to do well!" she cried in despair.

Sarah kept worrying over the natives' morals — that "foolish amusement" of surfing, "the source of much iniquity," because "it leads to intercourse with the sexes without discrimination." As a surfer had drowned, she hoped that would be a lesson to others to abandon such folly. Such simple native practices as "ornamenting the head and neck with wreaths of flowers and beads" bothered Sarah's sense of propriety because they cost time and did not last anyway. She made them tabu in her school. By the close of 1835 Sarah felt, "My heart is sad when I think there has only been one individual admitted to the church during the whole year...." The progress she yearned for seemed to come so slowly.

One success was "the tobacco reformation," especially to save them from their custom of swallowing the smoke, sometimes becoming so intoxicated they would fall into the fire or into the sea. The Lymans asked the people to surrender their pipes and burned the tobacco in a big bonfire.

Visitors Come — Some Good, Some Bad

Scottish botanist David Douglas, who had explored the forests of Oregon and California, stayed with the Lymans in January 1834. With Thomas Honolii as a guide, he spent ten days exploring Mauna Kea to determine its height and to collect minerals and plants. A week later he made a two-week visit to the volcano and Mauna Loa, traveling through 17 miles of snow 5 or 6 feet deep to the summit crater. It was early February before he got back and returned to Oahu.

On July 12 the Lymans were expecting him, having heard he had sailed to Kona to hike across the mountain to Hilo. Two days later came word that "Mr. Douglas is no more." His corpse arrived in a canoe. He had fallen into one of the deep pits for catching wild cattle and had been gored to death by a trapped bull. Becoming lame on the day after he left Kawaihae, Douglas had stopped at the home of an Englishman, who warned him of three pits in his path. Evidently he had ventured to the edge of the third pit to observe the trapped bull and had fallen in. Two natives discovered a piece of his coat by the pit, saw what had happened and reported it to the Englishman. He came at once, shot the bull, took out the body and hired natives to carry it 27 miles to the shore. There he got a man to take the body in his canoe, while the Englishman headed to Hilo over land with Douglas' belongings.

From their native house, the Lymans moved into their "little stone cottage" in March 1835 and by January 15, the next year, to their new wooden house — a neat one-story Cape Cod dwelling grand enough to warm the heart of eager Sarah. "It seems like being in a civilized land, to occupy a house built like those inhabited by civilized people," she exulted. Now she had even a spare bedroom for visitors. Two ships captains stayed with them and on one occasion they had 12 people at their long dining table. On May 21, 1837, the Lymans held an English service in their dining room for men from "Calcutta, Scotland, England, Wales, the United States, the Spanish Main and the Society Islands."

Sarah lamented the scarcity of "praying souls" among the seamen, feeling they above all needed "the support and comforts of the Gospel." She declared, "In the main they are an abandoned, hopeless class. They drink in iniquity like water and their feet are swift to do evil. Licentiousness and drunkenness are their besetting sins, and most of them are profane in the extreme. ... Pray then for the poor sailor, before you pray for us, or the benighted heathen."

Not even when the scientific expedition of the *U.S.S. Vincennes* with Lieutenant Charles Wilkes in command spent almost four months of 1841 making scientific studies of the volcano region was the Lyman religious attitude really satisfied. Sarah greatly feared that "the moral influence which they have exerted on these poor people has been deleterious in the extreme. Silly women have been led captive by the officers, ensnared and I fear are lost eternally..."

But, by late 1843, the Lymans could rejoice, "Our visitors, with one exception, have been gentlemen. — Some of them men of intelligence, others not." They invited ships' officers but not sailors, unless they called on the

Lymans and then, if at meal time, they always invited them to eat with them. The Lymans were pleased to hear reports such as, "Why they bow and speak to us when we meet them — invite us to eat and sleep at their houses, etc. Poor fellows, they are exceedingly blinded by the many, many false reports ... by wicked and designing men at Honolulu."

One visiting ship did produce bad economic effects — "a serious evil" caused by a profusion of American dollars, when the *U.S.S. Ohio* spent some time in port in summer of 1849. With $20,000 in cash distributed among the natives, they felt so rich they would not work. Food became scarce and high-priced.

By June 1851 Sarah could complain about the increase in foreigners, especially Chinese laborers marrying native women, even though they proved to be "industrious and enterprising" and made good husbands and fathers, but they were "as ignorant of true religion, as the veriest heathen in a heathen land."

Mainland cousins came visiting in 1857, and also "a good many transient visitors, guests for a day, a week or a month." Sarah now enjoyed more feminine society with eight "white ladies, permanent residents," and two others for the season.

Kings too visited. In 1873, newly-elected King Lunalilo had been entertained at the Lymans' home and that of their son Rufus "at great expense and to the great discomfort of both our families." But a year later, when King Kalakaua came, the missionaries remembered the previous royal visit "with real satisfaction." By then they could admire the refined tastes of the former monarch who "had too much culture to sympathize in the old *meles*, *hulas*, etc., and cared not for the adulation of the rabble." But, alas, for Kalakaua the people were preparing "*hulas* and *meles* and other heathenish practices."

Sarah, having reached her three score years and ten, found delight in the company of "some refined intelligent people" among the transient visitors, including "some of the most agreeable people in the world."

Coping With Nature

Earthquakes, tidal waves and volcanic eruptions are part of life in the Hilo area. Although not necessarily destructive, if severe, they can be frightening. The Lymans' first severe earthquake came in February 1834, scared them enough to make them dash outside for fear their fragile house would come crashing down, but no damage occurred.

The tidal wave of November 7, 1837, swept away most of the towns' canoes and 66 houses with the people in them. While most swam back, or were rescued by a ship's crew, 11 were drowned.

A terrible shaking of the house the night of January 29, 1838, aroused and quite unnerved Sarah. A series of quakes starting November 5th culminated in the heavy shock of December 12 that almost threw Sarah off balance as she ran out of the house. Even the Hawaiians became terrified. The year 1841 brought heavy trembling in the middle of the night of April 8, even "more severe than any former one." At two a.m., another shock cracked the plaster and chimney, and some stone walls went tumbling over — most severe shock the natives had ever experienced.

Mauna Loa volcano caused great anxiety during its long flow from August 1855 to February 1856, slowly advancing to within 12 miles of the town by November 1. In February, Sarah spent a night at the nearby flow, watching "the liquid fire flowing over a precipice." But the lava did not progress farther, although continued smoke revealed some action until late in October.

The terrifying earthquakes of the spring of 1868 caused great fear and destruction. As they had to restore the plastering of rooms, cupboard and closet, Sarah decided plastering was not good for walls where earthquakes occur. So she had all plaster cleaned off, covered the boards with cheesecloth, and dressed them with wallpaper. Then, the night of July 23, they "were waked and driven from our beds by a fearful shaking." Several more shakes came during the week, three of them quite heavy.

The most threatening Mauna Loa eruption came in May 1880. The whole summit seemed to be on fire, burning "so brightly as to light up the heavens to the Zenith." By July 26, 1881, the flow reached little more than two miles from Hilo, a week later getting so ominously close that families were leaving, some moving to Puna fearing "lava flowing down our streets like rivers of water" and filling Hilo Bay.

Prominent citizens from Honolulu came on the steamer to witness the awe-inspiring scenes. Sarah was religiously skeptical of the powers of "Luka, the old governess of Hawaii," to stop the flow by "incantations," referring to Princess Ruth Keelikolani, island governor from 1855 to 1869, who had been summoned from Honolulu by still faithful followers to induce Pele to desist from wiping out Hilo. The assault by lava miraculously ended. Whether it was by the grace of God or the playful fancy of Pele in response to the commands of a Hawaiian chiefess depended on believers' sympathies. But Sarah had no doubts as she breathed a sigh of relief after having been thus confronted by the angry fires "within half a mile of us."

Sarah made a distinct contribution to scientific knowledge of the volcano area by keeping a careful record of earthquakes and eruptions, the first person to do so.

No Easy Life For Wife and Mother

Sarah Lyman could not boast of robust health. Physical problems often beset her, but she possessed the resiliency to bounce back.

She attacked her school duties so intensely at first that by September 1834, her children's school had become almost "a hopeless task," as her pupils dropped out as soon as the novelty wore off. She reorganized with a school of 20 specially selected scholars from nearby homes of church members. At first they acted like wild goats, but then tamed down to be "quite orderly and quiet." Then Sarah's health failed her. For two months she suffered a severe fever from which she was recovering by the end of the year. Such had been and was to be her life — periods of declining health followed by recoveries and renewed spirit.

The heartening showing of her classes' skills in reading, arithmetic and Bible history in the January 1835 examinations spurred her on. By March 1835 she felt worn out again, as was David. After this feeling of depression, they got away to the general meeting in Honolulu to join in welcoming the eight members of the 7th company, arriving June 6. The Lymans became hopeful of a transfer to Maui, but were kept at Hilo although granted first choice of the newcomers as their associates. They chose the Rev. Titus Coan, the only ordained minister among the new arrivals, and his wife Fidelia.

On their return to Hilo three months later, the enthusiastic greeting of many people, including Sarah's school children, proved a cheering sight, indicating that the natives were coming to appreciate their teachers and the work they were doing for them. Attending another annual meeting in May 1836, Sarah became quite exhausted after three weeks of meetings and social affairs.

Then a far more serious trial and testing of her spirit began; her little David, born April 13, 1834, came down with dysentery. Encouraged by Dr. Gerrit P. Judd that the disease was checked and the voyage should prove beneficial to the boy, the Lymans a week later sailed for home. During the 36-hour trip to Lahaina on the bouncing vessel, Sarah's heart was "burning with anguish" as she felt her dear son suffering in her arms. For three weeks at Lahaina, David failed to respond to every remedy available. He finally expired July 28 and was buried there beside the graves of two other sons of missionaries with the 5th company.

After "a very seasick time" on the five-day passage back to Hilo, the saddened Lymans received a sympathetic welcome on shore by the assembled people in a flood of tears. Sarah and Fidelia Coan became so overcome by this intense mourning that they had to be carried to their home. And there "desolation reigned" as Sarah gazed upon the evidences of her lost son's childhood.

The Coans now took charge of the school and it became "quiet large and flourishing." The big problem was the lack of discipline in the children's homes.

Sarah's mother's love now turned even more fully to her baby boy Henry Munson, born November 26, 1835. Nine months later she had another son, Frederick Swartz, July 25, 1837. The fourth son came along March 27, 1840, named after her first one, David Brainerd. The last boy was Rufus Anderson, June 23, 1842. On September 27, 1844, came the first girl, Ellen Elizabeth, then Francis Ogden, August 9, 1846, and Emma Washburn, September 16, 1849.

After each birth at first, it usually took her four to six weeks or more before she recovered. By the sixth birth in 1846 she had learned to overcome debility — by taking cold showers. She took them morning and evening till the day of delivery and then resumed this invigorating method 12 days after, resolved to continue cold showers as long as they produced so much benefit. But the final birth in 1849 brought on "a long and tedious illness."

David Develops Manual Training School

David Lyman's concept of the Hilo Boarding School was a striking example of Yankee genius, combining idealism with practical ingenuity. Boys would learn and earn their way, acquiring skills and using them to provide for and improve their school and their own lives — the first manual

Hilo Boarding School (Boys) and Coan House — Source HMCS Library

96

training school —40 years ahead of those in the Lymans' native New England. The boys learned not only book knowledge but also manual arts and the vocational skills of agriculture and carpentry. In addition, under the Lymans' personal supervision, their characters were formed by daily habits of industry, thrift and morality.

At annual meetings, most missionaries seemed to favor the concept of such a school, but each felt too involved in his own work to tackle the extra commitment. At the 1835 meeting, they decided that Hilo should be the place for the trial. As Coan preferred preaching and Lyman had experience in organizing and managing local schools, he took over the project.

From August through September of 1836, the schoolhouse was built, providing schoolroom, dining hall, pantry, boys room, and a study for their teacher. Only eight boys enrolled that year at first, then four more later. This was probably just as well for the Lymans, who had to supply the native boys with bedding, shirts and pants. Sarah kept busy "cutting and basting shirts," then making pantaloons to preserve their respectability. Each year she improved the process, later making a pattern for each size and having a native assistant cut out the trousers. She taught the boys to mend their clothes and finally to even make their own.

David became engrossed in this fresh enterprise. He rose at four o'clock each morning to shave, bathe and read his Hebrew Bible. He let his hard-working boys stay in bed until five o'clock before rousing them for prayers by lamplight. Then they breakfasted, went to work, bathed, studied and attended classes before dinner. After that, came "recreation, study, school, work, recreation, supper and prayers." Sarah spent after-noons assisting the boys in their study and classes and instructed them in singing. She even treated their skin problems — "tedious boils" — by dosing them with sulphur and molasses and applying an ointment sent by her father.

By July 4, 1837, their six older students were prepared to sail to Lahaina for higher training there. Though eager to advance, they became sad at leaving the family who had been making a home for them.

To help the Lymans, Abner and Lucy Wilcox arrived in 1837 to serve as teachers.

The Lymans soon learned how to handle unruly boys. They "toned down" those "at first quite wild," and the boys learned to submit to school rules and made "commendable progress in their studies." The Lymans would tolerate no deviation from righteous moral standards. In January 1838 David had to administer a severe flogging to a boy caught lying and stealing. The Lymans followed this by personal counseling and presenting the situation before the whole school. With only three such cases of corporal punishment in the first three years of the new school, such "a painful case of discipline" was uncommon.

The year 1839 started in a rush of activity to get the carpentry work on their new house and school buildings done. Six professional carpenters were engaged and, as they could not get much native help, they had to make use of all available manpower among students and domestics. In spite of the customary abundance of deluging rains for several weeks, they managed to put together the new buildings. They built "new houses to accommodate 60 or 70 boys on a higher site nearer the school farm..." Besides the boys' dormitory and the schoolhouse, they had a cook house and "marvel of marvels, an infirmary in case of contagious disease."

The Lymans were delighted to move into their new home by April 22. "The new dwelling was almost a reproduction of our former [Cape Cod] habitation," Henry Lyman recalled, "though it had a larger and steeper roof thatched with sugar-cane leaves after the native fashion." It had also two dormer windows.

When David left for the Honolulu meeting that May 1839, the school closed early because of a famine that made people depend on wild products for food. Sarah remained at home "to do something to promote the good of the school." Lack of food caused deprivations for home and school again two years later. Sarah wrote in August 1841, "No eggs, no fish, and no melons. We are entirely destitute of both fish and pork for the school, and have over 60 boys."

Sarah's musical ability expanded from singing to instrumental harmony. Having harbored the ambition of organizing a school band, she mentioned this to a sea captain, who gave her an old flute. She mastered the technique of playing the instrument and taught it to the boys. They eagerly produced their own fifes and flutes from bamboo. With the later addition of an accordion and violoncello, the school band could offer an ample supply of music.

By the 1845-1846 school year, 60 boys were enrolled, 37 of them new ones. In 1848, all 50 boys became prostrated with the first attack of measles in the islands. Sailors aboard the visiting frigate *Independence* had brought in this disease, so far unknown in Hawaii but considered insignificant by the frigate's medical officers, who allowed natives thronging aboard and the recently ill crew members to enjoy their liberty among the people.

"Like fire in dry grass, the pestilence spread throughout the population until every one had experience of its direful effects," Henry Lyman remembered. "With no other assistance, because none could be obtained, my father medicated and fed the whole troop, while my mother took similar care of her family, without a single fatal result in either group. But among the natives outside, the disease raged all over the Islands, and destroyed a tenth of the population.... [because] the ignorant sufferers rushed into the water to cool their fever, and fell victims to pneumonia and dysentery, thus superinduced."

In July 1849 the Lymans had to expel seven pupils for misconduct — "a sore trial" as they were "much attached to the boys" and one had been with them for eight years. Sarah was inclined to blame the girls as "the greatest transgressors."

That same year the king granted the school 40 acres of land, which at once provided greater agricultural opportunities for student training as well as supplying the school with its own food.

A temporary set back occurred in November 1853. Some "fiend" set fire to and destroyed the schoolhouse. The community came to the aid of reconstruction with gifts of $200 from the native church, $300 from foreigners, and contributions from all the islands. The kingdom's legislature appropriated $4,000.

David then kept extra busy to get materials to build the new one. He bought a full load of west coast lumber from the *California Schooner* when it stopped in 1854. His boys were busy collecting coral for the lime, wood for burning it, sand to make the mortar, and stone to wall the basement. They used a curious-looking cart — "a clumsy thing," Sarah thought, with the drag made of the crotch of a tree — and three yoke of oxen to pull it.

The school now became increasingly a constant drain on David's strength — so much so, Sarah felt, that she expressed her wonder in March 1855 that he survived so much toil and trouble. "It is enough to kill one man," she asserted.

By the next year, Sarah happily could report, "Our new school house is commodious, airy and convenient." The basement provided space for dining room, storeroom and farm tools. The first floor had the school-room and two rooms for native assistants. The boys used the second story and attic for sleeping quarters.

The Lymans' 1839 house had been enlarged at this time, its second story raised to form higher rooms and a spacious attic above, the thatch roof replaced by galvanized iron and a wing added to provide study and library for David. In 1932 this Lyman home was moved to allow an extension of Haili Street and restored as a museum to serve as a perpetual reminder of the Lymans' unremitting labor on behalf of the people. It was dedicated July 16 that year, exactly one hundred years after the arrival of the Lymans, and still reposes proudly as the Lyman House Memorial.

In 1860 David was still busily occupied with his school and serving as land agent and school treasurer for the Hilo and Puna districts. Looking back a decade later in 1871, Sarah declared it had been "a sore trial" to her that David, because he "was so entirely devoted to the school," had had "no time to enjoy his own family," as she had.

The school seemed to be prospering under a native principal, though the student ranks were diminishing. But, as five years under native guidance failed to keep the school progressing, the Rev. W.B. Oleson, "a live man and is working for the Master," was placed in charge. David kept on as treasurer and assisting the new man as much as he could.

Sarah's love of the beauties of nature raised her spirits. She now spent more time beautifying the grounds with trees, shrubs and flowers, feeling that her health needed such open-air exercise. Later, Sarah found an invigorating pleasure in riding her donkey. This way she rejoiced, "I

The Lymans at their 50th wedding anniversary (Nov. 1891) — Source: **Lyons-Van Dyke Collection**

break away from all my cares occasionally." As age crept up, Sarah found it hard to believe in 1876 that she was past 70 years old. She felt her memory and eyesight failing. But, more happily, she could report a total of 19 grandchildren.

On November 2, 1881, the Lymans celebrated the first Golden Wedding anniversary on the island and the second in the kingdom. The first had occurred on Maui October 1st that year for the Rev. William Patterson Alexander and his wife Mary Ann, also members of the 5th company. The Hilo ceremony marked the half-century devotion of David and Sarah to their missionary work, the births of eight children and the present glory of 31 grandchildren, as well as the development of all the Hawaiian youths whose minds, bodies and souls had been nurtured by their teachers. Their "practical idealism and heroism" shone brightly in the memories of all.

David and Sarah, now in their middle seventies and no longer very strong, were getting along with help from the boys. The school, Sarah knew, had kept her and David "so long in the ruts, and...used up my husband's energies all too soon." It had indeed been "a hard life" that left them in their declining years "nearly exhausted." Yet they both had the satisfaction of feeling "quite free from those aches and pains with which so many old people are afflicted." Even up to April 1884, Sarah reported they still enjoyed "comfortable health," though unable to walk far or attend evening meetings.

The Lymans had unflinchingly devoted their hearts, energies, and long lives to improving the physical, mental and moral qualities of the people. Worn out by his long labors, David lingered on during two years of failing health — weak, partly deaf, and with poor eyesight. Then in June 1884, nearly at age 81, his infirmities developed into a "severe and protracted illness" that confined him to his bed with much suffering. He died October 4, 1884.

Sarah valiantly took care of her treasured partner for four weeks before wearing out and becoming confined to her own bed for seven weeks. Her strength was weakened by this siege and her great loss. She lived on another year, dying peacefully on December 7, 1885, at age 80.

David had achieved laudable success in establishing and carrying on his boys' boarding school. He was, as his brother missionary Elias Bond of Kohala knew him, "steadfast, patient, modest, of rarely excellent judgment; quiet and even in his methods of discipline, and thoroughly understanding the Hawaiian boy." The state minister of public instruction, in 1854, considered his school "the very life and soul of our common schools on that large island."

The kind of school David Lyman had started spread to Waialua, Oahu, in 1837; to Waioli, Kauai, in 1841, a school which Abner and Lucy Wilcox then conducted for many years; and to Kohala where the Bonds opened a school for boys and one for girls in 1842. The first school for girls was the Wailuku Seminary in 1836.

Influenced by Lyman's educational achievement, the son of the Rev. Richard Armstrong, with the Lymans in the 5th company, established Hampton Normal and Agricultural Institute in Virginia in 1868. Major General Samuel Chapman Armstrong, who was with the Union army during the Civil War, applied Lyman's principles to the education of blacks. He is quoted as remarking that "when he wished to make the best kind of school for the freed-man, he took Father Lyman's school in Hilo for his pattern."

Later he influenced Booker T. Washington to initiate industrial training at Tuskegee Institute.

The Lymans' educational efforts produced capable men who became judges, lawyers, politicians, educators, ministers and policemen. They established a dynasty that includes innumerable descendants today, many prominently active in the affairs of Hawaii and in other parts of the world.

15

TITUS COAN —
LEADER
EXRAORDINARY

Titus and Fidelia Church Coan — Source:
HMCS Library

The Voice of God Calls

Titus Coan with great energy pushed forward the work of the Hilo Mission. An indefatigable traveler and talker, he toured the territory and preached and taught with vigor.

Unlike David Lyman, Titus had not been directly destined for this role in life. Born on Sunday, February 1, 1801, at Killingworth, Conn., he first learned from his upright father Gaylord, a paragon of New England virtues — "a thoughtful, quiet, and most modest farmer, industrious, frugal, and temperate, attending to his own business, living in peace with his neighbors, eschewing evil, honest in dealing, avoiding debts, abhorring extravagance and profligacy, refusing proffered offices, strictly observing the Sabbath, a regular attendant on the services of the sanctuary, a constant reader of the Bible, and always offering morning and evening prayers with the family."

Titus was the youngest of seven, all boys except one. His mother was Tamza Nettleton, aunt of the Rev. Asahel Nettleton, distinguished evangelical preacher, who later returned to his home town to wage a devastating crusade against sin. Though Titus was away, he returned "just in time to see 110 of my companions and neighbors stand up in the sanctuary and confess the Lord Jehovah to be their Lord and Saviour, and pledge themselves to love, follow, and obey Him."

But Titus was not yet ready for such a pledge. In 1826 at age 25, he joined four brothers in western New York at Riga, west of Rochester, to teach in a large school near the Presbyterian church where his brother George was pastor and Titus served as Sunday school superintendent. Titus, in 1828, joined another brother in his mercantile business at Medina, west of Riga, working in the store, teaching school, and again serving as Sunday school superintendent. He debated his life's work— business, physician, teacher or minister, deciding "to be an active and devoted layman; to return to Connecticut, finish my business there, and then settle down to mercantile life in Medina."

Leaving Medina in April 1829, he went to Rochester to meet "an old and faithful friend, the Rev. H. Halsey," and join him in attending sessions of the General Assembly of the Presbyterian Church at Philadelphia. On the canal boat, Titus suffered from ague that kept increasing in intensity until they reached New York. There Titus had to give up the trip and instead sailed up Long Island Sound to Madison, Conn., just seven miles south of Killingworth. There he could go no farther and stayed with friends, prostrated for four months. He "wasted to skeleton," so weak that he would faint in an easy chair sitting up while his bed was being made.

It was autumn before he was able to make the trip home, "carefully in an easy carriage." By October he was well enough to teach in the local school. Then "a cheering revival" caused many of his pupils to be "hopefully born again," bringing about "the best year of my life up to that time." This proved to be his "turning point, the day of decision." "It was the voice of God to me," he rejoiced. "I could no longer doubt.... I said,'Lead me, Saviour. Tell me where to go and what to do, and I will go and do.'" Friends advised him to "pursue a short course of preparatory study, and enter Auburn Theological Seminary" in Massachusetts.

Back to western New York he went to spend the summer studying and laboring in the revival there with a pastor he had known. That winter and spring he spent in Knoxville,"continuing my classical studies, and assisting the pastor, and conducting evening meetings in surrounding villages." At Auburn Theological Seminary, he was licensed to preach April 17, 1833, having spent his Sabbaths teaching classes at the Auburn State Prison and serving as superintendent of the prison Sunday school. He was invited to preach that summer during a Rochester pastor's absence. Then, in response to an earlier request of the ABCFM, he went to Boston to be ordained and to sail on a mission of exploration to Patagonia, embarking in August. After his return, he published his *Adventures in Patagonia*.

Titus Coan was a man of action. He reached New London, Conn., May 7, 1834, reported to the Board at Boston, then hurried home to Killingworth "to surprise with joy my aged and mourning father." But his goal was Middlebury, Vt., there to realize at last his young man's fancy by claiming his chosen one, "who had waited patiently and without change of object or purpose, for seven long years to welcome this glad day."

At Riga, N. Y., Titus had often ridden past a little schoolhouse to glimpse through its windows an impressive face "that beamed on me like that of an angel." She was Miss Fidelia Church of Churchville. Titus attended church, for there he "often saw her sunlit face in the choir" and listened entranced by her sweet voice. That summer of 1827, Titus opened a select school and rejoiced when this admired one applied for admittance. Of his courtship, all he mentions is "it gave me a good opportunity to mark the character of her mind, which proved bright and receptive, and to become acquainted with her moral and social characteristics."

At Middlebury, Fidelia was teaching in the Female Seminary. After Titus arrived, the couple went directly to her father's house in Churchville, where they married on November 3, 1834. Next day they were off to visit friends in Connecticut and New York on their way to Boston. In Park Street Church on November 23 they met their traveling companions of the seventh company and received their instructions.

The merchant ship *Hellespont* took them on their way December 5th. As usual in the Atlantic, "the tempest raged" for a time, then the voyage turned pleasant. Titus had hoped to see "the wild coast of Patagonia," where he had "roamed with the savage tribes, or found more comforts among the whalers and sealers." But such views were denied him. After rounding Cape Horn the ship stopped for about three weeks, first at Valparaiso, Chile, on March 8, and then at Callao, Peru, on April 6, giving the adventurous Coans a chance to travel by carriage to Santiago about 100 miles inland and to enjoy a visit to Lima. By the 5th of June they spied the mountains of Hawaii and landed at Honolulu the next day.

At the general meeting then in progress, the Coans met the "veteran toilers" with whom they would join forces. "Some looked vigorous and strong," Titus observed, "others seemed pallid and wayworn." Here were their "brothers and sisters, with flocks of precious children." The Coans were eager and ready to forge into the wilds of Hawaii and add their energy and abilities to the tasks awaiting them at Hilo.

Harrowing Hazards of Mountain Traveling

Boarding an island schooner falsely called *Velocity*, Titus quickly realized the revolting conditions and uncertainties of this mode of inter-island travel. "The schooner was small, a slow sailer, dirty, crowded with more than one hundred passengers, mostly natives, and badly managed. The captain was an Irishman given to hard drinking." They sailed Monday, July 6, in a rough sea that made almost all dismally seasick, headed for Lahaina, Maui, 80 miles away. On Wednesday morning the captain announced the landing at Lahaina, just ahead, in about an hour. Alas, the inept captain had lost his bearings, turned about in the night and was back at Honolulu. They felt "a shock of agony" as they had endured for three days such extreme seasickness as never before experienced. Titus lamented, "Many of us had tasted neither food nor water from Monday to Wednesday, and all had lain crowded on a dirty deck, exposed to wind, rain, and wave."Yet nothing could be done but head for Lahaina again."

Nor did Coan's revulsion at such sea-going travel diminish over the years. Those poky, dirty, leaky old schooners took often four to six days to cover the 200 miles from Honolulu to Hilo, "sometimes lying becalmed ... for a whole week, in a burning sun..." Avoiding the small, filthy cabins, the missionaries slept on deck along with one hundred natives with their dogs and pigs. He remembered, "Mothers with four or five children, including a tender nursling, would lie miserably during the hot days under a burning sun, and by night in the rain, or wet with dashing waves, pallid and wan,with children crying for food,or retching with seasickness. I have seen these frail women with their pale children brought to land, exhausted, upon the backs of natives, carried on litters, and laid upon couches to be nourished till their strength returned." And why so often endure all this? All for the comradeship and cheer and enlightenment of their fellow workers at what Halford refers to as their "annual social debauch," the general meeting.

They finally managed to reach Hilo by July 21. Titus reveled in the grandeur of the "scene of surpassing loveliness" that the town by the bay with its towering mountain background offers. He was highly delighted with their assignment and ever after thanked the Lord for being sent there.

The Coans lived with the Lymans until November when the Goodriches left the house that they had built and Henry Lyman remembered as "a neat little two-storied wooden house, painted red, and famed all over the islands as the perfect reproduction of a New England farm house." Tackling the new language, the Coans went ahead "teaching a school of about a hundred almost naked boys and girls," at the same time being "pupils of a good man named Barnabas, who patiently drilled us daily in the language of his people." Within three months Titus was able to preach his first sermon in Hawaiian. Tours through the district also aided him greatly in learning to talk with the people.

As the Hilo Boarding School progressed and demanded all of David Lyman's time, he resigned as joint pastor to turn the preaching over to the eloquent Titus Coan. Titus battled the forces of nature, in spite of all terrible hazards, to deliver his God to the hearts of the 15,000 or so people along the 100-mile coastline of the Hilo district. He must teach them to drive away their superstitions, ignorance, hypocrisy and lower vices. To reach the widely separated points of population north from Hilo, he had to manage to cross over many of the 80 cataracts that cut deep, dangerous channels as they plunged from high mountains down to the sea over perilous precipices.

For many years Coan traveled on foot three or four times annually, with no roads, no bridges, and no horses, spending from ten to 20 days each time. He followed the winding trail down and up precipices "by grasping the shrubs and grasses, and with no little weariness and difficulty and some danger." The simplest way to cross streams was to skip from rock to rock, aided by an eight-or ten-foot-pole, which also helped him climb, let himself down steep banks, and to leap ditches up to eight feet wide. He waded across shallow streams, crossed swift ones on the shoulders of a sturdy native as he clung unto the fellow's bushy hair. His bearer carefully picked his away, slowly feeling his footing among the slippery boulders. As the native landed Titus safely on the bank, he would let loose with a relieved shout and laugh. This was a fearful way because "the cataracts are so numerous, the waters so rapid, and the uneven bottom so slippery that the danger of falling is imminent, and the recovery from a fall often impossible, the current hurrying one swiftly over a precipice into certain destruction." He knew of both natives and foreigners who lost their lives in those roaring streams including three from his Hilo church. Coan later abandoned this method because it was so dangerous.

Another method was to have strong men lock hands on the bank and then carefully and slowly move into the stream until the head man had a strong foothold near the opposite bank. "With my hands upon the shoulders of the men," Titus explains, "I passed along this chain of bones, sinews, and muscles and arrived in safety on the other side." The way to cross a swollen, raging river was to throw a rope across, fasten it on both sides to trees or rocks, and, hanging onto the rope with both hands, swing along the line to the opposite bank. If he did not remove his garments and shoes, he would push right on to the next station, preach in wet clothes and continue with his journey and labors in this condition until night. Then he would change, sleep well and get up ready for another full day of work.

Once it took Titus three hours, as the river was so wide the utmost skill and strength of the natives could not throw the line across. The raging waters rushing by and over a 20-foot drop just a short way downstream were enough to make even Titus shudder. One bold man on a rock up stream took the rope in his teeth, figured his chances, leaped into the torrents, and was swept violently down, struggling until he managed to set foot on the opposite shore but a few feet from the precipice. Coan would have forbidden it had he known of the plan earlier.

After some years and the building of a few rude roads, Coan tried crossing streams by swimming or hauling his horse over with ropes. This too had its hazards as the horse's hoof got caught between two rocks and over went steed and rider, "saved only by the energy and fidelity of the natives." One time his horse fell backward down a steep precipice and landed head down and feet in air, wedged between two rocks. Coan escaped instant death by his agility in sliding out of the saddle before the horse struck between the rocks. He summoned natives to rescue the wounded animal which he left behind to recover.

Journeys back by canoe at night were none the less perilous. On three occasions he barely survived "stormy winds, raging billows, and want of landing places along the lofty seawall of the coast." Once he and his companions ran into "a strong head-wind, with pouring rain and tumultuous waves in a dark midnight." They could not move against the storm for five hours, just "keep the prow of the canoe to the wind, and bail."

After much shouting and signals of distress to natives who gathered on the cliffs, four men came down, plunged naked into the towering waves at the mouth of the roaring river, fought their way through the raging waters to the canoe and told the crew to swim to land. Familiar with such dangerous conditions, the four men held the canoe in readiness for the dash into the river mouth until those on the cliff signaled the coming of a less furious wave. On the crest of the wave, with paddles beating the violent waters, they "rode triumphantly into the mouth of the river amid shouts of joy from those on land." Coan concludes with, "Praising the Lord for His goodness, and thanking the kind natives for their agency in delivering me, I walked the rest of the way home."

Father To Them All

Titus Coan carefully planned his tours to villages sending ahead his preaching schedule. Having mastered the language, he could "converse, preach, and pray with comfort" quite effectively, speaking with a charm and preciseness that captivated his audiences. On his 30-day tour of the Big Island starting November 29, 1836, he preached up to five times a day and held many personal conversations about the kingdom of God and examined 20 schools with about 1,200 pupils. Coan kept a notebook record of every Hawaiian, checking on each person he had listed.

Titus was supervising the studies of about 2,000 pupils in more than 50 schools until 1837 when the Wilcoxes came to relieve him. He served also as doctor until a missionary physician was assigned in 1849. In the meantime, he found that "the sick and afflicted multitudes... begging for remedies for almost all kinds of diseases" overcame his capacity of time and knowledge to provide the cures they needed.

Fidelia opened a boarding school for twenty girls from seven to ten years old in 1838. The people erected a comfortable thatched building with a partial floor for the teacher's chair and desk, open cells with beds of straw, and a diningroom with table, seats and eating equipment. This school lasted about eight years and "sent out a company of girls... distinguished among their companions for neatness, skill, industry and piety." Fidelia, weakened by domestic cares, then had to give up this added responsibility.

Henry Lyman, with "Father Coan" on one of his tours in 1848, tells of Coan's work among some more isolated people, still somewhat primitive but "not utterly degraded. Religion had taken possession of their lives," Henry noted. "The periodical visits of the missionary were the great events of their life... He knew them all by name; he examined the progress of the children in their lessons at school; he prescribed medicine for the sick, even going so far as to enter the realm of minor surgery with his jackknife.

"He visited the widows and orphans, counseling them with regard to their welfare in this life as well as the next; he was interested in the output of the salt pools and bestowed words of commendation upon the last new canoe or the latest fishnet. With the elders of the church, he reviewed the roll of the congregation, marked off the names, counted the number of births, ascertained the present abode and occupation of every member of the flock; so far as possible, he made it a point to see and exchange a few cheerful words with everyone in the throng."

Cases of discipline also demanded his attention. His "ecclesiastical tribunal" must examine the "row of penitent sinners" — hardened tobacco users, those hard drinkers "befuddled with fermented potatoes or other equally primitive intoxicants," unrighteous gamblers, giddy girls too "lavish of their charms." But "the judges were lenient." The sinners repented, received "a solemn admonition from the pastor," shook hands and returned to the fold. Coan then performed the rites of baptism and admission to the church and the celebration of Holy Communion with a morsel of wheaten bread and a cup that contained molasses and water.

At the next village, Coan, indefatigable and "cheerful and radiant as the sunshine," enthusiastically joined in a big Sunday school celebration. The people gathered about him in the evening, lit huge candlenut torches, ate and then eagerly took part in an evening prayer service. Coan read to them from the Bible. "How these simple people hung upon his lips, listening with eyes aflame and faces all aglow!" Lyman observed. Though Coan was tiring by then, Henry noted, "The teacher never wearied nor flagged, but overflowed like a fountain of beneficence till the evening was far spent and our eyes would remain open no longer."

So they continued from village to village. "Everywhere was the same cheery welcome, the same abandonment of wordly occupations, the same fervid interest in things spiritual and eternal. For these simple islanders, religion opened their only avenue to literature, poetry, art, morality, and the higher life — their all in all. The missionary moved among them as the messenger of God, and his remarkable personality rendered his influence irresistible."

Coan met one notable exception to such generous hospitality. In one small village 18 miles from Hilo, he "had taken special pains to tame and Christianize the people." But they failed to warm up to his presence, even showing reluctance to bringing him a cup of cold water from a distant spring. On his return, he stopped, "preached and conversed with the villagers." Though they declared they had no food to give him, that night he heard the family outside eating heartily. Exasperated with their hardness of heart Coan held a meeting, telling them since his words to them had borne no fruit, that he would let them reflect now on what he had advised them. Then, whenever they would "repent and desire to hear the Gospel again," he told them, "send for me and I will hasten to you with joy." But they never sent.

Then, in 1840, a lava flow swept through Puna, devasting their village. They settled in another section. In 1853 smallpox wiped out most of the population of the village, the only place in Puna so afflicted. Coan visited "the stricken remnant of the sufferers, spoke words of condolence, and encouraged them to come with their sins and sorrows to the Saviour." Though Coan vehemently proclaimed the demands of the one true God, he treated the people individually as his children, teaching them, advising them, encouraging them as a father and winning their grateful love.

This spirit of helpfulness extended also to the seamen who came to Hilo. He invited them to his home, provided religious books and tracts and held a church service for them every Sunday afternoon until the Coans turned their old stone house into a Seaman's Church with a reading room. All this filled his Sabbath, with Sunday school at 9:00, preaching at 10:30, meeting for inquirers at 12:00, preaching at 1:00 and again at 3:00 in English. His crusading cordiality influenced a number "to forsake all sin and to lead godly lives," some becoming church members and even ministers. Several ship officers gave up whaling on the Sabbath and held religious meetings. Coan formed many "precious friendships" among these seamen, including "noble specimens, not only of generosity and fine natural talent ... but also many choice Christians."

The Great Evangelist

Coan was increasingly fulfilling his role as the great evangelist. He had much admired the work of his famous cousin Asahel Nettleton, participated in evangelistic work in western New York, and had recently been stirred by the explosive revivals of the famous Charles Grandison Finney of Oberlin, Ohio. He noted that "like doctrines, prayers, and efforts seemed to produce like fruits among this people," who loved his flashing, fiery way of making the power of God fill their hearts with both fear and love. They responded with emotional outbursts as substitutes for their former joyous customs this new religion denied them — their *hula*, their poetic chants and their games.

In Puna, people "rallied in masses" at his meetings and followed him, seeking "to hear more of the 'Word of Life'" until late into the night. One Sabbath he preached at three villages between daylight and his ten o'clock breakfast, and his listeners followed him from village to village until at the fourth he had a great congregation. Another Sunday multitudes thronged to hear him. "The blind were led; the maimed, the aged and decrepit, and many invalids were brought on the backs of friends. There was great joy and much weeping in the assembly." He preached ten sermons in two days and carried on conversations with the crowds that pressed around him.

He made converts of even the high priest and priestess of the volcano. Coan turned this stately man from "an idolater, a drunkard, an adulterer, a robber, and a murderer" into a "penitent, [who] appeared honest and earnest in seeking the Lord." His sister, "tall and majestic" but "more haughty and stubborn," for a long time held out against Coan's appeals "to bow to the claims of the Gospel; but at length she yielded, confessed herself a sinner and under the authority of a higher Power, and with her brother became a docile member of the church."

The people from outlying places thronged into Hilo to live there and hear more and more of the divine messages of Titus Coan that so exuberantly enriched their lives, increasing the town's population to about 10,000 souls. They crowded into the great native house of worship, 85 feet by 200 feet, packed "almost to suffocation."

The natives planned a larger church where Coan could preach to the people of Hilo in the morning and to the people of Puna and Ka'u in the afternoon. At the same time the other group would meet for prayer in the smaller house. In about three weeks the men and women cut and hauled down from the forest some three to five miles away, "through mud and jungle, and over streams and hillocks," great quantities of timbers to build the great church, which filled with "a joyful crowd of about 2,000" on the Sabbath. Wilcox thought as many as 5,000 could crowd into this vast structure.

After the terrible tidal wave of November 7, 1837, that swept about 200 unsuspecting people and their houses and possessions into the tumultuous waves, drowning 13 of them, the people felt this catastrophe showed "God speaking to them out of heaven." They crowded more and more into Coan's meetings.

These Hawaiians found physical release by intensely displaying their emotions in response to Coan's rousing speeches. He tells of one man who suddenly "burst out in a fervent prayer, with streaming tears, saying, 'Lord have mercy on me; I am dead in sin.'" This display of great agitation as he wept loudly and trembled greatly, turned the congregation into a "weeping, wailing, praying multitude." While Coan was gratified at such showings of the power of the Lord, he "warned against hypocrisy, and against trusting in such demonstrations" and told them "that their future lives of obedience or disobedience would prove or disprove their spiritual life."

Coan's great "day of days" arrived July 7, 1838, when he dramatically baptized 1,705 natives specially selected from the roll of names to be called from the villages of each district, Hilo, Puna and Ka'u. They formed and sat in long rows. Then all former members of the church were seated on the side opposite them. After singing and prayer and an explanation of the rite of baptism, Coan strode back and forth between the rows sprinkling each individual from the basin of water he carried. From the center of the congregation, he pronounced the customary words of the rite. " All heads were bowed, and tears fell. All was hushed except sobs and breathing." The ceremony closed with the Lord's supper for all 2,400 communicants present.

Those baptized that day had survived Coan's careful process of tabulating their spiritual progress as registered in his notebook as individuals who appeared to be "sincere and true converts." He kept watch over those registered for from three to 12 months and then selected some for examination, eliminating those who sinned or seemed doubtful. The "hopefully converted" ones then spent several months at the central station, carefully instructed and watched over, "sifted and resifted with scrutiny." Coan finally selected his 1,705 from about 3,000 listed, limiting the number lest a higher count "might stagger the faith of others" with its unbelievable size. Each church member had to swear on the Bible "to abstain from all that is forbidden, and to obey all that is commanded therein."

Coan rejoiced that "thousands of habitual smokers abandoned the habit at once." Some did go back to this evil habit, but Coan claims he was more lenient with them than with those who broke the more specific biblical commandments. "I have never excommunicated or suspended members for this indulgence," he asserts, "but have taught them, by precept and example, a better way." Henry Lyman's memory of Coan's attitude was rather different. He observed, "No matter how upright and virtuous their lives, men and women who would not forsake the pipes were bundled out of the congregation of true-believers and handed over to the tender mercies of Satan and his host." Henry felt kindly toward the Catholic priest who accepted "the devotees of tobacco and other loose livers whom Mr. Coan would not tolerate in his church on any consideration whatever." The saintly priest welcomed "such hardened sinners.... This was naturally very galling to an imperious spirit" such as Titus Coan's.

Though many heartily approved, some less exuberant missionaries expressed doubts of the final effectiveness of such wholesale conversions. But Coan was the king of evangelists, and his mighty personal powers held sway over his people. Though others who flourished in the reaping of converts had added hundreds to their rolls, they later saw many drift away from the fold or revert to their former sins. Those whose hearts Coan had won over to the Lord held on to their faith more steadfastly. His record showed no more of his people dropping by the wayside than those of more conservative churches.

Builder of the Church

The large Hilo church, like others of native construction, succumbed in 1840 to "a mighty wind." Men with axes felled trees and hewed timber for their first framed church. Coan worked right along with the natives in dragging the heavy timber down to Hilo "through mud and jungle, over rocks and streams," encouraging the people with his energetic leadership. They loved and eagerly worked for their friend and pastor who was one with them in body and spirit.

He joined in this labor with the "hundreds of willing men and women, provided with ropes made of bark of the hibiscus, with light upper garments, and with leggins of the Adam and Eve style, such as never feared mud and water.... Arranged by a captain in two lines, with drag-ropes in hand, ready to obey the command of their chosen leader, they stood waiting his order.... 'Grasp the ropes;bow the head; blister the hand; go; sweat!'" And away they all did rush, "shouting merrily, and singing to measure. Then comes the order,'Halt, drop drag-ropes, rest!'...repeated at longer or shorter intervals according to the state of the ground," through "the trees, the jungle, the mud, the streams, and the lava fields."

They "employed a Chinese carpenter at a reasonable price, to frame and raise the building, all his pay to be in trade," as money was not yet available. "The natives, men and women, soon covered the rough frame with thatching. There was no floor but the earth, and the only windows were holes about three feet square ...on the sides and ends.... This, the first framed church edifice built in Hilo, and ...capable of seating about 2,000 people," was dedicated in June 1842.

Imagine the excitement in this simple church when the people heard their first concert played by the brass band from the frigate *United States*. "After playing several sacred songs which delighted the natives beyond all music they had heard before, the band, at a signal from the commodore, struck up 'Hail Columbia.' An electric thrill rushed through the great congregation, and all sprang to their feet in amazement and delight."

As this building "became old and dilapidated," they started "a year's hard toil bringing stones on men's shoulders" to construct "an edifice of stone and mortar." Such labor and the failure to reach bedrock after digging a trench six feet deep for the foundations made them decide to build a wooden church instead. They laid the cornerstone November 14, 1857, and dedicated the building April 8, 1859. "It was then the finest church edifice on the islands," Coan boasted.

Coan and his people had determined that no dedication was to take place until the last $600 debt of the $13,000 cost was met. The plan and hope was that the people would donate that amount on the final day. That day, alas, was "stormy, the paths muddy, and the rivers without bridges." But such conditions failed to deter the faithful followers of Titus Coan and the great Lord God.... They came "flocking in from all points until the house was crowded to its utmost capacity." Coan's well organized congregation came forward quickly and smoothly with their offerings. "A shout of joy went up to heaven" when Coan declared the contributions to be over $800. By three weeks later, the faithful added another $400, making the dedication offerings $1,239. This generously filled treasury expanded to provide several thousand dollars more for a large bell and for keeping the church and the grounds in good condition.

The severe 1868 earthquake proved how wise they were to have built of wood. A stone church could not have survived. The wooden building is the present Haili Church in Hilo, named from Haili Kalamanu, meaning "Paradise of the Birds," that place being eight miles away from which they had dragged the great mass of timbers.

Coan's ready workers for the Lord in other parts of his domain also labored to enjoy more stable church buildings. Seven were ready by April 1853; more were in progress. The people had spontaneously provided also smaller houses for social gatherings, prayer meetings and conferences. Seven branch churches were established in 1867 so that people could avoid the "unwieldy" crowds at Haili and the inconveniences of travel.

Coan directed groups of ten to forty to go forth two and two, seeking out hundreds in every out-of-the-way corner, "the sick, the ignorant, the stupid, the timid" to teach them "to give up their sins... [and] to see that the call of love and the offers of life were heard by all."

Practical Titus Coan sincerely regretted "controversies among Christians." The churches should spend their efforts fighting sin and Satan, he felt sure, and not in conflict with one another. "The many and different church organizations,with their external rites, rules, and preferences, never offend me where there is 'the unity of the spirit in the bonds of peace,'" he agreed. "All Christians are bound, by the supreme law of heaven to love one another, not to bite and devour, nor to indulge in 'envy and strife.'"

This Christian tolerance in Coan's mind, however, did not extend to Catholics, Mormons and Episcopalians who came trying to compete with this grand master in his own territory. His Catholic opponents especially irritated him. These bold and defiant priests confronted him everywhere. Worst of all, they "perplexed and vexed the simple natives" with accusations that they were doomed to perdition because they were outside the true church and living as heretic Protestants.

Once a French priest and his 200 followers blocked Coan's progress through a narrow pass, demanding he debate with them. Coan refused and tried to push his way through the crowd. The difference between their views was whether Peter or Jesus Christ is the head of the Church. A powerful native finally pushed the Catholics aside to make way for Coan to continue on his way. When the Mormon priests sought to have him join them, he refuted their beliefs, as he knew the Book of Mormon and its doctrines well.

The Episcopalian Bishop Staley twice visited Hilo to set up an effective branch of his church there. But Coan's loyal followers spurned his arrangements, and the development of an Anglican Church in Hilo was held up until 1903. And yet Coan declared, "We wish to be liberal and to labor in loving harmony with all who love our Lord and Saviour, and who pray heartily for His coming, but we pity all who are exclusive, and who vainly set themselves up as the only true church."

Adventures, Travels, Other Interests

Coan's interests ranged far beyond his own Hilo district. When the Mission felt a strong need for its own vessel to carry men and supplies to the Marquesas and Micronesia, it was Titus Coan who proposed to meet the cost by having the children of the United States contribute the money in shares of ten cents. The Board agreed, the appeal proved popular, the children contributed the needed funds, and the *Morning Star* was built, manned and provided. It received a jubilant welcome from the people of Hilo when it stopped there two days on its return from the Marquesas in July 1857.

In March 1860 Coan took a two-month sail on this *Morning Star* to survey the missionary field in the Marquesas. The scientific interests of Coan produced a clear historical, geographical and anthropological report on this savage region and the efforts of England, America and France to develop it. He questioned the need for the French to have tried "to propagate the Christian religion by the use of fire and sword." He visited the Hawaiian missionaries sent out first in 1853. One was the Rev. Samuel Kauwealoha, a native of Hilo. These devoted and courageous leaders faced "bloodthirsty cannibals" and tales of their terrible killings were told wherever Coan visited.

A meeting of the missionaries from the three Marquesan islands brought together eight, with wives and delegates, representing about 3,000 Marquesans. Coan got the figures on the meager accomplishments: 34 church members, 221 pupils.

The ever-adventurous and energetic Coan picked a dangerous journey by foot to meet the ship at another port. He climbed up a steep trail along sharp ridges to 3,500 feet for "two hours of exhausting toil and heat," and then an even more difficult descent of three and a half hours over a rough, rocky trail where a false step would have plunged him to certain destruction. This hardy missionary was back in Hilo by mid-May.

Again he sailed to this desperate field of missionary endeavor in April 1867, garnering more information about these strange islands. Ready to be a brave knight to the rescue, he ignored danger and went to visit a missionary's wife who had been seduced by two brothers. Though he "found her forlorn and desiring to return," she knew that she would be killed before the men would let her go. In came the two abductors, armed with sheath knives. Coan pleaded with them to let the woman return to her husband but to no avail. As the odds were against him, he had to leave without her. She died soon after. Ending his 23-day visit in the islands, Coan returned to Hilo in June.

His next long journey was to visit his homeland in 1870 especially to provide medical skill for Fidelia's precarious health. The Coans reached San Francisco on May 5, spent 14 days in California and then took the train to Salt Lake City to visit the Mormon institutions. They met several of the

Mormon missionaries that had been in Hilo. The tabernacle service left Coan further convinced that the Mormons' bold assertions lacked proof. The Coans stopped in Iowa, then went on to Chicago, where they saw two of the Lyman boys, Henry, a physician, and David, a lawyer.

Back east, Coan was in his element visiting places and people, addressing meetings, conventions and churches of various denominations. He was pleased by evidences of church unity of purpose and the possible increased efficiency through religious cooperation. He enthused over his week in Washington. He visited Howard University, Andover, Bradford, Vassar, Union, Auburn, and Princeton with "great enjoyment." He was especially delighted to attend the annual American Board meeting in Brooklyn and to meet other missionaries from all parts of the world, presenting to his eager mind "intelligence, culture, piety, beaming like sunlight from human faces."

Tears wet his eyes as he, now 69 years old, viewed again after 44 years the scenes of his childhood at Killingworth. The old homestead lay there but the cottage was gone as also many trees from the orchard. All his brothers save one lay beneath gravestones in the cemetery. Titus was to be the last to go.

Cordially welcomed back at Hilo, Titus still felt saddened. The journey had failed in its hopes of restoring Fidelia's health and she "was growing feebler day by day." His home lost "the dear one who had been its light and joy for 36 years" on Sunday, September 29, 1872, at the age of 62. Hers was the first grave in the Prospect Hill cemetery.

Titus extolled his lost one as "an extensive and eclectic reader, a clear and logical thinker ... a peerless helper." Her marvelous self-denial had sent him off to Patagonia when he had doubts of leaving her and later on to his trips to the Marquesas. She assured him that she was not afraid to remain alone. "To her tender love, her faithful care, her wise counsels, her efficient help, and her blameless life," he declared, "I owe under God the chief part of my happiness and of my usefulness ..."

Titus Coan became familiar with all the Hawaiian islands and with the missionaries and their work. Only once did illness delay his active life. A fever kept him from the pulpit for two Sundays when he once visited Waimea, Hawaii. He hiked with Lorenzo Lyons over the northern hills to Kohala; with Elias Bond he "descended into the deep and grand valley of Waipio" and climbed mighty Mauna Kea. He visited the Maui stations and "ascended to the summit crater of Haleakala." He also visited Molokai. The distance to Kauai delayed his visit there to 1874.

At the time Coan wrote his book in 1881, he reported the existence of 56 Hawaiian churches with only five foreign pastors, the other pulpits filled by Hawaiian converts. This was not a favorable situation, as the Hawaiians were still lacking in knowledge and experience to dominate the churches as their Puritan teachers had.

"Nearly all of our native pastors have been slack in church discipline, indiscriminate in receiving to church communion, and remiss in looking after wandering members, so that our church statistics are in so confused a state as to be past remedy," Coan regretted. "Out of more than 70,000 who have been received to the churches, our last report returns only 7,459, or about one in ten of those received."

Coan had high ideals, wide interests, a mind that carefully organized facts and a determination to do his best in every respect. Having lived a full and rewarding life, he closed his career on December 1, 1882, the year his autobiography was published, *Life in Hawaii*.

16

THE WILCOX
WOES

Abner and Lucy Hart Wilcox — Source: HMCS Library

From Poverty To Perplexities

Abner Wilcox, a slim farm boy at Harwinton, Conn., looking for honorable service in the work of the Lord, applied for a place in missions in 1836. In his letter to the American Board, he confessed having "found the Saviour" seven years earlier. At that time, he explained, "I was convinced that I had committed the unpardonable Sin and that my eternal damnation was sealed," for he felt "as if Satan with all his Legions were turned loose upon me and had come to convey me down to the yawning Gulf." Believing "God is a very merciful Being," he "groaned out a feeble prayer" and "a flood of light and glory burst upon my soul," he wrote. Thus he held "an earnest desire to wear out in the service of the Redeemer among the Heathen."

His pastor at the Harwinton Congregational Church wrote as recommendation to the Board: "Mr. Wilcox is a young man, unmarried and free from matrimonial engagements, and of a sound practical judgment." Abner had been a member of his church for five years and was teaching in the district school. The pastor added that Abner "has uniformly sustained an excellent Christian reputation, and, notwithstanding a considerable natural diffidence, is now exciting a salutary and sanctified influence among my young people."

Of course Abner did need a "matrimonial engagement" and found one with Miss Lucy Eliza Hart of Norfolk. She was described as an "amiable, intelligent and pious lady" and of a "sprightly, laughing nature." Since she was a poor farmer's daughter with even less of worldly goods than Abner, they both had to depend on the Board for "pecuniary assistance." Abner could buy his own clothes but must depend on the Board "for books, furniture, etc." Lucy needed "the means for buying articles of dress, sheeting, etc."Abner explained that Miss Hart's parents "are in somewhat indigenous circumstances; have a somewhat numerous family; and will be able to render very little help." Three months later Abner had to request "some more pecuniary assistance."

It all worked out well. Abner and Lucy were married at Cairo, N.Y., November 23, 1836. They arrived with the eighth company at Honolulu April 9, 1837. The *Mary Frazier* enjoyed a "quick and easy passage," in fact the quickest any missionary transport had made. One of the wives on the voyage noted that Abner could write good poetry. "His natural disposition is rather quick and impatient," she decided and that "Mrs. Wilcox is much like her husband."

After two months with the Bingham family, the Wilcoxes sailed on a small schooner, June 19. On the crowded deck all became seasick. The ship was becalmed and they roasted in the scorching sun. On Maui, they enjoyed a land trip to Wailuku. They reached Hilo on June 28, 1837.

As Abner's school had quite a fluctuating attendance, he had to go out to hunt up scholars. He disliked that extra labor. He found the children to be wild, rude and uncultivated as wild cattle and would take years to tame.

He went on tours with Titus Coan. He found the lava so rough that it could wear out a pair of shoes in a day. The native needs and demands amazed him. "The People pressed, literally upon us to hear the word of God. O this dying people!" he cried in anguish, "perishing for lack of — vision? O, no, perishing I fear because there is so little faith, prayer, holy living, and effort on the part of the missionaries."

Then Lucy was expecting. A flurry of letter writing by her missionary sisters offered all kinds of helpful advice on the problems and joys of becoming a mother. Chamberlain dispatched a schooner to bring the Wilcoxes to the doctor at Honolulu.

Four days later Abner was rejoicing in Honolulu at the excitement of receiving letters from home. "None but those who have had the experience," he proclaimed, "can know the satisfaction and pleasure, mingled indeed with melancholy, and the excitement of the nerves which the receiving of letters in our circumstances produces."

Charles Hart Wilcox was born April 10, 1838. The Wilcoxes spent three months in Honolulu, leaving May 29. Abner ably provided all he could for the hard journey back. To ensure milk for the little one, he brought along a goat with kid. Then he learned that goats get seasick and would give no milk. So he also got a native nurse to go along, including her husband and child. They continued from Lahaina June 25 for the long week's trip to Hilo.

"The voyage was a tedious one," he reported. "The vessel was crazy, but the natives trying to manage it seemed more crazy still…. The goat was sick as well as the other two nurses, Mrs. Wilcox and the native woman, so that I was under the necessity of cooking arrowroot twice a day for the child."

The Wilcoxes struggled on with the problems of reconciling their New England upbringing with the often uncooperative ways of the natives. Lucy found her pupils "slow learners with the alphabet" and saw that much "patience, perseverance and wisdom [were] needed."

Returning from the general meeting in Honolulu on June 23, 1840, the party spent three days at Lahaina. After leaving there on Monday, they found Tuesday "a somewhat boisterous day, the sea very rough." That was enough for Abner. He decided to leave ship at Kawaihae, "preferring to take a land journey home to enduring the sufferings of the voyage." With men and horses the family started in the afternoon for the station at Waimea, 12 miles distant. From the coast they experienced oppressive heat. At the higher elevation they met a "cold, damp and unpleasant atmosphere more like November than July." Snow still remained on Mauna Kea from the previous winter.

They rested two days with the Lorenzo Lyons family and left July 4, reaching Hilo on the 8th, only two days later than the vessel they had left. While Abner felt the journey had been "in some respects unpleasant and laborious," he declared he "by no means regretted our having left the vessel," knowing what they would have had to suffer on it. But the Wilcoxes were yet to experience the most excruciating of journeys back from Honolulu to Hilo.

That Frustrating Journey

As Lucy became pregnant and ill early in 1841, the Wilcoxes went to Honolulu to get the help of Dr. Judd. They spent seven months and five days there. Perhaps to keep them active and occupied, the doctor first sent them on a tour of Oahu. Lucy and the children were carried in two *maneles*, swung on poles carried by the natives. First, 12 miles to Ewa, to stay with the Artemas Bishops, then another 18 miles to Waialua to stay with the families of Edwin Locke and John Emerson, next a two-day trip to Kaneohe, home of the Benjamin Parkers, and then back to Honolulu by the inland route, only 10 or 12 miles.

For three or four weeks they had to stay in a little mud-walled one-room cottage. They moved to a larger two-room house and then stayed in a small house owned by the Benjamin Parkers. Abner was kept busy for two months conducting writing schools for boys and men, girls and women. Their third son Edward Payson was born September 1, 1841, and in October they moved to the Levi Chamberlains' house to stay while the Chamberlain family were on Maui.

Though knowing well the sufferings of a passage to Hilo, they little suspected what was in store for them. When the schooner departed from Honolulu on Tuesday, November 9, they crawled into a small cabin and lay there seasick. A brief stop at the Dwight Baldwins' in Lahaina, Friday, and next day they were being buffeted by the angry waters of the channel. Sunday they rounded the Kohala coast of Hawaii Island and stood off Waipio valley by Monday.

Tuesday and Wednesday the small ship still battled squally weather, " the schooner rolling and pitching with great violence," and the Wilcoxes "in constant fear [the vessel] would capsize, as the helmsman would frequently fail asleep." By Thursday the wind blew almost a gale. A leak in the boat set the men to frequent pumping. The captain and three men landed at Waipio for supplies. The Wilcoxes trembled with fear that the vessel "would be blown to pieces and sink," as the two men and a boy left aboard could not manage the sails. At night the captain returned with 12 more passengers to go to Hilo, a Chinese and his family of Hawaiians.

By Friday night the frightened Wilcox family felt sure that their lives were in jeopardy. The crew had used Abner's fuel for cooking so that he had just enough to boil a couple *taro*, their "last and scanty meal aboard." The fierce winds tore the rigging apart. The captain decided to turn back to Mahukona on the leeward side, "a small hamlet of fishermen built on the rocks." Next morning, Saturday, November 20, they landed, hungry and exhausted, after having endured a nerve-wracking imprisonment of 11 days.

When the captain decided to sail on, Abner refused to continue such a life-endangering voyage. He determined to head overland to the mission of Elias Bond at Kohala. Natives carried the three boys and led enfeebled Lucy to a small grass house they found at Mahukona. Food was so scarce they could get only a few pieces of potato.

On foot in the burning sun, Abner bravely set out to Father Bond's, ten miles away, but the first seven were all uphill so that he had to halt his speed often to catch his breath. On the way he hired six men to help him on the return and made his way to Kohala by 2:30. As Bond had no *manele* for carrying the family, they took an old arm chair and rigged it up with ropes and a pole. After hastily swallowing some food and sticking some in his handkerchief for the family, Abner started back on horseback, two natives carrying the chair.

As the horse proceeded slowly over the rough and rocky trail, Abner met the two native boys. Either eager to be helpful or enjoying a bit of mischief, they thought they would speed up the languid steed by putting a bush on his tail. Frightened, the horse "reared and ran furiously over the rocks and stones," Abner relates. Expecting to be thrown off any moment and suffer broken bones as he was dashed against the rocks, Abner managed to hang on "by the grace of Providence," and pulled the panicked horse to a stop.

Reaching the shore at sunset, he got his family ready for the hard travel up ahead. He had hired the men at their own price of 25 cents, but now they demanded more. His arguments proving futile, he had to pay the extra price or they would not budge. It was now the cold of night as they plodded on till 10:30 before they reached the haven of Bond's house. Next day was the Sabbath. As Bond had not yet mastered the Hawaiian tongue, Abner had to preach for him all that day.

They rested Monday. Abner took off on Tuesday eager to reach Hilo to get their goods off the vessel and dry them out. He headed first for the Waimea station and the hospitality of Lorenzo Lyons. On Wednesday he hastened off on horseback to the precipices and then on foot to Hilo to retrieve their wet belongings. When he reached there Friday evening, the vessel still had not arrived nor by noon the following Monday, the 29th. Back to Waimea he hurried to get his family arriving Wednesday evening.

His family had reached Waimea Friday after pushing their way mostly through woods for 30 miles. A few miles on their way, these natives also demanded double pay. But Lucy would not give in. She told them to take her back to Kohala, where she would complain to the governor there. That settled the strike.

Abner's men, due Thursday, did not get there until Friday. The group started Hilo-bound about 10:00 a.m., Abner riding the horse. As they came to the great swamp, rain descended in torrents, drenching and chilling all. The horse had to plod through mud up to its knees. Then a sudden thunderclap sent the horse plunging wildly, and the wind turned Abner's umbrella inside out frightening the horse even more so that Abner was nearly thrown off. But the same Providence that had saved him before preserved him again. It was 2:00 p.m. by the time they had stumped several miles across the swamp. Happily they found a native house, where a fire gave them a chance to change to dry clothes.

Next morning greeted them with a bright Hawaiian day and the route favored them with easier traveling. As they grew thirsty, Abner remembered an orange tree he had seen before. He went off and found it, returning with a couple dozen oranges to provide a cool and refreshing thirst-quencher. That Saturday night they reached a village where they rested over the Sabbath, and Abner held services at the meeting house morning and afternoon.

Monday they had to make their way over deep ravines and precipices, spending that night and the rainy next day in the deep valley of Laupahoehoe. There they expected to have a double canoe from Hilo meet them, but the sea was too rough. They had to negotiate the precipitous land route.

The greedy natives now demanded "an exorbitant price." Abner managed to strike a bargain with them, and they pushed on to cover the remaining 30 or 40 miles with this family of five facing the dangers of climbing down and up again many precipices and crossing about 75 streams swollen by heavy rains. For such passages across Abner explained, "The 12 natives would plant themselves in the deepest places in a phalanx, and the pole, to which was suspended the chair in which Mrs. W. lay, was passed through their hands, and the children and baggage passed from one to another till we all got over."

With this organized procedure, they finally reached Hilo by December 9, after suffering "a captivity to fear of 30 days." They got there just as the schooner they had started on was entering Hilo Bay. Their goods aboard the vessel suffered much damage. Their strenuous overland trek had cost them $15 as well as all that agony.

*   *   *

By that time the government was paying teachers and the schools were doing better, according to Abner's later reports. When Abner learned that Coan had written the Board "that the teacher of Hilo schools had long been playing truant from his labors," he responded to the Board with eloquent indignation.

The Wilcoxes had lived first with the Lymans in the house they built in 1835. Then they moved across the road to one end of the "Little Stone House" built by Jonathan Green. For their last five years Abner's family occupied the Cape Cod cottage. Lucy was ill for about two months beginning the first of December 1843. Their fourth son Albert Spencer was born June 24, 1844. They transferred to Waialua on Oahu that year, Abner directing the Manual Labor Boarding School started by Edwin Locke while Lucy conducted a females' weekly prayer meeting.

The Wilcox fame as missionaries rests chiefly with their work for over 20 years at Waioli on Kauai after they were stationed there in 1846. There Abner taught a boys' school and preached. While he and son Albert were on a trip to Boston from December 9, 1850 to April 4, 1852, Lucy took charge of the school. In broken health from their labors and from illness incurred on a trip home in 1869, they died within a week of each other at Colebrook, Conn., after 33 years of devotion to their work in Hawaii.

Their fifth son Samuel Whitney was born September 19, 1847, and married the Lymans' daughter Emma on October 7, 1874.

17

CHARLES WETMORE —
HILO PHYSICIAN-
DRUGGIST

Charles and Lucy Wetmore (1848) — Source: HMCS Library

Dr. Charles Hinckley Wetmore came as Hilo's first physician in 1849, the first of 12 individual arrivals after the twelveth and last company landed in 1848. He was the ninth missionary physician, and the third on Hawaii, following Dr. Dwight Baldwin at Waimea (1832 to 1835) and Dr. Seth Andrews at Kailua (1837 to 1848).

Wetmore, born at Lebanon, Conn., February 8, 1820, was proud to claim he hailed from a family known for their "longevity, piety, hasty tempers, love of kindred ... spoken of as honest, upright, philanthropic, public minded." He worked his way through Berkshire Medical Institute from 1843 to 1846 by teaching school winters and studying summers. At Pittsfield he won his medical degree and the daughter of the farm family with whom he boarded, Lucy Sheldon Taylor. Charles was a tall, handsome fellow, Lucy a pert, slim lass with sparkling eyes and a fetching smile. They both enjoyed an active interest in nature—its plants and minerals, and, of course, the stars at night.

Fate or the will of God sent Charles to Hawaii instead of India. He did not appear before the Board on the date set for the India appointment because of a black eye one of his arrogant students had given him. He married Lucy just three weeks before they sailed for Hawaii on a pleasant voyage of 146 days, arriving unexpected at Honolulu on March 11, 1849. Notice of his appointment sent three months before they left the States, reached Hawaii six months after the Wetmores landed.

Hilo welcomed them on Friday, May 18. By August, Lucy was happy in her new home with its large yard rich in rose bushes and fruit trees. A trip to Waiohinu in Ka'u was pleasant and interesting, but the sandstorm and then heavy sleet that pelted Lucy on the return trip made her feel worse than the coldest winters experienced in Connecticut.

Lucy felt lonely while Charles was off on tours with Coan to visit the other five stations on the island. Avoiding the strenuous land travel that had worn out Dr. Andrews, Wetmore traveled by canoe first to Waimea and on to Kohala for the birth of Ellen Bond's son, then from Mahukona he sailed to Kealakekua Bay. One night he suffered from flea infestation when he stopped overnight on shore south of Kawaihae. The next night with Father Thurston at Kailua proved more pleasant. He reached Kaawaloa just in time to avoid being on the furious seas stirred up by the most severe storm ever witnessed. He continued on horseback by way of Waiohinu and the volcano. A strong native carried his clothing and medicines.

Dr. Wetmore's duty was first to Mission families, then to natives and finally to foreign residents and visitors. In his first year he was kept busy by an influenza epidemic. Then, realizing the havoc caused by smallpox among the American Indians, he started vaccinating the people as a wise precaution.

The Wetmores' grief after their first child was stillborn in 1850 prompted them to open a school for children of mostly Chinese fathers. Lucy delighted in these young pupils with skins of a different hue realizing that they had "affectionate hearts, inteligent minds and deathless souls."

Lucy's loneliness while Charles was away made her decide to go along, but she "found going rough afoot over sharp lava, steep passes, by donkey and *manele* borne by two men" over narrow trails and through heavy brush. As natives gathered to watch them eat, she felt annoyed at having every movement eyed although she realized that it must be the first time these isolated people had seen a white woman.

On March 3, 1853, their first live baby, Charles Jr. was born. "He is indeed the light of our eyes and joy of our hearts," Lucy happily declared in September, when making short dresses for the boy to free him from the sweat and encumbrance of his flannel petticoats.

When smallpox struck the islands in 1853, Dr. Wetmore's foresight in starting vaccinations in his first year paid off. These vaccinations, combined with what Dr. Halford credits "his prompt, efficient methods of counterattack," cut deaths in the Hilo district to 75. On a Saturday, Wetmore got the people together to build a hospital. "You may judge somewhat of my surprise," he reported, "seeing a house 58 feet long and 15 feet wide entirely before night the following Tuesday." Working to quell severe outbreaks in Hilo and Puna, Charles himself caught the disease but only in a mild form that kept him quarantined only 11 days. He pushed hard to complete the vaccinations, training two natives to aid him.

More generous support for the Mission allowed the doctor now $650 a year, of which he was expected to earn $300. He proudly reported he exceeded that by $56.40 and saved enough to buy a horse.

Young Charles in December 1854 was a continuous delight to his parents "with his round fat face and laughing blue eyes," Lucy wrote, "not that he never causes us sorrow, for he already shows that he is born of corrupt stock; he is warmhearted and affectionate but impulsive in his feelings." On June 29, 1855, their first daughter arrived, Francis Matilda, "a delicate bud, so fair as to look pale to her mother when she feels a little anxious about her," Lucy admitted. And she added, "I would not have believed I could love a second child so well."

Modern Times

As a missionary doctor had charge of dispensing medicines, and by this time knowledge of aids and cures was advancing, Dr. Wetmore soon found a great demand from whalers and resident foreigners for his supply of simple household remedies. Lucy helped get them packaged for sale. By

1854 the doctor was disposing of most of his medicinal products to ship masters. In March, when the whaling fleet was preparing for summer action, he took in nearly $50 in eight days and regretted his supplies were so limited. Spirits of nitre, iodine and potash were especially in demand. Lucy had to direct boys in putting up powders and pills to meet the demands. In 1856 he invested close to $1,000 in building a drug store and office on the beach, where he could serve his seafaring trade more easily. His services at Seamen's Hospital also paid, to help him support his family now that the Board, as of July 1, 1855, no longer paid him as a missionary doctor.

As a doctor, Wetmore was "not for making a medicine chest of the human body. I assure you," wrote Lucy, "few families take less medicines than we." His policy was to give remedies only when he thought they were really needed "to assist nature in throwing off disease." Charles believed also in the value of exercise and relaxation. He wished Lucy would take to fast-horseback riding as Fidelia Coan did and insisted his reluctant wife make the trip with him to the volcano. She stuck on her horse until within a few miles of their destination, fell off and had to be carried the rest of the way. But the "glorious sight" of the active Kilauea volcano was her reward. Though the doctor believed getting away from one's cares annually was "better and cheaper than medicine," he failed to apply it to Lucy's confinement in taking care of children and helping him with his work. In nearly ten years, she complained that the volcano excursion was the only long trip to take her away "from the same old round."

Contact with America was being speeded up. Lucy wrote her sister in Massachusetts on July 24, 1856, marveling at receiving her letter in only 51 days. The first paddlewheel ship had reached Hawaii May 22, 1846, and the first screw propelled vessel, April 19, 1849. These advances and the short cut by land across Panama or Mexico made such a marvel possible.

By November 9, 1860, when their fourth and last child, Lucy Taylor, arrived, the Wetmores were really established. Little Charlie, now age 7, was starting to learn how to help put up powders in his father's store and looked forward to becoming a clerk. To replace his clerk, who had left, the doctor hired a medical student missionary son, Theodore Gulick, 23, son of the Rev. Peter Gulick, then retired.

Wetmore was advancing in medical skills, Lucy reported in 1861, telling how Charles had successfully treated a severe case of sore throat so that the man was up and out in four days and how he had made his first amputation of a man's leg. The doctor faithfully attended the general meetings in Honolulu to confer with other physicians and find fresh knowledge and inspiration from his frequent visits to the newly founded Queen's Hospital "to remove rust from my Aesculapian armor." He was especially interested there in the process of forming a new nose on the face of a Chinese man.

Financial matters now involved larger sums, such as his $15 for getting a boat to take him to Laupahoehoe to save a foreigner's life by amputating his arm and providing him hospital care. The man never paid him a cent. As his hospital's bad debts built up to $600, he closed it in April 1865 and leased the building for $120 a year. With his family assisting, his drug store was doing very well. He had a press to print labels and to take in other jobs. Payments from a boarder, "a professor of religion" in search of health, helped lighten the financial strain, and the man's companionship seemed to improve the pleasantness of home life. Delivering "the missionary baby crop" also helped keep the doctor going.

Charlie was growing up determined to become a doctor too. "If he lives," Lucy added, for she had a premeditated fear expressed in earlier letters. The doctor was proud to see Charlie, age 12, and daughter Fannie, then 10, help him in his drug store. Two years later, in July 1867, Charlie, now an active fellow of 14 and a daring horseman, joined his Hawaiian *paniolo* (cowboy) friends at a cattle ranch during his summer vacation. As he started on the 35-mile trek back home on July 24, he seemed well enough. Five miles down, Charlie "was seized with pains in the bowels and stomach, and in great agony he rode from Kilauea to Hilo," as recorded by Titus Coan. He took medicine and went to bed. Next day he had a strong fever and seemed feeble. That night he was delirious. In the morning, the boy's face lit up when he heard his Uncle Coan had been sent for. When Titus arrived he saw the boy was dying. He hurried back to get his wife and daughter, but by the time they got there, Charlie lay dead in the arms of his father.

Fannie, feeling the untimely loss of her beloved brother, pledged herself to devote her life to the medical profession he had sought to follow. Charles and Lucy now sometimes referred to their daughter as "Frank" instead of Francis or Fannie. As she at 15 had acquired all the education and training available at home, her parents sent her to New England in April 1870 with Fidelia Coan.

Joyously, the next year, Lucy traveled with Charles and her two daughters, Katie (Catherine) and Lucy, back to New England. How marvelous to travel in just 22 days, 5,700 miles straight eastward by steamship and train. Back in his friendly homeland, the doctor began to wonder whether to stay, as friends advised, "and take care of my aged parents and educate our children?" How badly was he needed back in Hilo? Could he expect Lucy to return with just one child? And who would take care of the two older ones that they would leave behind? One cold New England winter removed such doubts. After 23 years in the balmy climes of the islands, the Wetmores decided Hawaii was their best home and returned, along with the doctor's brother Edwin.

In July 1875 Lucy got another absence from home duties — a getaway to camp in the forests of Mauna Kea. The Wetmores set out with their three daughters and brother Edwin on July 15. The parents rode horses, while the other four rode mules up a rough and jagged trail. They found pleasure on a Saturday picking two quarts of strawberries. Then on the Sabbath morning, came the seemingly inevitable call that summons doctors to duty. Consumptive Mr. S. felt very poorly and wished the doctor to come at once. Not wanting to make the rough return trip without her husband's assistance, Lucy went back with him. Poor Mr. S. passed away peacefully three hours after they reached him.

Katie was helping the teacher at the Foreign School. Fannie taught at the Hilo Boarding School for four months in 1878. Then, the next July, she left again for the States to augment her already substantial medical knowledge. People had been sending for her to doctor them, and she had worked steadily for her father in the drug store. He felt her proficiency with the needle would be of more value in surgery.

Charles rigged up the first telephone on the island in July 1879, and at Honolulu in that year the Hawaiian Bell Telephone Co. was organized. The doctor had seen the first one in the Islands at Wailuku, Maui, the year before, built by a son-in-law of missionary William Alexander. He had stretched the line three miles to Kahului. Soon after Wetmore's telephone line, Kauai had one from Lihue to Dr. Smith's at Koloa. Wetmore delighted in the personal contacts his phone afforded him. "I would not be without it for many times its original cost; it helps me greatly to bear Fannie's absence," he rejoiced.

Fatherly pride grew at news of Fannie's good grades at medical school, learning so much more than he did at school. But his experience had convinced him that it was "not always ... the amount of medical and surgical knowledge acquired that makes the best practitioners; but the tact and ability to put into practice what one has learned both in the schools and from lessons in experience." "Dr. Frank" returned in 1882 with her superior medical education and people now called for her special attention to their problems.

Tragedy and Triumphs

The doctor's inventive abilities prompted him to install a big bathtub connected to the soft water brook that flowed past the house. This provided refreshing cool comfort on torrid days. "July 23, 1883, was a hot, stuffy day," Dr. Halford relates in his book, "and Mrs. Wetmore, now 64 yet always busy with her housekeeping, sought its cool solace when the day's chores were done. When Dr. Wetmore came home, no cheery voice returned his hail. Behind the closed bathroom door, silence...in the tub, submerged, his Lucy...dead. Apparently she had slipped, fallen, hit ther head on the rim of the tub, and, unconscious, drowned."

131

Such a tragedy left the doctor in a daze for months. Through the enjoyment of his namesake presented by his daughter Katie 15 years after the loss of his own Charlie, Dr. Wetmore recovered his pleasure in life and resumed his work by the start of 1884. "Little Charlie is a darling little fellow," he wrote, "loves to ride with grandpa of course..."

The Hawaiian Board sent the doctor "on a visit of friendly counsel, medical assistance and cheer" for a year among the Marshall and Caroline Islands in 1886. After his return, he had the pleasure of his daughter Lucy's marriage at Hilo on November 30, to Charles Sumner Lewis. The following year he returned to his old home in Massachusetts for a happy visit with relatives and old friends.

"Dr. Frank" had become just as popular as he had made himself during 40 years of practice. In 1888 he mentioned that she was "off attending to lepers, a duty which she greatly dreads."

Dr. Wetmore, "sprightly at 69 and one of the six missionary survivors" then, still attended the annual mission meeting in Honolulu for what Halford refers to as "his habitual yearly postgraduate work." In 1889 he found himself the only missionary present who had been there 40 years before. Three others of the six older missionaries still living were also from the island of Hawaii: John Paris, 80; Elias Bond, 76; and Edward Bailey, 76.

Honolulu was a growing city with "large blocks built of brick, stone, or wood," a horse-drawn railway (rates 5c in town or 2 miles out, 10c for the 4 miles to Waikiki), "a great bathing place and a sort of summer resort", brilliant electric lights and numerous telephones.

Hilo had been progressing in its own ways. The doctor had invested in some of the developing sugar plantations and then in the city's first soft drink plant, Hilo Soda Water Works. He still tended his drug store and started writing his autobiography, which he never got further than a few pages. His home showed his avid interest in many subjects, for he had "cabinet upon cabinet with specimens of everything from bugs to boulders." But his great love was for children. How he enjoyed his merry frolics with his grandsons and neighbor youngsters.

He held faith in the Hawaiian people disbelieving that the race was doomed as other missionaries had claimed. He defended the native ministers declaring they were "a very respectable class of men" and that they could discuss and vote intelligently. He passed his 78th birthday on February 8, 1898, in fair health and proud that the Wetmores were a long-lived family. In April, feeling tired, he accepted the advice to rest in bed. On Friday morning, May 13, they found he had peacefully entered his eternal rest. He had devoted an intelligent, energetic life to the land of his choice.

18

DWIGHT BALDWIN AND HIS DIFFICULT MISSION

Dwight and Charlotte Baldwin — Source: HMCS Library

Aesculapius or Jehovah?

Dwight Baldwin, born, September 29, 1798, at Durham, Conn., was brought up at the pioneer town of Durham, N. Y., in Catskill Mountain country,working on his father's 70-acre farm. His childless Uncle David provided for his higher education at Williams College for two years. He taught for a year and graduated in 1821 from Yale, where a professor instilled in him his lasting interest in religion. Dwight became a teacher, serving first as principal of the Academy at Kingston, N. Y., then at a select school in Catskill.

Attracted to the medical profession, he studied at a medical college while teaching two years at Durham. As the powerful preaching of the Durham Congregational minister stirred him to devote his life to religion and mission work, he entered Auburn Theological Seminary. After his second year there, he applied to the American Board for service abroad. Not immediately accepted, he completed another year at Auburn to graduate in 1829.

The Board, realizing the extreme need for physicians in the Sandwich Islands, had Dwight complete his medical training at Harvard that year. But, because his medical diploma did not get signed before he had to sail, he had to accept a Master of Science degree instead. This lack of documentary proof of his medical training kept him from getting a government license in Hawaii although he carried on 27 years of exhausting practice there. Finally, in 1859, Dartmouth College granted him an honorary medical degree. He could go as a full-fledged preacher of the gospel, having been ordained by the Presbytery of Utica, N. Y. Thus he became the first missionary formally equipped to care for the Hawaiian bodies as well as saving their souls from perdition.

While he might go without his medical license, he had to have a matrimonial license. Handsome Dwight had won the affections of a fair New England lass but not her consent to be shipped far away to help care for dreadful savages. Like Asa, Dwight sought help from a special classmate friend, a New Haven lawyer. A friend of his, Emeline Fowler, had a cousin Charlotte so heaven-bent on a missionary career that she had already refused other suitors. So, four weeks before sailing, Dwight with his two friendly mate-matchers drove off in a sleigh to the home of Deacon Solomon Fowler at White Hollow near Northford, Conn., for Dwight to win the hand of the deacon's youngest daughter.

Dwight modestly explained his purpose and plans and quietly suggested she accompany him on his mission as his wife. No response. Instead,Charlotte withdrew upstairs where Emeline found her crying. She had misunderstood Dwight's delicate proposal and thought he was taking her dear cousin Emeline away with him. Induced to return downstairs, she still felt confounded by the sudden and unexpected offer from a stranger. She requested a week to think it over and get guidance from friends and from God.

Charlotte Fowler was then 25. Devoted to an active Christian life since she was 16, she had been trained at excellent schools in New Haven and New York. Then she had started in mission work in New Jersey, teaching children without pay and later joining a group of Christian workers in New York City.

Dwight left with Charlotte ample assurances of his upright character as recommended by a friend who advised her he himself was also "a friend of missions" as well as "to domestick peace and happiness." Dwight, he declared, was fitly qualified for the role of missionary by "his ardent piety, decision of character, fortitude and patience, and literary and theological attainments," also mild-tempered, "frank, open, and honest" and "peculiarly kind and affectionate." He felt convinced that Dwight would make an ideal husband — "kind, indulgent, sympathizing, and truly affectionate."

When Dwight reappeared, Charlotte was willing to tie the knot at her home on December 3, 1830. Three weeks later they were off on the whaling ship *New England* from New Bedford with just three other missionary couples including two of Dwight's former Auburn Theological fellow students, Sheldon Dibble and Reuben Tinker. Dr. Baldwin arrived in time to assist at the birth of the Judds' second baby, Elizabeth Kinau, born July 5, 1831. As the Baldwins remained at Honolulu the rest of that year, Dr. Judd could return the favor by helping at the birth of David Dwight on November 26.

During those months, Dwight started his missionary service by preaching twice on Sunday to local residents, sailors and ships' officers. Though "a goodly number of sailors" attended, the preacher had to admit that "the greatest part of those in port" doubtless were at the 14 "wretched grog holes." Baldwin was learning "a lot about the morals and maladies of whalemen ashore and of their toxic effect upon the natives."

Charlotte too kept busy teaching sewing and studying Hawaiian. Dwight was looking after her health. He had been concerned that the fruit "would not be salutary." But he was relieved that "no hurt seems to follow" her almost constant eating of "oranges, lemons, tamarinds, *ohias* [*ohia loke*, rose apple], watermelons, muskmelons, pine-apples." One affliction she did suffer was from the "very industrious" fleas "& to her very person."

Waimea Health Station

Waimea had already been established as a health station in 1830, a cooler retreat for missionaries suffering from the heat at lower elevations.

Bingham's aim was "to resuscitate invalids, and partly to increase the amount of evangelical light and influence in that part of Hawaii." Three missionaries, Judd, Ruggles and Bingham, had enjoyed rest, adventure and refreshment and laid the foundations of a permanent station. Dr. Gerrit Judd and family, Kapiolani, the William Richards family, Mary Ward, a missionary teacher, and the Samuel Ruggles family tested the beneficial effects of "the cool, retired, lofty, and long-neglected heathen solitudes of Waimea."

Governor Adams arrived to go hunting wild cattle and commanded that a large meeting house, about 120 feet long and 50 feet wide, be built on a pleasant spot near the road. Judd established a church and school for native teachers. He was pleased at finding a congregation steadily increasing to at least a thousand when the governor addressed them. Crowds flocked to the doctor's house to confess "they are wicked and wish us to instruct them in the word of God."

Bingham and Ruggles, "nearly prostrate" from the continuous heat, came to enjoy the "relaxation, change of scene, air, and temperature" there. Arriving at Kawaihae in early July, they started that evening to make the climb to Waimea. Climbing from the oppressive shore heat to the more than 2,000-foot elevation, they met there "a slight rain and a chilly wind, which made our muscles shiver," though 25 miles from Mauna Kea, still snow-capped. The Judds welcomed them at midnight.

Dr. Judd set off, April 22, on one of the governor's mules with John Honolii and other natives to gain the summit of nearly 14,000-foot-high Mauna Kea. A violent thunder storm drove them into a cave about 2:00 o'clock and kept them there overnight. Starting early next morning, they reached the snowcap by noon. Judd, too fatigued to press on to the summit, returned to the cave to get his mule at 5:00 p. m. and make his way home at 9:00. He took a large bundle of snow, a novelty for Governor Adams, who enjoyed tasting and handling it.

Bingham eagerly welcomed the young king and Regent Kaahumanu to Waimea early in September. Kapiolani also came as did about 60 members of churches at different stations. When the king with more than a hundred men decided to ascend to the summit of Mauna Kea, Bingham determined to go "to watch over and instruct my young pupil, and to benefit my health." This became a nearly five-day excursion. On the fourth day they reached the snowbanks and icy shores of Lake Waiau, now the loftiest lake in the United States at 13,020 feet. The boyish king had great fun tumbling in this strange white stuff and vainly offered a piece to his unappreciative horse. Then he cut out blocks of snow to present to the regent and other chiefs.

As the sun was starting to set, the king decided not to scale the summit and hastily descended with his men. Not so Hiram Bingham. He, with a native who had braved the rigors of New England, pushed on up "to the summit of the loftiest peak." Bingham, panting for breath in the rarefied atmosphere, had to stop often to gasp for air and rest his exhausted muscles. They then descended hastily and reached the king's camp about midnight.

Soon after, Bingham joined the royal party at Waipio to meet the people of Hamakua. They had to descend a steep, 1,000-foot precipice sliding rapidly down the lower part on bundles of leaves, "not without fear on the part of the ladies." Judd had previously found there a large meeting house and interested and better-informed people. Bingham's descent was made by sitting on a basket of bushes and branches sliding on *ti* leaves with "six wakeful and sure-footed natives, two before, two behind, and one on each side." He delighted in this charming valley with its 1,200 or more inhabitants but, as was his custom, lamented their "heathenish darkness" which had been "never cheered by the voice of salvation or the sound of the church-going bell."

The leaders called the people together to advise them to follow "the commands of God, and to serve the Lord with gladness." They took canoe trips along the coast to show Bingham the impressive scenery. Ready to leave for Hilo, they put their energies to "ascending the great steep" with heavy, up-hill toil. Such was the wild, mountainous territory the Baldwins were to travel about to convert and civilize its widely separated people.

A Long Productive Life

The Baldwins set off to Waimea, January 2, 1832, enduring crowded decks and seasick, exhausting days to Kailua where they rested a few days with the Thurstons, then sailed up to Kawaihae. With the Artemas Bishops they struggled uphill to Waimea, Charlotte with her baby, and Delia with the two young Bishop children were carried on *maneles* over the 12-mile ascent. The Bishops stayed until Dwight, who quickly picked up the language, could deliver sermons in Hawaiian.

Dwight felt they were "very comfortably situated" and was pleased with the two thatched mission houses and the great grass church into which 3,000 could crowd. In spite of considerable rain, he reported the weather was mostly delightful and the climate invigorating, with temperatures between 58 and 70 degrees. The people provided them with generous supplies of food, and five goats gave plenty of milk.

The Baldwins eagerly tackled the task of providing aid to body and soul for such a scattered population in places of difficult access. While Waimea had some 2,000 people, 8,000 lived in Kohala and about 5,000 others in Hamakua. Charlotte loved these "pitiful" children, "ragged, filthy, lousy," taught and clothed about 30 of them and trained them to wash in the brook or elsewhere before coming to her school. They had classes for native teachers. The people built a large schoolhouse in Waimea, a large church in Kohala, and a road from Waimea, cutting travel time to three hours. Dwight went to Waipio and preached one weekday at the small meeting house and also at "a good house of worship" at Hamakua.

But all was not rosy. They had to deal with some natives intoxicated from fermented potatoes, vile foreigners hunting wild cattle, a party of 20 or 30 natives running off from their lands to the mountains "for the purposes of idolatry & vice," mourning customs of mutilating the body, and indolent habits. Dwight, like others, felt his hardest battles were to overcome "the degradation, pollution, thick darkness, which still cover the minds of multitudes of the people." It was hard to make them think as New England Puritans. It was a period of change as population declined. School attendance became discouragingly irregular as the wild cattle business increased. Classes had to be abandoned for people to carry heavy loads of beef, hides and timber to the shore and bring back salt.

The Baldwins found their native house more and more inadequate to protect them from the elements. Dwight wrote to Levi Chamberlain for glass for the house and church windows and for turpentine, as "the fleas seem to be afraid of it some." The damp climate left his "books, papers, shoes, & some other articles" in such a mouldy condition that he decided it would be "neither comfort nor health, nor economy" to keep occupying this station in a home of such unprotective quality. To build him a stone house, two masons later arrived, but the tools they needed did not. They left. Baldwin finally did get a horse for his travels to outposts of his territory. He had less success in procuring a wagon.

When the Peter Gulick family came to visit, the Baldwins turned over to them the comfort of their large house and moved into a smaller one, only 17 by 14 feet. It was there, in what Charlotte called "our palace," on her birthday, November 7, 1833, that her second child Abigail Charlotte was born.

Dr. Baldwin's responsibilities to missionary families kept him traveling long distances to take care of cases of childbirth and severe illnesses. He too found the journey from Waimea to Hilo an extremely difficult one in March 1834 to get there for the birth of the Lymans' first child. Starting on horseback with two natives, he became lost in fog and rain but finally found a fair shelter. Next morning, as they wandered about in rain and fog again, they found some beef hunters who led them back to the trail. The doctor sent his horse back the next day and then found the 20-mile-long forest path "a perfect slough hole" made worse by continued rain. They had to give up traveling by moonlight and "stopped under a shelter of leaves & slept very well through the night." After a stopover at a sawmill, where eight foreigners had him hold a meeting for them, he had to wade barefoot the remaining eight or ten miles.

Dwight regretted having to be called away like this from his pastoral duties, for he had expected to attend chiefly to spiritual needs. He felt unhappy about having to devote so much time to practice medicine for "the unusual number of sick" missionaries then. He told the Board he had come without any instructions from them "on the subject of practicing medicine." Doubting he would "ever be called on much," he had come without much-needed books and instruments that he now did need.

Such a "health" station became unfitted to Dr. Baldwin's constitution. In the summer of 1834, he kept on tending to the sick in steady bad weather even when he had a hard cold that left his lungs in such a delicate state that he could not preach. Still suffering from a fever, weakness and a long-lasting cough, he had to go to Kaawaloa to attend Kapiolani and deliver Rebecca Forbes's second child. That winter, Dwight's throat and lung trouble persisted so that he sought relief at Lahaina in February 1835. That failing, the mission sent him on a health trip to the Society Islands from July through September.

Restored in health, he was permanently stationed at Lahaina in a coral stone house and took an active part in the health, education and spiritual welfare of the people for the next 35 years. Lahaina was a busy port with hundreds of whaling ships a year. It served also as the kingdom's capital, as the king and high chiefs enjoyed its beauty and comforts.

In 1855 he and Charlotte made a visit to the United States, remaining until the first of 1858. He served as mission delegate to the Marquesas Islands in 1862. From 1872 to 1877 he taught at the Theological School in Honolulu.

Charlotte died at Honolulu on October 2, 1873. At age 87, Dwight was still blessed with his six children and 23 grandchildren. He died January 3, 1886, at the home of his youngest daughter, Harriet, wife of Samuel Mills Damon. Sereno Bishop conducted the funeral service at Kawaiahao Church remarking that Baldwin, in his long span of life, had outdistanced all other missionaries by residing in Hawaii longer than any other then — fifty four and one-half years.

When the Baldwins had left the Waimea Mission, the work there was being capably taken care of by Lorenzo and Betsey Lyons. Dwight and Lorenzo remained devoted friends. Five months before he died, Dwight wrote to Brother Lyons recalling their early days together. In 1832 they had considered their situation as in "a dark missionary field. ... There was often doubtless much in our doings that was awkward and wrongly planned," Baldwin admitted. "We had hardly begun to study human nature in this dark part of the Globe, but I am persuaded there was no lack of earnestness.

Neither you nor I ever came to this land to fill our coffers with silver and gold. We were in dead earnest to save some of the people, and therefore God often heard our prayers."

Dwight felt the missionaries had ample opportunities "for placing themselves in easy and comfortable circumstances, not to say of getting rich." He cited "the liberal manner in which the mission is supplied from the Board" and "money and other articles" from private friends, plus presents "sometimes extravagant" from the chiefs. "Most stations," he added, "have flocks of goats and herds of cattle [and] every missionary may cultivate as much land as he pleases."

He expected to see "self denial and piety advance" and hoped the extra resources acquired would be "used to further the progress of the gospel..." He referred to one recent missionary to whom he had commented on the lack of "self denial for the cause of Christ" in missionary sermons. This man confessed, "'I must get rid of some of my stuff, before I can preach of self denial.'"

This was the dedicated character of Dr. Dwight Baldwin who fought to ensure the good health and the spiritual welfare of the people. He was a practical man with the idealism of faithful service to his fellow man without regard for gaining wealth. His notable works are remembered, and his impact on the life of Lahaina and of Hawaii is recorded at the Baldwin House in the town to which he devoted most of his life.

19

LORENZO LYONS — HE LOVED HAWAII AND HAWAII LOVED HIM

Lorenzo Lyons — Source: HMCS Library

"The Very Children Are Coming"

One of the most loved Christian missionaries to Hawaii was Lorenzo Lyons, as his granddaughter Emma Lyons Doyle reveals in her biography of him, *Makua Laina — Lyric Poet of the Mountain Country*. Unlike other partner-hunting missionaries, Lorenzo had his own beautiful true love to whom he devoted his expressive talents in love letters "beautifully permeated by tender affection, by deep spirituality, and by poetic thought."

Sadly, no picture remains for us to enjoy the features of Lorenzo's sweetheart, Betsey Curtis, a real beauty in her day as testified by a hired workman who declared, "That one oughter not to go. She's too purty. Them savages'll EAT her!" Lorenzo's respect and admiration for Betsey exceeded her physical beauty. She complemented him with her fine intellect, good education and spiritual interests and qualities. While at Auburn Theological Seminary, after his studies at Union College, Lorenzo had propounded to Betsey ponderous theological questions but could not "trip her up," as she had done well in the same subject at her school.

Betsey,"the shortest, the slimmest, the lightest of them all," on the voyage to the Sandwich Isles, weighed just 99 pounds. As Mrs. Persis Thurston Taylor remembered the arrival of the Lyons couple in Hawaii, when the crowd of natives caught sight of "the fair rosy girl and her scarce taller husband," they exclaimed, "Why, the very CHILDREN are coming to teach us!"

Perils and Pleasures on the Sea

Sadly saying their last farewells and raising their voices in prayer and hymns, the 19 members of the fifth company sailed on the whaleship *Averick* from New Bedford, Mass., on November 26, 1831. Among those with Lorenzo and Betsey were Cochran and Rebecca Forbes and David and Sarah Lyman. Though dismayed at sight of such crowded quarters, Lorenzo at once refrained from complaining. Such a positive attitude rescued Lorenzo throughout life from doubts and despair. Their berth, only two to three feet wide and close to the top of the cabin, was loaded with shelves of books, a writing desk, nails for brushes and looking glass,a large trunk used as sofa, a small trunk with travel clothes, a foot stool, hanging cloaks and towels. To retire, they pulled a curtain across their berth to separate them from the other three couples that shared the cabin.

Set sail—a storm — agonies of seasickness. Lorenzo escaped the worst of the malady, but Betsey's suffering distressed him.He ministered to her and other victims of the merciless motion. When he managed to get his Betsey up on deck four days later, she fainted in his arms. A terrible shaking one night sent dishes dashing off the table as lights went out amid a deafening and terrifying noise — nothing but the breaking of heavy sea on deck, a frequent occurence. At every meal, someone got "splashed by a social wave," or was frequently sent sprawling on the floor atop their dinner or a fellow victim, or their shoes becoming a receptacle for tea and coffee. Lorenzo, holding morning and evening worship, was once prostrated by a giant wave at the feet of his small congregation. Most uncomfortable "in garments soaked in brine," he continued the service below.

In the dead of night came the frightening cry, "The ship's on fire!" Soon came the reassuring report," The fire is discovered and will soon be extinguished." A missionary wife, left asleep when her husband went on deck, had knocked over the lamp and set the bed afire.

The ship, becalmed, was struck by a gale that sent passengers scurrying down to the cabin. Soon they were back enjoying the fun of watching porpoises. One harpooned by a sailor provided their dinner from the tenderloin and the liver and pancakes made from the brain, plus a gallon of fine oil from the blubber for much-needed light. The heavy rain supplied water for laundering. On Christmas they feasted on plum rice pudding and chicken pies. Then came a whaling expedition, the sailors harpooning three whales.

Suffering from "almost intolerable" heat, they reached Rio de Janeiro, January 11, 1832, to repair the decayed foremast. They passed Cape Horn in unbelievably benevolent weather. At Juan Fernandez, Lorenzo enjoyed wandering over vales and mountains through caves and by streams, the pleasant variety of food at the governor's, and the story of Alexander Selkirk, the real Robinson Crusoe who had spent four years and four months there. They sighted Hawaii, May 16, and anchored at Honolulu next day.

Winning the Wary, Weary, and Wretched

On July 4, Lorenzo and Betsey boarded the "somewhat crazy" brig of "rather deficient" size, prepared for the onslaught of seasickness by clearing away enough calabashes, dishes and bundles to make room for themselves amid "natives by scores lying all around us, goats bleating, pigs squealing; hens, turkeys, dogs, all making their various noises." Though this seemed quite obnoxious to the newcomers, the older missionaries claimed that it was little compared to what they had to endure on earlier trips. Then came two days becalmed in oppressive heat, the stormy night of the 7th, horrible, with terrific rocking, mattresses soaked from upset calabashes, frightening yells— far worse rocking than Betsey had endured in all her 18,000 miles from New England.

143

Landing at Kailua next day, Lorenzo and Betsey stayed with the Thurstons in their new wooden house for four days, Betsey enjoying the Thurstons "like home folks." She delighted in the trip in a double canoe to Kaawaloa with Cochran and Rebecca Forbes, the cart ride up hill to the Ruggles's home, and the moonlight sail back to Kailua. On July 11 they sailed on ship with about 150 goats, reaching Kawaihae about 5:00 p.m. on Friday, July 13, and spent the weekend with John Young, then 87 years old. He had landed on Hawaii about 45 years earlier, served as adviser to King Kamehameha, married a chiefess, had several children, had favored the landing of the first missionaries and supported their work since then. Lorenzo noted, "His wife is a very pious woman, a church member."

Early Monday they set off on the 12-mile climb to Waimea with the Baldwins, 22 natives carrying the baggage and the two wives in rocking chairs. Lorenzo and Dwight shared "an old worn out horse," but the light, lithe Lorenzo "walked most of the way ...all up hill, some pretty steep," until they reached their "grass house surrounded by shrubbery, a very comfortable place for us." But in no time rain and wind descended on them "and made it dismal indeed."

With all his kindliest intentions, Lorenzo found that he was not at first heartily welcomed by these suspicious and superstitious people. Many fled when he approached, as if he were "some destroying monster." Children would flee "like wild deer" when he tried to talk to them about school. Women mocked him ridiculously. One group treated him with "ridicule, shameless gestures, derision" or would "make sport in the basest manner of what they had heard told of the Christian God, whilst a great laugh went up among the others." Good-natured Lorenzo took their reluctance with some good humor, prayed for them, understood them, even when his soul seemed "tortured as with burning spikes." He saw "All were not alike of course. Some appeared decent and willing to hear."

He heard strange tales about their imagined fears. The missionaries wanted to get children to school to kill them by putting them in barrels. Some had come to believe that Baldwin killed people in their houses at night to get brains and blood for the sacrament. But what could one expect of a people suddenly confronted by "alien beings, with strange language, strange dress, mysterious motives, and weird customs?" asks Emma Lyons Doyle. "By hearsay," she concludes, "little by little, Lorenzo learned of your fears, and blamed not, but pitied; saw that the truth must be gently taught you 'by God's grace'; prayed for ability to be God's instrument." And when Lorenzo witnessed men and women loaded with food literally creeping up the precipice on all fours, his "heart yearned for them."

What a territory he had to cover! Forty miles to the most distant parts of Kohala and the same to Hamakua, not counting the mighty downs and ups of deep valleys, traveling over parts almost inaccessible via faint foot paths. It took him five or six weeks to make a complete tour mostly on foot to visit an estimated 16,000 people and check the progress of more than 100 small schools. The peoples' wretched conditions aroused his compassion. "The squalor of some," he deplored, "is almost incredible: — cats, dogs, fowls, men, women and children all mingling together." "The females," whose lack of proper clothing he lamented likely failed to miss the bonnets and shoes he felt they needed.

It was July 22, 1832, when Lorenzo reported a large congregation of about 1,200. On August 12 an uninvited guest entered the open-door church. A goat, "with a great deal of freedom and dignity, made his way through the midst of the people to the pulpit steps." Lorenzo seems to have accepted the situation with his usual good humor. A week later he preached his first sermon in Hawaiian. He admitted Betsey could talk and understand the language better than he. Two or three thousand came for communion service September 2. A common plate and tin cups provided the means of serving. Lorenzo feared that the people "arrayed in their best apparel" appeared with "some pride withal." The meeting was honored by the presence of "several head men and chiefs ... and Mrs. Young from Kawaihae" who had come that Friday with "offerings of *poi*, *taro*, watermelons, potatoes, fowls, *kapa*."

In a tour with Dwight Baldwin, Lorenzo observed, "We fell in with all conditions of men, the maimed, the lame, the blind, the sick and the dying, the naked and the maniac." Betsey saw how "wretchedly poor" the people were with little more than "worn mats on which they sleep, ragged *kapas* for covering, a few calabashes, their *kapa* pounders, and markers," all they had, "unless," she added, "we count families of kittens, puppies and pigs."

On another trip with Baldwin, Lorenzo found people burdened by heavy taxes, "as if some of the chiefs may be ranked with those that grind the faces of the poor." He found himself rebuked at the beef market with "There is no beef for missionaries." The great days of school examinations brought him some satisfactions. About 2,000 of the 6,000 could do some reading, whether the book was upside down or not. "But," he remarked, as he often did, seeing the better side of things, "the day of small things is not to be despised."

Challenges at Hamakua

A little Lyons named Curtis Jere blessed the missionary home on June 27, 1833, and Betsey at last could exult that God had "sustained me during the trial through which I have passed, beyond my expectations, and made me the happy mother of a fine son."

After more than two years of missionary labor at Waimea, the family traveled to Hamakua to advance the work in that section of their wide territory. The 40-mile journey was made "after a fashion" through roadless forests with Betsey "drawn part of the way in a rocking chair attached to the fore wheels of a wagon" or carried by natives and walking some, while a native carried little Curtis.

The Waimea home of Lorenzo Lyons (1888) — Source:
Baker-Van Dyke Collection

Their native house had low entrances, a bed of posts, poles, leaves and mats, a "humble table" made by Lorenzo. "To be without luxuries is no trial," he reassured himself. He taught the men, while Betsey worked with the women and children. So they made schools flourish, organized large singing classes, and were pleased to see people bringing in products to exchange for books.

To attend a funeral, Lorenzo had to make a "prodigiously fatiguing" climb up a mountain. On his return, he lost his way "in the wide wilderness" and attempted to descend "an awfully high precipice" but had to go back up and happily found the right route. When he took over Betsey's school of children one morning, he marveled at her patience trying to teach "such wild creatures day after day."

One of their greatest personal trials was the illness of baby Curtis. He had a high fever with flushed cheeks, difficult breathing, languor.

Lorenzo despaired. Then his courage told him, "We will do as well as we can. We have medicine and will use it to the best of our ability."

In February 1835 Lorenzo was having his students read the Hawaiian newspaper to learn to understand its contents. On the 12th he made a trip to the great valley of Waipio, preached "under a scorching sun" to a company of men preparing to plant, "but the Lord sent a cloud once in a while," he added.

Waipio Valley (1887) — **Source: Baker-Van Dyke Collection**

His visit to a lonely school teacher, far inland with towering mountains on every side, was the first by a missionary there. He prayed with this isolated man and his family, held a brief meeting with just eight people and then another with nine, then "conversed at several houses and held three meetings, attended by about 100 people in all." He kept on in moonlight, telling those in other villages of meetings in the morning. That night he "ate a very coarse supper — attended family prayers and retired" so tired he could sleep but little on his hard bed. Out he started at 3:30 in the morning moonlight, to hold a meeting at 5:30 for about 60, ate breakfast, a slice of cold taro and salt attended prayers and returned home.

Walking several miles to another unvisited place, he tried to get the children to tell him the letters, but they refused to respond to him or to the "laughing, scolding or hollering" of their parents. So he took his staff and made letters in the sand. This drew people to him, curious to see what he was doing.

Impressed by his visit to Waipio, he figured how to get the many inhabitants of the beautiful valley up to his regular meetings and save him "such tremendous ascents and descents" which demanded of him such "considerable exertion of muscular power and mental strength." He decided that, after morning service, he would "take a little refreshment then go down the dizzy precipice into the valley," hoping the people would like his preaching and follow him up the *pali* to his service "at the usual place." That did work, though at the close of the Sabbath he felt completely exhausted. He enjoyed the excuse of one man for not coming to the afternoon meeting — he stayed home to repent of his sins.

"A faithful tour through this field would require several weeks," the weary Lorenzo noted, "also strength, patience, self denial. Sometimes you ride horseback. Again you will find it necessary to crawl on your hands and feet. You will look above, and lo! a high precipice will threaten to exhaust your strength. You will look below and wonder how you will reach the bottom. The unruffled ocean will be on one side. On the other, desolation in its drearest form. Night comes on. You spread your table on a mat. Sit on the floor. Eat. Perchance you may be in an old tottering school house. Perhaps in a neat dwelling. Lying down, you sleep sweetly."

After the few months there, Lorenzo and Betsey felt quite "contented and happy" that the people "almost all said they had 'new hearts,'" They started back to Waimea on May 25, Lorenzo on foot, Betsey on horseback, little Curtis carried by a native. At their leaving, the peoples' very affectionate farewells and the pathos of their weeping made their departure quite a sad occasion.

Hardships and Despair

Alone in his expansive and isolated station when Dwight Baldwin left, Lorenzo pleaded with the ABCFM to send him help. The burden of so many thousands of souls weighing upon him was more than he could bear, he wrote them May 8, 1835, pointing out that Kohala needed a permanent missionary and Hamakua expected them to return. He cited the pernicious influence of foreigners and that the Waimea station "is the most difficult and uninviting of all stations now occupied" and no other missionary was willing to come to aid him. And none came in answer to his pleas.

In December 1835 Lorenzo summed up his feelings: "Distracted and vexed with the world." "A comfortable frame dwelling house" now provided "no small addition to our convenience and comfort in this cold, damp, windy region. We have in progress a stone cook house." In Dr. Baldwin's absence, Lorenzo had to provide medicines for "poor perishing bodies," his home "thronged from morning until night with those who need medicine, or must relate their difficulties of all kinds, or ask advice." He had supplied "about 5,000 books of one kind or another."

Lorenzo and Betsey, anticipating another birth, felt "somewhat cast down" because Dr. Baldwin decided "it not prudent to come on account of his health." So they left Waimea on April 8, 1836, to reach the Baldwins then at Kaawaloa. Lorenzo preached on the 27th, and about sundown they and the Baldwins boarded a ship for Lahaina. In an adverse current, the ship took 24 hours to make the 15 miles to Kailua. Lorenzo cried in agony that night of the 28th: "All night beating about against wind and current — have not sailed 6 miles — All of us very sea sick — hot sun pouring down, vessel rocking as if wishing to dip us into the sea. About 5 o'clock... my dear wife was suffering ... —All seasick — the cabin not much larger than a bread trough, a score of natives under our feet—the vessel tossed most unmercifully." They gave Betsey some medicine that prevented further progress of the birth.

At Kawaihae, Betsey landed very feeble but comfortable, though unable to proceed until May 3rd, carried in a rocking chair and the children in a "kind of litter." Dwight and Charlotte rode horseback, while Lorenzo plunged ahead on foot through prodigious rains and strong winds. The others had to stop four miles from Waimea. They got there on the 5th. "Poor wife had almost given out," Lorenzo sympathized.

The expected delivery came June 4 — a son Luke. Betsey devoted herself to her two boys. But Luke became sick on October 19 and died two days later. Betsey, "the bereaved little mother of 23," admitted it was the Lord's will but remained unconsolable. "How empty the world looks! How like vanity."

But their work must go on. Lorenzo took Betsey's schools in the mornings, she in the afternoons. Taking Curtis along, they visited a school, January 3, 1837, and on the 13th journeyed to Hamakua again, pleased to find that "some whole schools of children have given up smoking tobacco." The people showed their joy at their return by giving them many presents of cooked pig, fowls, potatoes and bananas. Lorenzo was back there again by April 4 to examine 346 children and 230 adults in 14 schools.

Betsey now missed Lorenzo more than ever when on his tours, sometimes for 10 to 14 days. Betsey, "fair, and beautiful, and scarce more than 20," remained perfectly safe at home alone even though "foreigners of no very virtuous character" lived nearby. Loving friends would protect her. Lorenzo kept plodding along. He made trips to Kawaihae and about five miles down the coast to Puako, and, there again, October 3, 1836, he spent a night in a canoe shed, "annoyed not a little by mice running over me and on to me," until he got up at 2:00 a. m. to walk back to Waimea by moonlight and reach home as the morning star was disappearing.

Even more fondly Betsey nourished little Curtis, "a tender plant" whose "little body needs much care." She too was waging a heroic struggle against ill health and her consequent sense of melancholy prompted by her bodily weakness, her sadness at the loss of her child, and her concern for her delicate son Curtis.

Then unexpected news brought her great joy. Mail from Honolulu announced that among the large reenforcement of 32 missionaries in the eighth company was her sister Emily, wife of the Rev. Isaac Bliss. Betsey held fond memories of her dear sister — "the former idol of my heart," whom she had thought she would never see again. The happy reunion occurred in Honolulu, Saturday, April 29, 1837. A week later on Sunday, Lorenzo preached twice at Waikiki and reported Betsey was taken sick. Next day she was so ill she could not leave the house. By Friday her condition was considered dangerous, as the medicines did not help her. All hope for her was gone by Saturday. Her friends gathered, prayed, read scriptures and left Lorenzo and their little son alone with their fading companion.

Lorenzo recorded his painful last moments with his greatly beloved Betsey. "She said a few words to us both as her dying counsel. Left a message for the children of Waimea. Near sundown, after praying for a while in a whisper, she broke out in an audible voice. At one time she repeated a verse of a hymn with great distinctness. At candle light there was singing and prayer in which she seemed to take great delight. I took her cold hand in mine, and placed my lips to her cheeks, and bid her farewell, and she did the same. The same with respect to her sister Emily. Her soul seemed dead to the things around her, and absorbed in the things of heaven. Just as Sabbath was commencing she fell asleep. Oh saddest hours of my life!"

And then on Monday: "Funeral of my dear wife at 3 1/2 PM at the native meeting house. Sermon by Mr. Baldwin — burial in the mission yard. I have taken the last look. The coffin — the cold earth — conceal her from my view. But I shall see her again. The Lord take care of the bereaved husband and the motherless little one. My plans are broken up."

Lucia Smith Lyons

As Lorenzo knew God had decided, "It is not good that the man should be alone," he felt the need of another helpmeet. Knowing that two unmarried Smith sisters had come with that eighth company and that Lucia Smith was teaching at Lahainaluna, he made "a tedious voyage of five days" to Lahaina in May 1838 and came away June 24 with the Lymans, Emersons and Miss Lucia Smith, all bound for Hilo. He reached Waimea the 28th. "All was dismal." Next day: "Left for Hilo and the volcano, tho a wife was the principal object."

He reached Hilo by July 2, preached to about 3,000, proposed to Miss Smith, and started to the volcano with the Emersons and Titus Coan. On Saturday, July 14, he was married to Miss Lucia G. Smith by Mr. Coan, and he preached again on Sunday to a great multitude. Tuesday the bridal couple took a canoe up the coast, there "took horses and reached Waimea about sundown." Lucia, born at Butternuts, N. Y., had previously taught on the Tuscarora Reservation in New York. Her sister Marcia, two years older, was teaching at Kaneohe on Oahu.

Lucia efficiently and lovingly took the place of Betsey as the mother in the family. Though Curtis throughout his life held "a deep and affectionate reverence for the memory of his beautiful girl mother," he had such respect and love for Lucia and her loving, motherly care for him that he would never allow anyone to refer to her as his "step mother." Emma Doyle admits that Lucia, being older than Betsey, was "sterner, more practical. In her bleak desolation, she bore three children, whom she cherished, nursed, reared, educated, with a giving of herself that must have drained her very being," while faithfully taking care of her little ones and "teaching the native women and children, taking three or four children at a time into the household to live and be trained," and carrying on her "cooking, washing, spinning, doing odd carpentry jobs, skinning and quartering sheep, whitewashing and gardening."

Her first child, Fidelia, was born September 4, 1839. Her son Albert, 1841, became an outstanding authority on Hawaiian flora, having had Lucia's love of plants instilled in him. The final Lyons child, born 1842, was named Elizabeth. Lorenzo was either busy involved in local activities or using up his strength on his wearying trips, such continuous exertions gradually wore him down until he could no longer "attempt anything that would strain his meager strength." Lucia then took over more of the physical work that such pioneer life required.

She started a family school for girls and supervised it until 1879. In 1887, after Lorenzo died, she maintained a school that included many children of people born after her arrival in Waimea. During her declining years, Fidelia and Elizabeth took care of her. Although suffering from heart trouble, she had such a hardy spirit and determination to keep active that she was confined to her bed only a week before her death on April 27, 1892, at the age of 84.

"Be Strong! Rouse up!"

The spirit of the frail, often weary, but determined Lorenzo seemed unquenchable. In May 1845, despite suffering from great weakness, he kept on with his tasks as best he could. In December, again he felt "lame and fatigued,but thankful to resume my labors." On a tour, January 12, 1846, he became "exceedingly tired and lame." But a new singing school aroused his interest.

A letter later that year told how he "had come home all tired out... had traveled that day over 20 or 30 precipices... reached home, all exhausted and almost speechless." Even the children's keen interest in the newly arrived box of foods from New England failed to stir him, until he finally took some supper, and then looked at the gifts of tea, chocolate and raisins that made his heart "glow with joy and gratitude." Of his four children, Curtis, then 13, and Elizabeth, 4, he commented, "None of them give evidence of piety. The Lord speedily convert them."

He well understood the natives' nature and their need for "some wise and good man to sit by them and tell them in the simplest way what to do. They are as children and must be led kindly along as children, and this for many years to come." His personal philosophy was "Let the body and mind be constantly active."

In the fall of 1848 he had to cope with a measles epidemic using up his time and energy visiting the sick, administering medicine and attending funerals. Then came diarrhea, dysentery, and whooping cough. Fidelia and Albert came down with the measles, recovered, but a month later all four had whooping cough, Fidelia suffering severely. In the cold and stormy weather, he reported "multitudes sick with coughs." Dreary reports go on day after day of deaths,funerals and more sickness. Next it was influenza, but "not fatal though very distressing." On December 16, Lorenzo estimated "60 deaths in Waimea, 300 in my whole parish."

Death threatened Lorenzo too in March 1849 — death by drowning. Thrown into the ocean by a tremendous wave while trying to land in a canoe at Waipio, he survived by the masterful efforts of his Hawaiian companion, who grasped Lorenzo twice, the second time bearing him to shore, much to the relief of the wailing natives, who considered him lost. "Oh most wonderful escape!" Lorenzo rejoiced.

Downpours could wreak havoc too. On January 3,1850, came the heaviest thunder storm he had ever seen — the meeting house and homes flooded. And for the first time in his 18 years of tours he was summoned home to take care of Lucia and his children down with influenza. That year he reported he and Lucia had set aside "a furnished room to seven Hawaiian girls, a Domestic Boarding school." He explained, "They sit around a table and eat after our own manner. When they stand with a choir of singers you might mistake them for a company of American daughters. The school is supported from our own salary with such donations as we can secure from American friends."

To meet the insistent demand for a class in English to help the children of mixed marriages learn their father's language, Lorenzo finally consented to open a school for just six pupils. Although he put a high price on books, 20 entered the class. "Some make good progress," he found. "Others, *Auwe!* [Alas!] Sometimes it is all I can do to keep my risible powers within proper bounds!" But, he hoped that, in due time, "those whose organs of speech are incapable of English may give up."

When the smallpox epidemic hit in 1853, Lorenzo got busy vaccinating. He had one case in Waimea, two in Hamakua, but many at Kawaihae, where he lamented that so many of the aged and young succumbed.

Waimea's battering weather had wreaked havoc on the old meeting house by April 30, 1855, and so it was abandoned. By June, the roof had fallen in, leaving a mass of ruins. They tore it down and put up a new clapboard building. On August 29 they laid the cornerstone. The new, present Imiola Church was dedicated in 1857.

As frail church buildings were always blowing down, Lorenzo wanted 14 new substantial churches built in his district. He took the lead, urged his people, planned their churches, made estimates, ordered lumber, and did much more. The people also worked hard and performed nobly. Seven churches were to be completed, and if paid for, dedicated, during 1860. Four more were to be built in 1861 and another restored, keeping him engaged in the building of 12 churches. These, with the two already in use, gave him 14 to take care of. For five of the churches, Lorenzo ordered bells from America. Financial help came from fund-raising affairs in America and some less-profitable feasts put on by the Hawaiians. By March 4, 1867, all 14 churches had been completed and dedicated.

In 1863 he had to give up making the tours in which he had so greatly delighted. "Native pastors have taken over the work, but my wish to visit and aid them has been denied me," he regretted.

Lorenzo in 1848 had contributed native hymns to the Hawaiian newspaper and sent off his first song book for publishing. In 1870 he prepared the *Hawaiian Hymn Book*, containing over 600 hymns. His *Robina Gula (Golden Robin)*, a book of songs for Sabbath and day schools, was put in use all over the islands. *Lei Alii (Royal Diadem)*, containing one hundred hymns, soon followed. "All these are works of love," Lorenzo happily declared. "I have no compensation but the joy and pleasure in doing good, and the hope that much good may result."

On July 16, 1872, people came from all around to celebrate the 40th anniversary of Lorenzo's coming to Waimea. Lorenzo reported on his 40 years of work. The bell rang out 40 times, and there was a dirge for those who had died. Then all joined in a procession to the big love feast and much shaking of hands and kissing. By the time Lorenzo got home about 6:00 p. m. he was "all used up."

Lorenzo summed up his present situation: He owned a simple house on about four acres of land. As postmaster and school agent he received $50 a year. He supported his wife, one daughter, and two Hawaiian children on means so limited he could afford hired help only to do the washing. He managed "by great economy" to keep his annual expenses down to one thousand dollars. He sent a package of writing to each of the native newspapers every week. He looked after seven schools, and an English independent school.

"Love donations" from the 1880 Sunday school celebration provided him means to prepare his new hymn book and a shingled roof to protect better his home from the rainy weather. Then in June 1882 he could announce "My hymn book, *Hako Ao Nani*, is being distributed all over the land."

Lorenzo Lyons 50th Jubilee (1882) — Source:
Baker-Van Dyke Collection

The jubilee of Lorenzo's arrival in Waimea came July 16, 1882. Declaring himself "feeble and weak," he requested no special observance be made by the Sunday schools. But the people held an appropriate celebration with "the presentation of various loving gifts, congratulatory letters, and poems, and congratulatory addresses by delegates from other places."

He was proud of his long endurance record, being "the first of all the Hawaiian missionaries from the pioneers in 1820 down to July 1882, that Providence was permitted to complete 50 years on the Islands." Other missionaries still living, he admitted, had lived 50 years in Hawaii, but some had retired and others had withdrawn from missionary work. He rejoiced and blessed the Lord that he had been able to labor "a full 50 years for the temporal and spiritual good of the Hawaiian race!"

More special gifts were presented two months later on September 16. The meeting house was filled with visitors from all over. "No better singing was ever heard," Lorenzo gleefully proclaimed. Then came a great feast at the courthouse. Lorenzo received almost $350 in gifts.

July 5, 1884: Lorenzo finds himself listed in the latest directory as "Rev. Lorenzo Lyons, pastor of Imiola Church, postmaster, school agent, and Government physician." He continued as pastor, he admits, though he is 77, feeble, partially deaf, and really not fit to preach or be pastor, but he still serves because the church is so small no one wishes to take his place. He is postmaster because no fault is found with him and no qualified person would take the job, or as school agent, a post held since his arrival in 1832, even though he is now unable to visit distant schools. Though not an M. D., he has served as doctor all these years and so earned the title, as nobody objects to his medical work and he carries on in it "out of love to Hawaiians — and others." To these titles he would add that of Poet Laureate, as composer of Hawaiian hymns, as "there is no other who writes hymns and songs for Hawaiians." He had published two books of hymns, the first in three editions, the second just out. He was still translating a hymn a week for the native newspaper to be printed in a book when he had completed 60 more.

It was August 25, 1884, when "the Lord arrested me suddenly in my work," Lorenzo noted on December 17. During that period he had not been able to preach or write. Recently two of his companions on the *Averick* had died—William Patterson Alexander, head of the Theological School on Maui, and David Lyman, whom he missed especially, as they had corresponded weekly for 52 years. But on this Saturday in December he managed "with staff in hand, and feeble step, to get up to my dear Imiola, house of God." On the second Sabbath of January he preached there again to a full house — "all Waimea, young and old and middle-aged, Catholics, Mormons, Protestants, unbelievers." The communion offering of $50 was donated to Lorenzo as an expression of aloha from this "mixed assembly composed of a majority of outsiders."

About a year and a half later, on March 7,1886, he suffered another breakdown, reporting it to the Board, July 29 as from "your broken down missionary." He had earlier offered to resign because of deafness and debility. During September 1886, he was suffering nightly from neuralgic spasms like shocks of electricity, though spared during the days. He died October 6.

The Rev. C. M. Hyde in his "beautiful tribute to Laiana" quoted one of Lorenzo's last utterances: *"E Hooikaika! E Hoala!"* ("Be strong! Rouse up!") So had he commanded himself to push himself up in spite of his weakness so that he might not call others away from their work to wait on him.

Children of Lorenzo Lyons - Lyzzie, Albert, and Fidelia. Photo by Stangenwald — Source: Baker-Van Dyke Collection

With his "deeply affectionate and idealistic nature," he was devoted to his native land and held the same strong patriotic ardor for the adopted land he had served faithfully. Emma Doyle reflects," It is well that Lorenzo did not live to see and weep over Annexation." For, when "his son Curtis wrote an article for publication, pointing out that annexation to the United States was the logical and ultimate destiny of the islands, paternal reprimand, swift and severe, came by the first mail from Waimea."

The burial was near the Lyons home, where lay Betsey's baby Luke and later Lucia. A marble shaft marked the spot, the funds for it contributed by Sunday School children in Hawaii *nei*. The three graves were moved, placed in one, beside Laiana's much-loved Imiola Church in April 1939. There the white shaft marks the spot of the final resting place of one of the most dearly loved men of Hawaii. Beside it stands the old church bell.

Many paid tribute to his greatness. He was extolled as "the most beloved of all the missionaries," for "his abounding faith and winsome personality," and as "a man of loving nature, of saintly simplicity of character, an indefatigable worker ... Enfeebled by the infirmities of age, his spiritual life was strong, patient, cheery to the last."

So Hawaiian had Laiana become that he even encountered the spirit world of Hawaii — the dreaded Night Marchers, ghosts of past chiefs. Riding slowly up from Kawaihae, he saw far ahead a multitude of people coming towards him. These, he saw soon, were a great company of chiefs with their warriors and food bearers. When he failed to recognize any, he realized they were spirit people. They came close, looked at him, but passed on without harming him. "They were people of the spirit," he explained in relating the experience."God has given both material and spiritual forms."

His loving spirit became manifest in the volumes of Hawaiian hymns into which he poured the poetry of his soul. At any Hawaiian gathering, Hawaiians rise and join in singing the beautiful, soul-inspiring strains of Laiana's *Hawaii Aloha*, that so poignantly expresses the spirit of love the missionary had for his adopted home and people and their "heavenly righteousness." Such a contribution makes Makua Laiana forever memorable and loved.

157

20

FORERUNNERS IN KOHALA

Artemas Bishop visited Kohala in 1823, preached there in 1825, traveled through there in 1826 with Queen Regent Kaahumanu on tour, returned in September 1828 to perform marriages, examine schools, and preach. Even after Lorenzo and Betsey Lyons joined the Baldwins in July, the two families found that trying to cover Waimea, Hamakua,and Kohala was beyond their capacity to do justice to all. Kohala was the largest district, with 8,000 people, and had a church that would hold 4000.

Lyons made a brief visit to the Kohala church on January 19, 1833, greeted by eager natives with their *aloha* and a feast of baked potatoes and fowl. Sunday, he preached three times to large congregations in a church "exceedingly large," but, having no pulpit, he had to stand on the matted floor and try to send his voice way back. This "exercise of speaking almost completely exhausted my lungs and my strength," he admitted.

The Baldwins, in the fall of 1833, spent four months in Kohala, "perhaps the happiest of our lives," he declared, pleased at this opportunity of "imparting the gospel to such needy souls, while there were so many ready to hear." He reported the people had "long ago," built a house to accommodate the missionary. The head woman sent 20 or 30 natives to Waimea to carry Charlotte and the baggage on the eight-hour trip. Charlotte took charge of the children for Sabbath school and a class of 40 during the week. Dwight had day schools and made tours in the district. Though he found clear evidences of idolatry and iniquity, he felt encouraged that "some few appear to be the children of God, and the gospel had some hold on the consciences of others."

In late 1834 he and Lyons preached in Kohala, supported schools there, and were delighted to have Governor Adams order the "tumbled into ruins" schoolhouses be rebuilt. But Baldwin had little hope "of having any efficient schools, unless we can live on the ground and qualify efficient

158

teachers," asserting later, "The 8,000 in Kohala have claims which lie painfully on my heart by night and day." Seven months later Brother Lyons emphatically echoed the need, but Kohala had to wait two more years before Lyons's prayers for an additional missionary for Kohala bore fruit on August 7, 1837, when two new missionaries arrived to his rescue. He took them on a tour to select a spot for a mission station at Kohala.

Cruel Kohala Discourages the Edward Baileys

Edward Bailey with wife Caroline came in the eighth company to Honolulu, April 9, 1837. He was a teacher, having been a student in various schools, a farmer, a teacher, and then a language student at Amherst College. Juliette Cooke, a companion traveler, wrote she considered Mr. Bailey "a natural genius... something of a musician, writes very good poetry, has taste and ingenuity about drawing, has cut profiles, and, too, is very intelligent and pleasant, gaining the love of all." She added, "Mrs. Bailey is equally agreeable, possessed of peculiar sweetness of disposition, calmness and fixedness of purpose."

The Baileys settled in Kohala on September 26, 1837, but soon found Kohala too harsh — "cold, damp clothes" and bed chilled them, and, along with books, everything else in the house, turned mouldy. Fearing the constant wind would blow down the house, they begged for materials for a more permanent building. Supplies sent "went to the bottom of the ocean in a whirlwind" that capsized the canoe.

Other discouragements came. Bailey felt the people were "wild, heathenish," although he admitted earlier missionaries had helped remove "the darkest features of heathenism." He had to close his boarding school because the king took the students out to work for him. To help people earn money for books, he tried to get them to raise cotton or start a sugar mill. Finally, his family (first son Edward born 1838) could endure this debilitating climate no longer. Afflicted by fever in 1839, they transferred to Lahainaluna on Maui, and helped conduct Wailuku Female Seminary from 1840 to 1848. Two years later they left the mission and remained active in teaching and sugar work until moving to California in 1885.

In Hawaii, Bailey demonstrated his wide range of abilities. As a physician, he aided with smallpox vaccinations. He planned and directed the building of the church at Wailuku. He also designed and built a mill and manufactured sugar, directed road work and bridge building, did surveying, settled land claims, helped develop and maintain Maunaolu Girls' School at Makawao. As a first rate musician, he taught music. He wrote a synopsis on Hawaiian ferns and a long narrative poem, made sketchings for engravings at Lahainaluna, and did delightful landscape painting.

When Edward died at Alhambra, Calif., March 31, 1903, age 89, he was the last male survivor of all missionaries the ABCFM sent to Hawaii between 1820 and 1850.

Isaac Bliss — Wrong Kind of Missionary

Isaac Bliss with his wife Emily Curtis, fellow arrivals with the Baileys, joined them at Kohala six weeks later.The Rev. Isaac, born at Warren, Mass., August 28, 1804, came as a graduate of Amherst College '28 and Auburn Theological Seminary '31, and had served as pastor at Victor, N. Y. As his first wife lived less than a year after marriage, he married Emily Curtis, sister of Betsey Lyons, August 14, 1832, at Elbridge, N. Y.

Isaac Bliss — Source: HMCS Library

When Bliss and Bailey visited Hilo in early 1839, Abner Wilcox found them quite discouraged about their isolated location. He reported also he "was quite pleased with Brother Bliss' manner of preaching. He is emphatically an itinerant preacher; i. e. in his preaching he continually travels all about the house, seizing hold of the heads or hair of men and women and shaking them to gain their attention. I think he is not yet very *akamai* [well versed] in the language ..."

On their return to Kohala, they found their meeting house blown down and were pleased to have the chief's permission to relocate nearer the shore. About late 1839, a house site three miles down to a place two miles from the shore was selected. After Baileys left, the Blisses suffered loneliness as well as the trials and hardships of their position. Isaac urged that a pair of shoes be sent him from Honolulu, as he had worn out his on his first tour of Kohala. He and Emily needed clothes warmer than cotton or linen, and he could not make a pen until he received a good penknife. Although their flour was "musty and wormy," they had "good *kalo*, some butter and milk and most of the time good breadfruit, also sweet potatoes and Irish potatoes, and eggs ... a large lot of fowls, some turkeys ..."

Having to live under such toilsome and deprived conditions, it is perhaps "small wonder ... that Brother Bliss developed strange tendencies" and often treated Emily quite erratically. His chief preoccupation became the building of his stone and timber dwelling, assisted by a carpenter, and made ready to sleep in by January 1841. Soon they were "quite comfortable" but needed a sheet of zinc for the roof and shoes for little Mary, born in 1837, their only child. Emily, probably pleased at being away from her eccentric husband, was helping at Waimea and expected to go to Kailua soon to assist at the birth of Parnelly Andrews' second child.

Samuel Ruggles, back in the United States, had met Bliss there and wrote to the brethren, warning them against his odd nature. His moodiness and sometimes too merry demeanor had become occasionally too familiar on the voyage over. He beat his wife while on a visit to widowed Lorenzo. "Wild, indiscreet and fickle," one writer diagnosed him, adding "he turned out to be wholly unfitted for the ministry or for missionary life. The mission sent him home." The Missionary Album says only that "severe illness forced his return to the United States."

At the general meeting in 1841 he asked to return to his native land. Elias Bond was appointed in his place. The Blisses invited the Bonds to live in their house, but Bliss "soon followed them in one of his most erratic and unaccountable moods, and settled in the house with them, claiming everything as his own." Bond wrote to Honolulu to remove Bliss, "who extracts great stores from the natives, is most abusive in his dealings with them, and is a constant source of menace to the health of Mrs. Bond." Finally Bliss left, to the relief of all.

Bliss was released from the ABCFM soon after his return in 1842. He died at Moline, Ill., August 9, 1851, less than three weeks before his 47th birthday. Emily continued there until her death on January 3, 1866, at age 84.

21

ELIAS BOND — STRONG MAN OF KOHALA

Boy of Great Promise

If ever one was reared to become a missionary, it was Elias Bond, Jr., "born of good Puritan godly stock," August 19, 1813, at Hallowell, Maine, the ship-building port on the Kennebec River.

His father had been an active Universalist, not a true Christian in the eyes of his wife, brought up with "best Puritan training." So she held to her strong faith that her husband would be "brought into the fold." Nearly a year later Elias did renounce his faith and joined hers as another faithful follower of Jesus Christ. This change of heart came about after both suffered during bereavement over the death of "a beloved daughter to whom they were devotedly attached."

Soon after, Elias, Jr., arrived in this family that "steadily aimed to make their Lord and Master's service the predominating service in their domestic, social and secular life." As the ABCFM had just been organized, the Bonds became "saturated with the Missionary Spirit" and, with "undying, all absorbing interest," followed news of missionary work in distant Ceylon. To his enthusiastic mother young Elias became her "little missionary." The Bonds' hearts filled with such abounding joy when the first letters from Kaahumanu and other chiefs arrived from the Sandwich Islands in 1821 that the elder Bond paid to have the letters printed to present copies to his neighbors.

This great cause inspired such an exuberant joy in the eight-year-old Elias that he "took a boyish pleasure in working to earn money ... to contribute to the cause of Christ" and, he proudly claimed, "many is the dollar I earned and with loving heart gave to the Missionary Cause." In those days when earnings for a boy came usually as a mere copper cent, a dollar was a whale of a lot of money requiring many jobs to earn it.

As the Bond home became "a place of habitual resort for Ministers and Christian people," young Elias was continually listening to "discussions of Bible Doctrines and points in experimental religion" and conversations about "the Kingdom of God, at home or abroad." Thus he "came to imbibe an abiding love for Ministers and the Missionary Service." When a Sabbath School was introduced, Sundays consisted of morning service at 10:30, Sabbath School at noon, afternoon service at 2:00, Sabbath School again, then a final meeting at 7:00.

To avoid the possible "contaminating" influences of the public school, his parents, after a trial period there, sent Elias to the academy, supposedly with "a cleaner class of boys," from the most respectable families. But what Elias recalled was "the battles with shovels and tongs and clubs in school hours between the larger boys and the Preceptor, — the breaking out of the whole chimney back, — the tearing down of the out buildings and the frequent disfigurements of the Academy building and property." Elias saw "The main end and aim of the Pupil was to annoy the Teacher with endless tricks, whilst the Teacher with his big ruler in his hand was ever on the alert to head the boys off." Such schooling, with only "the dullest routine work," proved of no great value to Elias.

Just a regular boy in those pioneer days, bewitched by the river that flowed past their house, Elias dared its waters on fragile home-made rafts or its thin rubber ice on skates, being rescued from drowning an uncounted number of times summer and winter. Handy with tools, he made his own skates, sled, fish line or other play items. He willingly sawed, split and piled up in the wood house all the wood needed.

When Elias was 13, his mother died, April 18, 1827, after more than a year "going gradually, gently down to the grave" with consumption. Grieving at her steady illness, Elias labored to earn 75 cents for a bottle of patent medicine, labeled "British Oil," declared sure to save. When it failed, he learned one of the bitter truths of life — not to believe everything you are told.

His 19-year-old sister Elizabeth, serving as housekeeper for the two remaining Eliases, caught typhoid fever but recovered. Then Elias caught it. "For three weeks I lingered between life and death, while she nursed me tenderly, and in her weakened condition this brought on a relapse that was fatal." About three weeks later, Elias's father, "now, bereaved and cast down, having no house-keeper," on the advice of friends, married. This wife became a faithful and devoted mother to the boy, helping him through college later.

Finding a Place in the World

When Elias reached age 16 it was time to choose a career. He declared "A sailor." "Oh, no," his distressed parents objected. Then a hatter he would be, like his father. "But," he decided, "only in a first class Establishment, not in any country Manufactory." So he went to Chelmsford, Mass., as an apprentice, receiving board and 75 dollars a year. Elias spent his evenings reading books from the library at Lowell, a muddy two-mile trip away.

A year later, seized by a severe cold and sent home for several weeks, he attended revival meetings, "but did not turn to the Lord." Back at Chelmsford, he was seized as if in "a giant's grasp" with the realization that "all the great privileges of the Gospel" he had enjoyed had done him no good. Then home again with a renewal of his cold, he gave his heart to Jesus; his pastor urged him to study for the ministry, but Elias felt "it was impossible for me, so unfit, to entertain the thought for a moment."

He then became manager of a new hat store at Lowell. Boarding at Deacon Davidson's, he found a companion from New Hampshire who had also been urged to study for the ministry. They agreed to hold "frequent discussions and prayer for guidance, and then make a final decision" at the end of a year. Elias and his friend determined to study for as long as they could live on their money. If that gave out, they would return to their trades.

His bosses agreed to let him go and take him back within two years if he wished. As he became discouraged at his lack of progress, his teacher at the academy advised he was really making rapid progress but trying to do too much. So he "pushed on with fresh zeal." Later he spent "a pleasant and profitable two years" studying with the new teacher at the academy and then passed entrance examinations for Bowdoin College at Brunswick. Lacking funds, he took his freshman year studies with the academy teacher.

At Bowdoin in 1835, he had among his professors the poet Longfellow. While his college classmates showed grander destructive talents than had those at the academy, Elias put his energies to earning his way, ringing the chapel bell, sawing and splitting wood, making fires at college and teaching school in winter vacations and for one term out of college at a select school in Poland, Maine. Though he found this "a wretched way," he had no other course until, in part of his last two years, he borrowed from the American Education Society. Dissatisfied with getting further in debt, he preferred to go "patched and poorly clad" until he could earn money for new clothes.

He taught school then to get the needed funds. On his first job he proved his ability to come through difficulties "honor bright and authority unimpeached." Full of theory for using "moral suasion," he forgot his pupils were "uncouth country boors" in school just "to have some fun." After two days of not getting results from his proposed honor system, he was warned that the big fellows planned next day to put him out the window, tie him to a load of wood and haul him thus to the village, about two miles off, as they had done to the previous teacher.

Next morning he held up a big ruler and declared," This ruler henceforth governs this school, and he who breaks a law of the school will know it." Looking the large fellows square in the eye, he saw them wince and knew he had won the battle.

Just once he had to punish — "a little roguish fellow" that he caught whispering and playing and so had to administer ten strokes on his open palm. But the boy's old grandmother, fired by this chastisement of her pet, went "on a Crusade through the District [and] declared that every bone in her darling's hand had been broken ... and vowed [Elias] should never teach another day in the School House." At a district meeting, however, the people voted to keep Bond. A few days later at his boarding house he found an old lady who was sour and sharp, but he was ready to excuse such attitude in old people and treated her very attentively and kindly. Later he found that she was the disgruntled grandmother who had come to vent her spite on him. His generous attitude had won her over completely, and she became one of his warmest friends.

At Bangor Theological Seminary in the fall of 1837, he lost three or four weeks nursing a chum suffering from typhus fever. The food at the boarding house was so poor that the students rebelled and got permission to provide the meals themselves with Elias in charge. He carried on that task successfully for two years.

In an 1896 letter to the Bond children in Hawaii, Elias's roommate, "chum and cousin," the Rev. George W. Field, attested to their father's executive ability in this matter and added that Elias had so much surplus energy that "he threw up with his own hands the walks which today connect the buildings on the seminary grounds and planted the trees which now border these walks.... He was by nature exceedingly quick and somewhat impetuous, though he mastered this trait..." Elias was developing qualities invaluable to him as a missionary at isolated Kohala.

Decision, Bride and Journey

His keen interest in his theological studies fortified Elias's inclination to become a foreign missionary. Aware he must have a feminine partner, in his middle year at the seminary he met at a party at the home of the Rev. Cyrus Hamlin, Ellen Howell of Portland, who had studied at Gorham Female Seminary and expected to be a foreign missionary. Cyrus arranged for Elias to see Ellen home afterwards. On the long walk, they shared their interests and hopes, and, finding themselves "in accord as to the great questions of life," they "soon agreed to join hand and heart in the Master's service," applied to the Board and received appointment to the Ceylon Mission, later changed to the Sandwich Islands because of the pressing need there.

After graduating in 1840, Elias attended a meeting of the Board, hurried home for a short visit, bounced down to Portland, got his marriage certificate and arranged for a minister to marry them at 5:00 A.M. the next morning (with apologies for getting him out so early). After the ceremony they "jumped into the stage and started for Hallowell." He preached one Sunday in Augusta and, the next, at his "dear old South Church in Hallowell." They visited Poland where he had taught school, then to friends for a week or so at Portland until they were notified that their sailing date would be November 14.

They hastened to Boston to purchase their outfit for their future home across the seas — two bedsteads, two rocking chairs, a small birch dining table, a work table, bureau, cook stove, a few kitchen utensils and "a very narrow stock of clothing and bedding," conscientiously economizing because "the Board was desperately pinched in its Finances." Such a small amount of equipment, Bond assures us later, caused them "no suffering and no inconvenience to speak of." He brought a few simple carpenter's tools to make the household articles that they would need.

Ellen was 23 when she married 27-year-old Elias at Portland, September 29, 1840. As a young girl, she had amazed people by the nimble way she went flying over objects and dashing up and down stairs like a streak, "as agile, deft, lithe, spry, as anything in fairyland." But, as the Rev. Cyrus Hamlin also recalled after her death,"When she gave herself formally to the service of Christ she was much less full of fun and merry-making. A serious and dignified air took the place of her normally frolic-some spirit. She had passed... to the higher life of a Christian woman, living for higher purpose than mere enjoyment.... Small in person, she was large in energy, capacity, life and loveliness."

They set sail from Boston on November 14, 1840, on what was to be the longest, and in some respects the hardest, voyage of any missionary group so far. With the Bonds were two other graduates of Bangor Theological, the Rev. John Paris, who would be sent to Waiohinu, and the Rev. Daniel Dole, also a graduate of Bowdoin College.

A terrible gale soon sent waves sweeping overboard most of their provisions — 18 of the 20 hogs, nearly all the vegetables and all the chickens, salt pork and beef. So they were fed "salt junk" all the way, with fresh fish only twice so that "the very sight of Salt Beef was like a dose of Ipecac to us. We went to the table only as the cravings of hunger forced us to after fasting till Nature would endure the strain no longer." They suffered also from bad water carried in impure casks, trying to doctor it up with "the application of sugar, Lemons, Sarsaperilla, Soda and French Claret," though they would have preferred pure cold water.

Bond tersely summed up the voyage as "a dull one, devoid of incident and comfort both." It took two weeks of battering the elements to get around the cape. "In fact," he explains, "the voyage was so protracted that our vessel was believed lost and numbers of the missionaries were waiting anxiously on the shore in Honolulu to greet us," when they landed there on May 21, 1841, after suffering 188 days in such miserable conditions.

About a month later, the Bonds were on their way to Kohala. It was a 10-day trip, as other families had to be landed at Lahaina, Kaawaloa and Kawaihae. When they let the Forbes family off at Kaawaloa, Mark Ives came aboard to help the Bonds get started at Kohala. A gale of wind prevented landing at Mahukona, and the mate lost his life trying to fix the jib when the heavy sea washed him overboard. Landing a few miles north, they returned by canoe. Two church members were waiting to carry Ellen overland in a *manele* while Bond and Ives hiked the 10 miles. Elias felt at first much too warm in his thin linen suit, but by the time they reached the high land he was chilled through by the strong, cool winds. He was glad to find a horse provided for him on the rest of the way.

They reached the house at dusk, "wet, cold, tired and hungry," grabbed a cold lunch from their bucket and went to bed. It was June 26, 1841. The next day being Sabbath, they ate again from the food they had brought, managed to get on their only partially dry clothes and went up to a meeting.

"King of Kohala"

Here Elias found himself with a small, barely finished house, grounds void of plantings or fencing, an old meeting house "very rotten, leaky every where, a wallowing place for hogs during the week." But it filled with people when Brother Ives preached that Sunday. The two men then made the tour of the district on foot as the mission owned only one horse. Elias prepared to take off his shoes and stockings to wade across a swampy place, but "a great strapping fellow" came from the other side, picked him up as though he were light as a feather, carried him across and accompanied them part of the way. Elias succinctly concludes with "The next day he was dead and we attended his funeral. I wonder the people did not think we had bewitched him."

Halfway through the tour, Ives was called home because of the sickness of one of his children. This gave Elias a break "to get up our goods and get things regulated in the house." Then he completed the tour with Brother Lyons, getting familiar with his district from Hamakua west to Mahukona "and down to Kawaihae, and 12 miles up in the woods."

From then on Elias relentlessly and religiously made four quarterly tours each year through the district. He had the church book with the names of every church member, called them, inquired into their lives and tended to any trouble anyone was having. After that, he gave "a more or less protracted exhortation with a hymn and prayer ..." Each school he examined there, then had all schools gather at the central meeting house at the close of the year for a general examination and feast. In recognition of such control over his people, King Kamehameha IV declared at the stone church in Honolulu, "Bond is King of Kohala." And so he became known.

About two weeks after his arrival, Bond started a school to train his 32 native teachers, thus creating a normal school, an innovation not known in his homeland. His method succeeded so well that the minister of public instruction declared later that Kohala schools led all others in the islands. Elias made blackboards for all schools, their use more vividly capturing the attention and interest of pupils and teachers.

All these special projects left him little time to become familiar with the vernacular as other missionaries had done. So, when Abner Wilcox reached his home in November 1841, exhausted by cold and hunger, Elias Bond rejoiced that the Lord had sent him a man capable of delivering an understandable sermon and urgently prevailed upon poor Abner to perform that duty all that Sabbath. Abner addressed a large congregation in the spacious meeting house that had been rebuilt.

Bond was slow in acquiring language ability because he missed having someone capable of correcting his attempts at speaking in Hawaiian. But by 1843 Elias found that his separation from other white people and constant contact with natives had gained for him "a good and accurate knowledge of the Hawaiian vernacular."

He regretted the wretched state of the mission in which Isaac Bliss had left it, claiming he "neglected his missionary work entirely" and had suspended between 300 and 400 church members for such minor offenses as "smoking tobacco" or "wearing garlands on their heads." Bond felt these were "simple pleasures [and] had no place in the matter of church discipline," especially considering "the great diversity of opinion and practice among the Brethren," since some used tobacco daily, while others were excommunicating church members for such a habit. Even worse, Bliss had used his position "for his own personal profit."

To give further educational opportunity to capable students, Elias devised a select boys boarding school and built a schoolhouse, two dwellings and a cook house. The school was free except that each boy had to bring his mats, *tapa* covering, and animal food. It opened September 12, 1842, and kept operating 36 years, until it merged with the government schools in 1878. During this period, Bond instructed each class two or three years and sent out over 300 boys, many to Hilo Boarding School. Most returned to become teachers, while some entered other employment, "and a portion of them were of no special use any where," Elias frankly admits. When he was off on his quarterly tours, he left his best boy in charge, "always exacting a full and minute account of the behavior of the boys" during the absence.

Like Lyons, Bond found some of his travels greatly fatiguing, especially one in December 1843, when he managed "by dint of much hard labor and some peril" to reach "the extreme village on our Eastern boundary, a place never before trodden by a missionary foot, though our predecessors attempted it." He had to climb "over 5 or 6 *palis* [precipices] and then ravines of great depth" to Awini, atop a precipice more than 1500 feet high. Under a burning sun that produced clothes-saturating sweat, he pushed his way upward "until almost completely exhausted." Refreshed by cold water and a short repose and his soul heartened by the peoples' "unaffected and joyful welcome," he examined the school of five members and conversed with his seven disciples there. The repast that followed consisted of "fowl, *kalo*, *poi* and a calabash of shrimps, direct from the water, which the natives devoured with great gusto, all alive as they were."

Family, Food and Friendliness

Ellen Bond's duties were taking charge of the household, raising a family, and working with girls and women. A healthy little daughter was born September 29, 1841, and named after her mother. Elias, having "no friendly hand skilled in such matters," spent the night before the birth almost overwhelmed by his magnified fears that he would be unable to "discharge the new and unexpected duties of midwife and nurse successfully." But he succeeded well, and Dr. Andrews, having been summoned "post haste," arrived five days later.

Only five months later, in February 1842, Ellen found the courage and energy to open a school for about 30 native girls to study sewing, arithmetic and Bible. Some of her eager students walked six to ten miles every day to school and back home. Ellen also taught Bible study to a woman's meeting every Friday and held a Sabbath school. Although part of the time she had native help to wash dishes and clothes, "and do the heavier part of the drudgery," she did the cooking herself. Ellen's increasing family duties later caused her to suspend school operations. As her brood grew, she had to see that the children were "fed, tended, washed, clothed, nursed and taught by herself." A son born prematurely on March 1, 1843, lived but an hour. Elias was thankful that Dr. Andrews had "very unexpectedly and providentially" stopped in on his way from Hilo. Dr. James Smith from Honolulu delivered a son, George Shepard, on May 21, 1844.

Providing food for family and school presented problems. A barrel of flour that arrived in 1842 was "horrible — a mass of life, sour and musty." Fresh food came from the garden which Elias paid his school boys to work. In 1843 they supplied "a superabundance of the finest potatoes." The next year their garden produced "string beans, shell beans, squashes, pumpkins, radishes, onions, tomatoes, sweet corn, cucumbers, melons, cane, bananas, guavas, pine-apples, mulberries, strawberries, potatoes and a small variety of flowers." As their chickens insisted on sharing in their garden, Elias eliminated them. "I therefore put the remaining fowls with *poi* into the stomachs of my boys," he explained, "where I presume they together furnish a very comfortable purpose."

Meats they got from others. In exchange for two legs of fresh pork from their pigs, they received sweetmeats and "a whopping great salmon." The fish was so big that the Bond family finally gave much of it to the school boys to relish with their *poi*. A free gift of beef was received from "one of those three Botany Bay convicts who stole a ship, came down here and destroyed the ship, and then scattered through the district."

In December 1848, Bond was lamenting how people were dying in great numbers from whooping cough — 100 within three weeks, 275 since the epidemic started. And during these weeks, the severe weather added to the difficulties and afflictions — "an incessant gale and the rain poured in torrents." All other activity had to give place to administer to the sick and dying. " This poor people are a doomed race," Elias grieved. Dr. and Mrs. Wetmore in Hilo, after the loss of their first baby in 1850, took little Ellen Bond for a year or so to help with her studies.

Three Years' Labor Lost

Dreams of a good, substantial meeting house had naturally inspired Elias Bond ever since he beheld the repelling sight of the original one — "an old, tumble-down thatched building, only a roof really, for the hogs had pulled off all the thatch on the sides, and inside was only rubbish mixed with water." A later writer added, "Fleas abounded, and the stench was sickening." They tore down that abomination and used a new sugar mill for church meetings until a new building could be made ready. The next church "was a common thatched building that lasted five years, although with our high winds and heavy rains, it was soon greatly dilapidated."

Elias, eager for a more substantial meeting house, aroused his people to gather timber. He watched them wield "two or three axes whose edges were no sharper than the back of one's razor" to fell mighty trees and cut them into timber a foot or more square and 40 to 50 feet long. Bond hired some "Botany Bay convicts and runaways from ships" to saw giant *ohia* trees, "so large that two men could not reach around one." One man stood in a saw pit and the other out of it and sawed away all day for 50 cents pay, which they spent on drink. It took 80 to 150 men and women all day to drag these weighty *ohia* logs ten or fifteen miles down and over precipitous banks through thick woods. Drenching rains in late 1843 made such labors practically unbearable.

Coordinating these operations so taxed Bond's strength that he felt such labor almost "more than human nature could bear. I had not a half day's rest for several months in succession and for two months of the time had not more than two or three hours sleep in 24, in consequence of the severe sickness of a child." Yet his "health suffered not at all because of it." He highly praised his people for performing marvels "of hewing and dragging, incessant and severe labor, such as they had never before been called upon to encounter, though visited during this period with famine and epidemic diseases, their resolution never flagged. They never seemed weary."

As the first carpenter proved incompetent, Bond had to get another in October 1844. Four months later he was still preaching in the dripping rain because the carpenter had not come yet. In July 1845, zinc plates for the roofing were set on so insecurely that Bond reported, "our gentlest winds raise the whole mass of roofing from ridgepole to the eaves and keep it thrashing up and down like a huge blanket but with a noise of thunder which can be heard a long way off. What our violent winds will do yet remains to be proved."

More anguish too: "Most of the 3000 feet of lumber... arrived split, torn and battered. Then the wind continued so high and the influenza so prevalent that the lumber could not be carried up [the ten miles] from Mahukona." It was a herculean task for men to bear such burdens. "One native carried on his shoulder two planks of lumber 32 feet long, in the face of a driving storm of wind the whole distance. Another brought from Waimea a keg of nails, weighing 100 pounds, that had been sent to that place by mistake, agreeing to carry the burden 22 miles for 25 cents."

Bond rejoiced when they had "an exceedingly strong frame up, wattled on sides and ends very neatly with *ti* leaf and thatched with cane leaf on the roof. Oh, what a palace in those days!" he rejoiced in later years and describes the labor of gathering, preparing and weaving in the *ti* leaves, just as they had built the chiefs' houses earlier. Only a few natives in Bond's time still knew the art of wattling. Then they made the building solid with *koa* boards for floor and ceiling and lining the sides. The *koa*, sawed by hand in Waimea mountains, had to be carried to Kawaihae, brought by schooners to Mahukona, and then on men's backs to the church site. As the wood came "unseasoned, green and tough," it was extra hard to work with it.

Having no carpenters then, Bond trained his faithful friend and teacher, Deacon Paku, "to the use of plane and saw, and he... generously left his school and gave himself unstintedly to this work with me for six months..." This was all free labor on Paku's part, as Bond had nothing left to pay him, having spent all he could collect and save to buy the necessary lumber and glass, though he did occasionally divide a piece of brown cotton with Paku, whom, Bond declared, "was one of the noblest souls that ever trod this earthly footstool."

He praised his congregation of two or three hundred, who, in scanty garments drenched by rain during a six mile walk and climb over precipices and ravines, came to sit on a stone and listen attentively to his sermon. There, "in the wet and wind and dirt," he thought of the comfortable New England churches and wished for one at least "as good as the poorest" there. By the first Sabbath in April 1846, just six months after the start of construction, the house offered sufficient protection for services to be held inside. By November it was quite complete and filled each Sunday with from 800 to 1000 worshipers.

The building measured 86 by 100 feet, surrounded by a *lanai* six feet wide. Two doors opened on each side, and 12 large windows with 35 panes of glass eight by ten inches, gave light to the interior. The natives made their own settees — 130 of them, all the same size. Some bought them for six dollars each. Those without such seating sat in the wide center aisle or one of the side aisles, the seats accommodating about 900 and the three aisles at least 500 more, "sitting closely as Hawaiians are accustomed to do."

The cash investment in building came to $1,580.33, plus $40 contributed by the people. On the first Sabbath of 1847, Bond proposed "raising a thank offering to God for his blessing upon our efforts to build His house." The congregation made a pledge to give money for benevolent causes each month for life. When puzzled church members came to Bond, wondering how thet could get any money, he told them to sell their products — a pig, or potatoes, or *kalo*, or bark ropes. The result was $200 raised in the first six months, far surpassing Bond's expectations of not more than $50.

After six years, Bond felt gratified by the great improvement in the peoples' clothing, their seating and orderliness, and their resolve to show no mercy to anyone caught "in the filthy and irreverent habit of squirting tobacco spittle over the floor" or of allowing "one of the canine race" to explore the house of God.

But, alas, heavy misfortune befell this promising community. Afflicting as the winds and rains had been, now, in July 1848, they became so excessive as to put an end to all enterprise throughout the district. By October, the measles epidemic laid low the entire population. "All Kohala was a hospital and every inhabitant was a patient therein," Elias sadly reported. He went visiting and caring for the sick until the illness of his own family demanded his attention. In the first two months of 1849, multitudes died or were carried off by an influenza epidemic that soon followed. Such a personal disaster weakened the people physically, mentally and morally.

Then came the final blow, one that might well have destroyed the spirit and ambitions of a man less courageous and determined than Elias Bond. A violent southwest gale on December 21, 1849, totally destroyed the beautiful meeting house. Built unusually strong with extra large and heavy

172

timbers, the church they expected would endure for a century served but four short years. One vital part of construction had gone wrong. Not a single pin had been put in the tie beams. The carpenter had sent a man up to pin them, but he had shirked this important task.

Build With the Help of God

After such a catastrophe, Bond had to admit "our anticipations are disappointed, our hopes are frustrated and we are bereaved and desolate." But, steadfastly relying on the Lord, he felt new strength charge his spirit with fresh understanding and determination. Just a week after the disaster, he and his faithful followers cleared away the remnants of their beloved church. Then they sat down, prayed and wept to relieve their anguished feelings. "After a sufficiency of talk," he reported, they resolved to "build a stone church with the help of God, and begin now to collect the material, stones, lime, sand, and wood." Also they declared they would "not beg aid of any kind from any one." And Elias proudly added, "These resolutions we carried out fully." The people did raise $800 in 1851, and, "without the slightest intentional hint," came aid from other Hawaiian churches and from New York and New England.

Bond's policy was to start building only after all materials had been collected. Men carried heavy rocks on their shoulders from neighboring ravines. Others dived from canoes into 18 to 30 feet of water to loosen large hunks of coral, tie ropes around them and haul them up to the canoe. Then they had to carry these to the church site, to which others had brought an equal mass of wood from eight to ten miles up the mountain to provide fire with the intense heat to break up the coral for use as lime. Women and children lugged in hundreds of barrels of sand from all along the coast, in any kind of container available — kapa, calabashes, rags, lauhala bags, old shirts or pants.

Again, the most severe task was "hewing the large timber in the hills and drawing it thence a distance of eight to twelve miles.... It was rough hauling, diagonally up and down steep ravines, over the roughest country imaginable." And, to supervise this work, he had to labor like a draught animal twice a week, getting home late and exhausted. The new stone church was to be the same size as the former building, 85 by 45 feet, and on the same site.

By May 1853, the walls of the church were nearly up, although its completion had been held up by "the immense floods of rain" pouring down so violently that carpenters and masons could work only ten days during ten weeks. A native mason from Lahaina, "aided by daily relays of the people for carrying stone, sifting sand and mixing mortar," put the walls up for $300. Two liquor-loving carpenters got the frame up with great difficulty.

Church members were still raising funds for this project but also contributing $400 for the Micronesian Mission, and the school children were expected to raise $150 for that cause also. By the close of 1853, contributions came to an unprecedented $666 for the pastor's support, $559 for the house of worship, and $358 for foreign missions, a surprising total of $1,583. Besides this, the peoples' work on the church building came to at least $1,000, Bond figured, far more than he had ever "expected of 1000 individuals living from hand to mouth as Hawaiians do and having no market by means of which to turn industry into cash."

By 1855 Bond could rejoice he had an edifice comparable to "no house of worship in the Islands, beside Kawaiahao." He beamed with pride at his handsome *koa* pulpit and pews. The previous church had a 210-pound bell donated by the Rev. Henry T. Cheever of New York, who had visited Kohala in 1844. As that bell cracked and became useless, the people collected funds for a new bell, later housed in a tower built on the church. Cheever did get his brother, the Rev. Dr. George B. Cheever, to deliver lectures and bring in $1,500 to add to the funds for church building.

Bond was surprised to learn that the king planned to come for the dedication. The day before the ceremony, the king with his royal court arrived and requested to hold a meeting at the new church at 10:30 A.M. the next morning. But Bond maintained, "The House was for the service of God, and God must be first in it and not the King." Thus rebuffed, the king next morning, "about an hour or so before the service, sent up Ruth Keelikolani, the Governess of this Island," requesting Bond send the people down that he might speak to them on some public matters, "promising that it should not interfere with our Dedication Service." Though the people saw it was a trick, Bond urged them to go and trust in the king's honor. The king postponed the speeches until the hour of the dedication service. Some heard the faint call of the bell and returned to listen to the service by Bond and Brother Lyons, filling the church but two thirds full. The king never came and hurried away early next morning to avoid Bond's courtesy call.

"It was this, what they called my needless Puritan stiffness," Bond confessed, "that made me always so unpopular with the chiefs, but I could not help it." He had no regret that the chiefs on Oahu utterly opposed his taking the pastorate of Kawaiahao Church. And, in spite of at least five other offers to carry on his work elsewhere, he preferred to remain in Kohala, his "first love," where his heart was among the people he served.

Though completed and dedicated, the new church building, of solid masonry three feet thick, had rain seeping through and running down the inside of the east wall. They tried tarring, painting, and cementing, but all proved in vain. So they built a protective shield of thatch about a yard from the wall to keep away the rain and left it there two or three years till the wall was thoroughly dried. They also removed the overhead plastering, this too

174

being damaged by rains, and put up a board ceiling. "Deacon Paku and I did a vast deal of work on the house outside and in," Bond recalled, "and the entire keeping of the house and grounds in order always fell upon us two, till his death."

What Price Missionary?

After donating both energy and money to his great building problem, Bond had now to deal with his personal financial position. In 1849 the Board had offered to give mission station land to any missionary who would pledge to remain. Bond was too independent and ambitious a man not to welcome this as an opportunity.

Elias's love and devotion were always first to Ellen and his family. When she became too ill in the summer of 1858 to get up from bed or settee, Elias, in spite of a painful infection on his finger, took over the household chores, doing all the cooking for his family of ten, acting as nurse and still taking care of his school and church duties. His mind made up to become an independent missionary, Bond, at the general meeting in Honolulu, found not another missionary was willing to free himself from the Board's support and "take the property and settle here." Bond listened to "all the discussions and bickering about dividing everything," and then declared he would accept the terms. His courage went unrecognized. "Instead of rejoicing, ... they were all against it," he found. One even questioned "what Brother Bond would get into, he might disgrace the Mission."

After his resignation, the Hawaii Mission would not give him even his house. A committee priced it at $500, and Bond, in his pride and independent way, bought it. In 1851 he reported that "we find no necessity of remaining longer a weight upon the churches and the Board, and hence we yield our salary, although we love the Board and ever shall, and have no wish to be considered separate from it. It is God's will that his work continue here ... We are now living with the strictest economy and we thank God and take courage for the future."

Although Bond saw the people were "miserably poor," being quite "destitute of all resources" for making money, he set a budget for church income — first one fourth, then one third to the service of God. He took but $450 for his salary, "the lowest figure at which we could live," and from that he also allocated ten percent to the Lord. Under Elias's good management, the church did pay him $450 on an average for the next decade, "the balance of our support," he adds, "coming from our own private means." Bond declared in 1860 that they had put "$3500 into the Lord's Treasury and have not only had a plentiful living, but have means sufficient with God's blessing to provide a decent education for our 9 children as expensive as this is found to be. This year the cost of 4 children away from home, has been more than $700." Outside of some work surveying, he had "never worked for nor sought pecuniary profit, a single day since our Missionary life commenced."

Bond, with all his energy, expertness and high inclinations, could have done much better in other mission fields. "The Mission repeatedly urged him to take a better paid cost at Lahainaluna, and he was offered a position at $3,000 a year in government work." That opportunity, he agreed, "would have suited my natural tastes precisely." But Bond was devotedly loyal to the people he had come to teach and help. "I love them still and expect to love them to the end. They have had the best years of my life as under God they shall have what remains. I have no other ambition than to lead these perishing souls to Jesus Christ." In spite of all the more lucrative offers he had had, he still felt "more than satisfied in this obscure district."

The Hard Road to Success

Elias saw his work was becoming futile about 1860. His people not only kept dying off but were departing to more attractive places. Conditions had changed much in the past score of years and so had the natives. His people no longer gladly made their laborious way many miles to church and sat "with all patience upon the ground through two protracted services and sometimes four." Bond disappointedly now beheld "a people well clothed, 'civilized,' and congregations already so delicate that without the aid of a horse, they cannot get to the House of God from the distance of half a mile, dare not think of coming out in a shower, and with nerves that by no possibility can endure more than one half day's service in the worship of God."

The natives could no longer sustain work projects. They vacillated from raising an abundance of food to neglecting the land and suffering from "merciless hunger." Some left home and land to gather *pulu* for export about 1859. This was the dense, brown, silky hair covering tree fern buds and used by the Hawaiians for filling the body in embalming, but, used by Americans, for stuffing pillows and mattresses. Some families left home to "live for months in a most heathenish and abandoned manner," with their "lands unplanted, houses desolate, schools neglected, the sanctuary forsaken..."

Bond could see the difficulty of really civilizing people as long as they lived in the same old crowded, unhealthy and corrupting living conditions of their native huts, with all family members lying together on the damp ground without "the slightest opportunity of privacy for a word or a prayer or any act in the performance of which nature itself dictates seclusion from the common gaze."

When on church salary in 1849, Bond bought 200 acres for raising vegetables, paying $300 borrowed from a friend not connected with the mission. His vision directed him to add more land in hopes of inducing the natives to stay to work it. Later, from Kamehameha IV, he purchased 1,200 more acres on both sides of his first 200 acres. In future years he would be accused with other mission pioneers of having "mercenary and self-seeking" motives in making such land acquisitions. He had earned some money from 1850 to 1862 by surveying for the land commission, urged to do so to protect the Hawaiians against the designs of foreigners. In one year he was paid $800. He saved some from his salary and he had also $400 given to him by his mother-in-law when he left Maine.

Seeing his people leave for greener fields of enterprise, he saw clearly that sugar cane was the only sure answer to this problem of "retaining our people in Kohala *nei*. There was no work in the District by which our people could earn a dollar." And he added emphatically, "This was the sole motive that led to the establishment of Kohala Sugar Plantation."

In spite of the failure of three small plantations, Bond became satisfied that proper management could pay expenses and keep his people from leaving. The question was whether he could convince any other man to invest in his plan. About 1860, he went to the partnership of Samuel Castle and Amos Cooke, two missionaries who were released by the Board in 1851 to become merchants to dispose of remaining goods in the mission depository. A committee examined the Kohala lands in late 1862 and reported favorably on the plan to acquire 3,282 acres at $2 an acre. Bond put in all his land except 500 acres reserved for his family and school.

His report of February 14, 1863, stated that the Kohala Sugar Company was organized and chartered with about 3,300 acres. He was sending to Glasgow for machinery at a cost less than in the United States and expected it would take about three years before returns would be coming in from the plantation. As Bond had to insist on "certain moral restrictions which might cause unfriendly remark," subscriptions from the general public were not sought. To Bond the chief objective was "the encouragement of industrious and virtuous habits in the people of the district, and I may say directly aiding the laborious missionary who has worn out 22 years of his life in exhausting toil for the spiritual and temporal good of the people."

By the following year local laborers were busy plowing fields and planting cane. Bond blessed God that his enterprise was not "pestilential morally or detrimental socially to our people." He steadfastly stood up for the rights of his people in every connection, sometimes to the consternation of the company's manager and the Honolulu agents who reminded him that "the business of the Plantation must go on, morals or no morals."

Bond set down his own rules: church every Sunday and prayer meeting once a week, no leaving the plantation without permission, "no card playing, no interfering, or intruding on any one's rights or sleeping place," no fighting, "no quarreling or whipping wives," and "no tittle tattling, ... or gossiping or running about from house to house interfering with other people's business." Management could not quite go for all that. Stockholders made some adjustments: no enforcement of church attendance, no prayer meetings during laboring hours, except if the men could be spared from work, church meetings after working hours, and laborers would not be hindered from going to Bond to talk over their troubles.

But a new manager in 1866 acted so severely that Bond declared that the man could return to the job only if he would refrain from floggings and allow the people to hold their regular weekly meeting and have a newspaper if they wished. "We must try to train men, not brutes," Bond asserted. "A man flogged for stealing, and rendered sulky by such treatment, undoubtedly set fire to the carpenter shop recently. This style of management must be abandoned." As Bond saw the plantations "carrying the people back to barbarism with fearful speed," the project became "the conflict of my life ... a burden of consuming care" for two years. "The people are treated as mere beasts of burden," he complained. All he could do was protest vainly and have his people join him in praying for deliverance.

"And it came so strangely!" he exulted. "Our new manager is a missionary son, a graduate of Yale, and a professor of religion." Dwight Baldwin, eldest son of the missionary, had taken over as manager, replacing the man whom Bond felt was so detrimental to the cause of Christianity. "It is my unceasing joy that religion is free and that all who will may now come to see the Pastor and may attend a weekly meeting for prayer!"

The financial situation was far from encouraging at first. The plantation debt of 1865 almost doubled the next year and then declined gradually until the first year of profit in 1872. The Bonds were struggling to make ends meet. The Board had kindly restored his salary of $450 in 1864. Now in 1868 Elias had to ask this be raised to $700, explaining he had to pay the expenses of eight of his nine children, at least $350 a year for his school of 16 boys and that he had no other income exceeding $180. He also suffered a sad loss of $200 from the burning of the schooner *Kohala* at the plantation landing. A careless sailor had lighted matches to hunt something in the hold. Of great personal loss to Bond was some of his old home furniture sent to him after the death of his father in Maine.

More cares were added. Because of the weakened condition of Lorenzo Lyons in Waimea, the district of Hamakua in 1867 was turned over to Bond, "a heavy increase to my cares and duties." Two years later he noted, "The last five years have taxed my brain to the breaking point. I can't sleep nor read nor write." Seeking to relieve the strain on his mind and body, he tried a trip to California late in 1869, but anxiety forced him back home within two months. In 1870 he wrote he had given up hope of getting any income from the plantation.

It was five years later when the Kohala Sugar Company declared a 25 percent dividend. Bond could at last reimburse the Board in 1877 with over $12,000. About 1885 he received $48,000 from the plantation, making him the largest individual contributor to the American Board, though his donations were always given unidentified as only from "A Friend."

To his children he bequeathed this high policy: "My design and wish has been from the first to give to the Kingdom of Our Lord all I have and all I am.... I am not my own, nor are my possessions my own." And so he urged his children to "keep this constantly in mind and use what may befall to them, not for personal gratification, but for the glory of God in the building of His cause in these islands."

Fresh Demands, Harder Struggles

Inspecting the Hamakua district when Lyons had to give it up in 1867, Bond, greatly disturbed by the "exceedingly low" foreigners, lumbering and making shingles there, but "wallowing in habits which the tongue would blush to record," he set to work to prod "the churches to the point of freeing Hamakua from the foul stains of drunken Christianity." Bond later got James Bicknell, son of a missionary to Tahiti, to take over this problem area.

As English-speaking workers joined the plantation, Bond felt the need of helping them also. First he befriended each and urged all to attend local worship services. Then he took on the extra heavy burden of starting a separate church, preaching at English services in a schoolhouse in 1865, after hurrying to them Sunday afternoons following a full morning of Sunday school and church services and hurriedly swallowed or neglected dinner. With funds from the plantation, its foreign employees, Bond, and a friend, and $100 from the Hawaiian church, a new house of worship was dedicated in January 1869.

It was such overdone activity that caused his break-down that year and his useless flight to California. Though the Board offered him a trip to Maine and a friend provided funds for Ellen to go, he steadfastly refused to leave again or to take a pastorate elsewhere. He declared, "I dwell, more than content, among my own people... with whom in unbroken harmony, I have lived as their recognized leader, for nearly 30 years."

When a later problem came up for providing a pastor for the growing foreign population, the Board suggested one of Bond's sons, then at Yale. Elias had to admit that the youth did not seem to have "the making of a pioneer missionary." Finally a minister consented to fill the post for

$1200 salary, a house, and $50 for teaching in a small school. So the Foreign Church became officially established in March 1879.

Bond became active in preparing and installing young natives as ministers and boasted of his leadership "in raising up so large a fraction of the entire number of Hawaiian preachers." In 1870 one of his former pupils was ordained in South Kohala, another part of Lyons' field.

Some Chinese workers needed Christian leadership. The first Chinese church in the islands was organized in Kohala in July 1883 and prepared to build a new church.

Bond vitalized his long-time dream of a girls' school by getting the support of congregations throughout the islands to provide the funds. He managed to open his school on December 3, 1874. With a hired carpenter, "assisted by good old Deacon Paku," Bond "worked with might and main in clearing the grounds, building stone foundations and fences, as well as carpentering... both as laboring mechanic and overseer," aided by boys from his boarding school. "He devoted his unstinted energies, body and soul, from early dawn to late at night, to the work... in a manner that permanently undermined his health," son Cornelius remembered.

Elizabeth Lyons served as principal of Kohala Seminary. Elias fervently sought in letters as an assistant "a genuine missionary spirit... a sanctified common sense in connection with a cultivated intelligence" and "a professed Christian and a steady worker for God's cause." Several came and did outstanding service.

As the one building became too crowded, a separate schoolhouse was added in 1878 for the 45 girls. After a series of setbacks — a typhoid epidemic, difficulties in getting proper assistants, Elizabeth Lyons leaving to take care of her aged father, and finally her retirement in 1882 — the school closed in October that year. In 1889 the Hawaiian Evangelical Association took over management until 1926, when the school became a boarding home for students attending Kohala High School until 1956.

As Ellen became feeble but valiantly tried to carry on what family cares she could, Elias built her a little summer house at the end of their lovely garden, a pleasant place to rest in her old rocking chair, with Bible in hand. Daughter Carrie remembered her toiling up the hill to hold meetings with the Hawaiian women in the little old schoolhouse, "when it seemed as though a breath of wind would blow her away." She kept on "the domestic harness" until her hands failed her after keeping the family home going over 40 years.

She passed away quietly on May 12, 1881. Though relieved at the peacefulness of her leaving, Elias felt this loss a bewildering blow. His one wish was to follow her immediately, but he was resigned to wait his turn, little knowing it would be another 15 years. Under the trees in the garden, they buried Ellen.

At first the loss made Elias feel it impossible to continue his work but he felt compelled to go on to make his 160th quarterly tour. "The wonted habits of 40 years and more resumed their sway, however, and all was well," he admitted, though far from easy in his condition — an acute bronchial affliction for years, torturing rheumatism, and in 1891 a fall left him practically helpless. After a long life of extremely vigorous action, he had to suffer 12 years of physical incapacity and great suffering. But, serene in his faith and clear of mind, he kept up his triumphant call, "The Lord reigneth. All is well." One new interest was his aid to the great number of Japanese then arriving. And he kept on his work as postmaster until nearly 1880.

In that year he finished his fourth revision of the *Hawaiian New Testament*. Elias was a true scholar and careful student of the native language, able to hold his Hawaiian audience for two and a half-hours of preaching. He kept noting new words and variations in his Hawaiian dictionary. His study was piled high with books on a great variety of subjects.

Carefully he considered the merits of each cause to which he donated dividends from the plantation. Avoiding personal luxuries, he directed funds to the American and Hawaiian Boards and to schools and colleges and many foreign missions. He refused to go to America just for the pleasure of the trip, considering such "an unnecessary affectation." Awarded the degree of Doctor of Divinity by his alma mater, Bowdoin College, in 1890, he refrained from using the title as he felt himself unworthy of such superiority over others in the field just as deserving as he.

As Elias saw his power waning, he eagerly sought capable persons to take over his service to his people. Finding a suitable man to serve in his place at his native church was most difficult, but, bowing to the inevitable, he conceded he must yield to a native pastor and resigned on his 71st birthday, August 19, 1884, turning over his pastorate at beginning of 1885 to one of his early pupils, the Rev. S. W. Kekuewa, missionary to Micronesia for ten years.

Ethel Damon sums up his latter days: "Hero and saint he was indeed, to the very end. Crippled and in pain for 12 years, almost helpless for five years, he was at last unable to rally from an attack of grippe. Murmuring the words, 'How long, O Lord, how long? When wilt thou take me home to thyself?' he fell asleep on the night of July 25, 1896. ... In his 83rd year, he had given 55 years to the life of Kohala."

"Hero and saint" were part of the appraisal of this mighty man by a much appreciative missionary son, the Rev. Oliver P. Emerson. "Father Bond was a man whose record places him among the foremost of the mission fathers... a man of great sagacity and force, practical and at the same time idealist, never satisfied with half-way measures. ... he was a royal host and charming companion. ...He lived an inspiring, exalted life...."

22

JOHN PARIS — LEADER WITH TWO MISSIONS

John and Mary Carpenter Paris and their children (1855) — Source: HMCS Library

New Home in the Wilderness

Accompanying Elias Bond to the Sandwich Islands in 1841 was John Davis Paris, born at Staunton, Va., September 2,1809, educated at Hanover College, Indiana, and, like Bond, a graduate of Bangor Theological Seminary, in 1839, the year before Bond. He married Mary Grant, born at Albany, April 27, 1807, in New York City, October 25, 1840, 20 days before they sailed on November 14.

Though assigned first to the Oregon Mission, they were sent instead, because of unfavorable reports from that area and a need for more aid in Hawaii, to open a new station at Waiohinu in the district of Ka'u, southern part of Hawaii Island, formerly under supervision of Titus Coan.

As they had to await the birth of their daughter Mary Aletta on August 1, 1841, they were sent to Ewa on Oahu to learn from Artemas and Delia Bishop, who had come there five years earlier from Kailua. Their first land trip in Hawaii was a "hot, sultry journey" of 12 miles, though it seemed more like 30 miles to these uninitiated travelers, as they wearily looked upon "the kind faces of Father and Mother Bishop and the shelter of their home."

Only three weeks after their daughter's birth, the Parises boarded a schooner for Kaawaloa and Kealakekua, where they were "hospitably entertained and cared for by Brother and Sister Forbes." There Mary and her babe remained, while John and Cochran sailed off to land at Kaalualu on the southeast coast of Ka'u about sunset on September 10. With them was Daniel Barret, an English gypsy ship carpenter left on the island because of a sickness, from which he had recovered. During that night all the Paris furniture, books and household equipment were deposited on the smooth *pahoehoe* rock, remaining quite safe there till morning.

A powerful, fierce-looking native, tatooed from head to foot and clothed only in *malo* girdle, lifted John from the boat to deposit him gently amid the waiting crowd on shore. There he received a most cordial welcome from the chief, Job Lilikalani, like his namesake "sore smitten with boils," and from the gathered multitude, many a joyful *aloha*. Their prayers for a teacher were at last answered.

All formed a long train to walk three miles inland to the chief's welcoming house so the "weary and worn" missionaries could recline, rest and refresh themselves,drinking from coconuts and eating bananas. As it grew darker, children came in carrying long strings of lighted *kukui* (candlenuts). Then two strong, tatooed men bore in a huge baked hog,while others followed with calabashes of fish, fowl, *poi* and potatoes, and still more, adding melons, bananas, sugar cane and little gourds with goat milk.

It was a colorful scene "in royal Hawaiian style, a dozen *kukuis* burning and *kahili* waving." John observed the native cleanliness of washing before attacking this bountiful feast. He took "a goodly portion" of pig meat but confessed he could not relish as much as Brother Forbes did. All remaining food had to be carried with them next day.

A section of this large canoe house had been curtained off and provided with couches and fine mats for the newcomers' comfort. But the infestation of roaches and lice played the devil with sleep. At dawn, the sound of the conch shell called them and they tramped off uphill to the next village, home of the head man, Paul. He offered another Hawaiian feast for breakfast, which the ravenous appetites of the walkers now much appreciated. Then, with a long train of natives, they "made haste slowly" to Waiohinu, the name meaning "shining water."

A man dressed in European style and sitting on a white horse soon appeared in the distance and greeted them with a hearty *aloha* as they met. It was Kema (Hawaiian for Shem), a native school teacher who had come to offer horsepower for John's travel. Only the animal preferred to back up at first and, over the sharp lava clinkers, danced delicately "like a hen on a hot griddle."

Kema had ready for the Parises a new grass house — about 15 foot square, with a doorway about four and a half foot high, no flooring, no windows, no ceiling, no partitions. It rested on a huge pile of lava, the ground covered with coarse grass and *lauhala* mats. The gypsy carpenter cut out two holes for windows and helped get the house ready by setting up the bedstead, table, wash stand, cross-legged stools and such. During his two or three weeks there, Paris visited his district with Forbes and Kema.

Forbes left first. Paris followed later in a large canoe with the district judge while the tax collector and a teacher did the rowing for the 70-mile trip. John found Mary and their daughter staying with Mark and Mary Ives. He made a one-day trip to Kailua to visit the families of Asa Thurston and Dr. Seth Andrews.

Success — Then a Tragic Loss

Off the Paris family set in a double canoe for their mission life at Waiohinu. A squall made them stop at Honaunau until late in the afternoon. Then, on a smooth sea, with six strong paddlers bending to the oars, they sped southward during a long night and until the next afternoon to Kailikii not far from South Point. After the family lunched and rested at a native house, four men carried the weary Mary in a *manele* up the precipice and the three or four miles to the home of Job Lilikalani. John found it "a hard walk against a strong trade wind through a thick growth of coarse grass and weeds, carrying our precious babe, who cried all the way for her Mama."

A great crowd of mostly nude natives eagerly welcomed the novel sight of a foreign lady and her baby and pressed as close as possible. Nor was this night less frustrating, as the cockroaches and fleas tormented "the wayworn and sleepless mother," never sparing the babe either.

They felt great relief to know they were to be on their way early next morning to their ultimate destination. Kema with his white horse met them atop the hill. There they rested and refreshed themselves, then proceeded with John and little Mary on the white horse, Mrs. Paris in the *manele*, and a long string of natives following. Happy and hearty was their welcome by a host of natives from the nearby villages, and kind and gratifying it was too, but how "killing to the weak and weary one." The peoples' intruding presence made it most difficult for the harassed mission couple to unpack their belongings or to prepare food until Kema finally shooed the inquisitive ones away to allow peace to reign for the night.

Early next morning back came the multitude to witness the white man's outdoor cookery in the open-top cook house built of lava rock piled four feet high. They marveled at the utensils and at "all the wonderful operations of frying fish, baking bread and boiling coffee." There the curious viewers stood continually watching, until Kema came to send them away.

The grass hut provided little comfort, its small area having to serve as parlor, bedroom, diningroom and study. For weeks gale-like winds swept beneath to raise the heavy floor mats, unless held down by chests or trunks. Through troubles and suffering, they had to make the best of it for more than six months. John knew they must have a more protective building.

An appeal for lumber to build a house was denied. Ever resourceful, Paris had his gypsy carpenter put up a small stone house for a kitchen but in which they could live until the natives could build a large grass house on land that Governor Kuakini had granted for missionary purposes. Using mats for partitions, Paris divided the quarters into a reception room, dining room and guest bedroom, making a simple bedstead and building a dining table on a center post in the dining room.

After he had the church organized, the marriage business boomed as couples who had lived together from 20 to 40 years came to make their union sacred, discarding extra spouses. Infanticide among them had been a common practice, one woman having buried 19 of her offspring.

The new grass house gave way to a frame house in 1843-1844. Paris considered it "finished in the plainest style with *koa*," now so admired for its rich grain but then considered "the cheapest lumber we could get from the native forest." Without carts or oxen, the workers had to drag the timber 15 or 20 miles. Henry Lyman, staying at the house in 1851, remarked that, since Paris was "a gentleman from Virginia," he "had, very naturally, reproduced the salient features of the Southern mansions among which he was brought up." He added, "The outlook over the native village and the surrounding territory was attractive, and in front of the house was a pleasant garden that contained many tropical plants and fruits."

185

When, in January 1843, the Paris family were visiting the Coans at Hilo, Mauna Loa erupted violently. Titus and John somewhat rashly decided to climb the great mountain to witness the happening. It proved to be a mighty dangerous expedition, with harrowing experiences. Staying too late to stare at the magnificent fiery spectacle, they suffered from hunger, thirst and despair as they rushed down madly, falling on the cutting lava clinkers, seeking their camp at night, "scaling ridges and plunging into rugged ravines, tearing our shoes and garments, and drawing blood from our hands, faces, and feet," fearful of stopping too long on the snowy heights, lest they stiffen with cold. Totally exhausted by the time they providentially reached camp, they fell prostrate, never rising till the next noon. It took them "three days of hobbling on lame feet" to reach home, two wearied but wiser men.

Another daughter, Anna Matilda, was born in 1843.

Sunday, August 23, 1846, Charles S. Lyman, the sometime Yale professor on a visit to the Sandwich Islands, attended services at John Paris's church — "a new one, a few rods from his house." Lyman admired the "beautiful mottled appearance" of the black lava blocks mortared with white coral and its thatched roof, making it "a handsome & commodious house." It could hold a thousand or more people, but only 300 or 400 were present because many others were attending newly established out stations.

Here again native strength had erected the essential missionary meeting house. Many of the stones came from Hawaiian temples in the district. Coral had to be carried seven miles from the sea to be burned down to lime for the mortar. Timbers had to be cut in the forests of Mauna Loa and dragged down to the building site. This building was destroyed in the great earthquakes of 1868 and replaced by the present Kauahaao Church, "a neat framed building, painted within and without, and well seated, with a steeple and a bell." The cost was $2,200, of which island churches contributed $700.

Lyman found the people attentive and "mostly decently dressed," except for their "hideous apologies for bonnets." He declared, "In their native headdress of full curling hair bound by a tincture of ribbon or a wreath of flowers they look free & in good taste, but an old fashioned, rumpled, dirty cast-off bonnet stuck crown-up hat fashion on the top of the head transforms them at once into hags, resembling the poorest dressed negro wenches..." He objected also to putting "these free buxom savages into corsets to make them "appear like a monkey in small clothes in agony & ill at ease."

Lyman assisted Paris and Brother Hunt in performing the marriage of a young couple, with old Jacob, who had come from his town 20 miles away, as witness. "Old Jacob," he added, "is a firm & consistent Christian, & his pastor always knows where to find him. Before his conversion he was a hardened opposer, & hated everything good."

The church filled the next Sunday for the communion service, offered from "a handsome set of brittania." The congregation, mostly church members, "appeared sedate & were generally well dressed, bating the burlesque old bonnets." Lyman found it a pleasant sight afterwards to watch "the people in their gay colored dresses wending their way home..."

Church at Napoopoo, Kona (1927), built by Rev. Paris (see p. 191)
— Source: Baker-Van Dyke Collection

In 1846 Mrs. Paris became so seriously ill that a runner was sent a hundred miles to summon a doctor, but he could give no help. Titus Coan reports that "she was stricken down with consumption." After no sign of improvement for months, she was carried to Hilo for medical aid, then to Honolulu for some months more without improvement. The Parises returned to the Coans at Hilo, where Mary Paris died February 18, 1847, her soul "wafted to immortal glory," Coan relates, quoting her continued "words of such triumphant faith."

Fidelia Coan took care of the two Paris girls, while John went back to carry on his work for two more years. In 1849 he returned to America to seek a new partner.

Others Carry On — Timothy Dwight Hunt

Timothy Dwight Hunt, graduate of Yale and Auburn Theological Seminary, arrived in Hawaii with his wife Mary Halsted Hedges with the

11th company on July 15, 1844, after a long voyage of 224 days. He was born at Rochester, N. Y., and she at Newark, N. J., where they were married November 1, 1843, 34 days before sailing from Boston, December 4. They were sent first to assist John Paris at Waiohinu from September 11, 1844, to October 28, 1845. Then they served at Lahainaluna until Hunt returned to Honolulu in 1848 to preach to a foreign congregation.

Henry Kinney

Henry and Maria Louisa Walworth Kinney were stationed at Waiohinu after arriving as the sole couple in the three-member 12th and last company in 1848. Young Henry Lyman, then a student at Punahou School, dreamily remembered the fond impression Maria Louisa made on the innocent swains there. When they beheld her "tastefully dressed in a gown of changeable silk, the like of which we had never seen before, and radiant with youthful loveliness, [she] captured the hearts of all the boys; and we worshipped her afar off," he recalls, "as a veritable goddess descended from heaven to illumine the earth with beauty."

Henry, on his first expedition as an independent surveyor at the age of 16 in 1851, stayed with Kinney and "his beautiful wife and two little children" in the house that Paris had provided — "a pleasant parsonage on the grassy slope of the foothills of Mauna Loa." The Kinneys had had a daughter born in 1848 and a son in 1850. Unhappily, Henry's health failed in 1854. He and his family moved to Sonora, Calif., where he died September 24 that year. Another daughter, born in 1853, died also in 1854. Maria Louisa returned to Hawaii and married a Benjamin Pitman at Honolulu, April 5, 1856. A daughter born in 1858 did not survive, nor did the mother.

William Cornelius Shipman

William Cornelius Shipman, with his wife Jane Stobie, came as individual missionaries, arriving at Lahaina from Boston, October 19, 1854. With their appointment to Waiohinu in 1855, the station once more had a resident missionary. William spent the rest of his short life there, dying at Punaluu, Hawaii, December 21, 1861. The Shipmans had three children. The youngest, Margaret Clarissa, born in 1859, married Asa Thurston's grandson, Lorrin Andrews Thurston.

When Dr. Rufus Anderson, foreign secretary of the American Board, visited Waiohinu after the Shipmans' stay there, he much admired the roads and was told they were the work of Kinney and Shipman. Anderson reported that "Mr. Shipman possessed a rare executive talent, and was regarded by foreign residents as a model missionary. I was told," he explained, "it was his own impression, as he drew near the close of life, that he had given an undue proportion of time and strength to merely civilizing influences, and the material prosperity of his people. This may account in part for their spiritual weakness when the supporting hand of their pastor had been withdrawn." It was the better part of a year before his successor arrived.

Orramel Hinckley Gulick

By now the generation of missionary children was beginning to take over. Orramel Hinckley Gulick was the second son of Peter Johnson and Fanny Hinckley Thomas Gulick, who had come with the third company in 1828. Orramel, born October 7, 1830, at Honolulu, attended Punahou School. He married a missionary daughter, Ann Eliza Clark, May 19, 1855. She also had been a student at Punahou and then at Mt. Holyoke Seminary in Massachusetts.

Her father, the Rev. Ephraim Clark, and her mother Mary had come also with the third company. He first provided services for seamen in Honolulu. Then the mission stationed the Clarks successively at Waialua, Lahainaluna and Wailuku before Ephraim became the third pastor of Kawaiahao Church from 1848 to 1863.

Orramel joined with his wife's older brother Alvah in starting a store in Honolulu. When that failed, he became second mate of the missionary brig *Morning Star* in 1857 and first mate two years later. When the mission decided to send Orramel and Ann to Waiohinu in 1862, David Lyman, Titus Coan and John Paris, known as the "Hilo Brethren," ordained him on October 12, when he was 32 years old.

Dr. Anderson, at Waiohinu in 1863 on his tour of Hawaiian missions,was impressed by seeing the stone church there filled with more than 600 people, some riding to town on the backs of about 200 horses that "stood fastened to lava stones in the adjoining fields." What concerned Dr. Anderson was that within the district population of about 4,000, "the Roman Catholics have obtained more hold than we could wish owing to past adverse circumstances." What he referred to was the impressive record of the work of Father Marechal. He had come to Ka'u in 1842,made strong friends with the people and a high chief, gone to Kohala to get the friendly support of Governor Kuakini, and returned to Ka'u to build up a strong following and chapels. Father Marechal, like the successful Protestant missionaries,was a powerful, active and attractive leader who won peoples' respect, confidence and support.

As the Gulicks did not take Shipman's place at Waiohinu until some months after his death, Protestant activity lapsed somewhat during that interval, Dr. Anderson felt. "Intemperance, an easily besetting sin of the people, made sad inroads upon the church while it was without pastoral care," he noted, "though the people kept up their public worship, and their usual collections for the institutions of the gospel."

At Waiohinu the Gulicks joined in starting a female family boarding school, which they "transplanted" to Waialua on Maui when transferred there in 1865, according to Elias Bond. There the Gulicks conducted the Waialua Girls' Boarding Seminary. In 1870 the American Board sent the Gulicks as missionaries to Kobe, Japan, until 1892. They returned to Hawaii in 1894 to work with the Japanese there. Orramel died at Honolulu on September 18, 1923, but Ann continued on another 15 years to October 9, 1938, "the oldest child of the mission."

John Pogue

The Pogues, who had served at the Kaawaloa station from 1848 to 1850 and then at Lahainaluna, came to Waiohinu in 1866 for a two-year stay. In 1869 they visited the Micronesian missions. Back at Honolulu in 1870, John Pogue became secretary of the Hawaiian Board until ill health directed his resignation in 1877. He visited the United States that year but died at Laramie, Wyoming, December 4, having had to leave the train there because of severe illness on his return trip. Maria Pogue died April 20, 1900, at Santa Clara, Calif.

Paris Returns, Revives Kaawaloa Mission

Back in Boston, John Paris on September 7, 1851, married Mary Carpenter, born January 21, 1815, at New York City. Still strong in his missionary ambitions, he arrived at Honolulu in the spring of 1852 with his new wife, along with Lucy Thurston, home from her second voyage to New England, and Abner Wilcox, also returning.

The Parises received the task of reviving the Kaawaloa Mission. Paris well knew that the climate there had been "exceedingly trying to the health of the missionaries." But John was a staunch, sturdy, capable character, now just 40 years old, and for him life was about to begin anew, involving him for another 40 years.

As the old mission houses of Ruggles and Forbes proved worthless, Paris set right to work to put up a stone kitchen and the Parises moved right in there. He then built a good house during the next two years, getting lumber for an *ohia* frame with *koa* clapboards and shingles. For his duties at the church below, he walked "up and down the steep, hot, rocky trail, since his one horse must be saved for more distant journeys."

Due to the "failure in health of the missionaries," Paris explained, he found "everything in this mission field was in confusion, dilapidated and demoralized." No usable house of worship or schoolhouse remained in South Kona. Though he found "many good Christians, they were like lost sheep without a shepherd." While his wife was wisely conducting the mission household duties and supervising women, John devoted himself to preaching and making tours of the district. He saw that the outlying schools and churches were erected, teachers prepared and books provided. With his experience in building, he took the lead in this work. He trained the best men in each village to conduct Sabbath services, weekly prayer meetings and catechising.

As the old church lay in such bad condition, Paris decided he must completely rebuild it. With his mastered building capabilities, Paris could serve as head carpenter and mason to supervise the work as he had at Waiohinu ten years before. As the multitude of worshipers in Kapiolani's days had dwindled, Paris made a smaller church, 62 by 56 feet, taking the width of the old building for the length of the new one. Again the natives dived for coral to make the lime in the kiln Paris built for them. Again they dragged down heavy *ohia* timbers from the mountain forest and *koa* wood for shingles, the pulpit and pews. This time the work took three years.

Paris gazed proudly at his finished church with its wooden tower, a landmark visible 30 miles down the coast, and with its little bell to summon the congregation from nearby villages. The bell came as the gift of a friend of John's wife in New York City. The builder of the tower and his native helper had almost lost their lives by falling from near the top of the roof when the tower they were building gave way because the man had worked with unslacked lime.

The missionary also financed the construction by borrowing money at 12 percent interest. His trusted native Christians repaid all. He called his new church Kahikolu, or Trinity Church. He established seven small churches and maintained them in his district. When Asa Thurston had to give up his pastorship at Kailua in 1861, Paris took over that care and had that church building fixed up and reshingled. He labored for nine churches in Kona until 1870.

That year, at age 61, he moved his family to Honolulu. Daughter Ella Hudson, 18, and son John Davis, Jr., 16, attended Punahou School, a two-mile walk from the mission house on King Street. As Paris was assigned to establish a theological seminary, he selected and purchased the Marine Hospital building, then spent the next two years repairing it. It opened in 1872 and Paris taught there till 1874.

Finding living costs too high in the capital, he then resigned, returned to Kona and resumed his work there for about six years more. When his son married, he sold him the Paris house and went back to

Honolulu with his wife and daughter. Mary injured her knee in an accident, and they found they could not manage to live on his meager mission pension. So back to pleasant Kona they went to spend his last 11 years there.

On the foundations of Kapiolani's old stone house, destroyed by earthquakes, he built a new house. There the Paris family enjoyed a matchless view of shore and ocean from their 1500-foot elevation. It was a place with royal and personal memories — where Kalakaua and his sisters Liliuokalani and Likelike had lived, and where Paris had conducted a Hawaiian school for years. And here John Paris devoted himself to working with the churches, visiting the sick and unfortunate and counseling the native pastors.

He continued to July 28, 1892, dying at age 84. He left many fond memories among the numbers of people he had served with his "strong Christian character, pleasing personality, vivacious manner and royal mien." He was a wise counselor, loved and revered by the Hawaiians.

His wife Mary Carpenter lived four more years after him to age 81. His daughter Ella Hudson is honored by a plaque at Mokuaikaua Church. It reads, "Ella Hudson Paris 'Hualalai.' Missionary daughter, loved and honored for her translations of Hawaiian hymns sung throughout Hawaii *nei*, great in Christian character, humble in spirit, faithful member of Kahikolo Church, Kona, Hawaii. 1852-1938."

Home of Rev. Paris at Kealakekua. Ella Paris, his daughter, in a white dress, is at the left (1926) — Source: Baker-Van Dyke Collection

APPENDIX A

Missionary	Co.*	Birthplace	Missionary	Co.	Birthplace
Alexander, William	5	Paris, Ky	Coan, Titus	7	Killingworth, Ct.
Andrews, Claudius	11	Kinsman, Ohio	Conde, Daniel	8	Charlton, N.Y.
Andrews, Lorrin	3	E. Windsor, Ct.	Cooke, Amos	8	Danbury, Ct.
Andrews, Seth	8	Putney, Vt.			
Armstrong, Richard	5	McEwensville, Pa.	Damon, Samuel	Ind	Holden, Mass.
Bailey, Edward	8	Holden, Mass.	Dibble, Sheldon	4	Skaneateles, N.Y.
Baldwin, Dwight	4	Durham, Ct.	Diell, John	6	Cherry Valley, N.Y.
			Dimond, Henry	7	Fairfield, Ct.
Baldwin, William	Ind	Greenfield, N.H.	Dole, Daniel	9	Skowhegen, Maine
Bingham, Hiram	1	Bennington, Vt.	Dwight, Samuel	12	Northampton, Mass.
Bingham, Hiram II	Ind	Honolulu			
Bishop, Artemas	2	Pompey. N. Y.	Ellis, William	Ind	London
			Ely, James	2	Lyme, Ct.
Bishop, Sereno	Ind	Kaawaloa, Hawaii	Emerson, John	5	Chester, N.H.
Blatchley, Abraham	2	Madison, Ct.	Emerson, Oliver	Ind	Lahainaluna, Maui
Bliss, Isaac	8	Warren, Mass.			
Bond, Elias	9	Hallowell, Maine	Forbes, Anderson	Ind	Kaawaloa, Hawaii
Brown, Lydia	7	Wilton, N.H.	Forbes, Cochran	5	Goshen, Pa.
			Fuller, Lemuel	6	Attleboorough, Mass.
Castle, Samuel	8	Cazenovia, N.Y.			
Chamberlain, Daniel	1	Westboro, Mass.	Goodrich, Joseph	2	Wethersfield, Ct.
Chamberlain, Levi	2	Dover, Vt.	Green, Jonathan	3	Lebanon, Ct.
Chapin, Alonzo	5	W. Springfield, Mass.	Gulick, Luther	Ind	Honolulu
Clark, Ephraim	3	Haverhill, N.H.	Gulick, Orramel	Ind	Honolulu

*Company

Missionary	Co.	Birthplace
Gulick, Peter	3	Freehold, N.J.
Hall, Edwin	7	Walpole, N.H.
Hitchcock, Harvey	5	Great Barrington, Mass.
Holman, Thomas	1	New Haven, Ct.
Hunt, Timothy	11	Rochester, N.Y.
Hyde, Charles	Ind	New York, N.Y.
Ives, Mark	8	Goshen, Ct.
Johnson, Edward	8	Hollis, N.H.
Johnstone, Andrew	4	Dundee, Scotland
Judd, Gerrit	3	Paris, N.Y.
Kinney, Henry	12	Amenia, N.Y.
Knapp, Horton	8	Greenwich, Ct.
Lafon, Thomas	8	Chesterfield Co., Va.
Leadingham, John	Ind	Arbroath, Scotland
Locke, Edwin	8	Fitzwilliam, N. H.
Loomis, Elias	1	Rushville, N.Y.
Lyman, David	5	New Hartford, Ct.
Lyons, Lorenzo	5	Colerain, Mass.
McDonald, Charles	8	Easton, Pa.
Munn, Bethuel	8	Orange, N. J.
Ogden, Maria	3	Philadelphia
Paris, John	9	Staunton, Va.
Parker, Benjamin	6	Reading, Mass.
Parker, Henry	Ind	Nuuhiva, Marquesas
Pogue, John	11	Wilmington, Del.
Rice, William	9	Oswego, N.Y.
Richards, William	2	Plainfield, Mass.
Rogers, Edmund	5	Newton, Mass.
Rowell, George	10	Cornish, N.H.
Ruggles, Samuel	1	Brookfield, Ct.
Shepard, Steven	3	Johnstown, N.Y.
Shipman, William	Ind	Wethersfield, Ct.
Smith, Asa	Ind	Williamstown, Vt.
Smith, James	10	Stamford, Ct.
Smith, Lowell	6	Heath, Mass.
Smith, Marcia	8	Burlington, N.Y.
Spaulding, Ephraim	5	Ludlow, Vt.
Stewart, Charles	2	Flemington, N.J.
Stockton, Betsey	2	Princeton, N.J.
Taylor, Townsend	Ind	LaGrange, N.Y.
Thurston, Asa	1	Fitchburg, Mass.
Tinker, Reuben	4	Chester, Mass.
Van Duzee, William	8	Hartford, N.Y.
Wetmore, Charles	Ind	Lebanon, Ct.
Whitney, Samuel	1	Branford, Ct.
Whittlesey, Eliphalet	11	Salisbury, Ct.
Wilcox, Abner	8	Harwinton, Ct.

APPENDIX B

PERSONAL MISSIONARY RECORD BY COMPANIES

Co.*	Year	Missionary	Position	Left	Years	Born	Married	Died	Age	Ch.**
1	1820	Hiram Bingham	Minister	1840	20	1789	1819	1869	80	7
		Sybil Moseley				1792		1848	55	
		Daniel Chamberlain	Farmer	1823	3	1782	1806	1860	77	7
		Jerusha Burnap				1786		1879	92	
		Thomas Holman	Phys.	1820	1/3	1793	1819	1826	32	3
		Lucia Ruggles	Teacher			1793		1886	92	
		Elisha Loomis	Printer	1827	6	1799	1819	1836	36	5
		Maria Sartwell	Teacher			1796		1862	66	
		Samuel Ruggles	Teacher	1834	13	1795	1819	1871	76	6
		Nancy Wells				1791		1873	81	
		Asa Thurston	Minister		47	1787	1819	1868	80	5
		Lucy Goodale	Teacher			1795		1876	80	
		Samuel Whitney	Teacher		24	1793	1819	1845	52	4
		Mercy Partridge				1795		1872	77	
2	1823	Artemas Bishop	Minister		49	1795	1822	1872	76	2
		Elizabeth Edwards			5	1798		1828	29	
		Delia Stone	Teacher		52	1800	1828	1875	74	0
		Abraham Blatchely	Phys	1826	3	1787	1821	1860	73	2
		Jemima Marvin				1791		1856	65	
		Levi Chamberlai	Supt.		26	1792	1828	1849	56	8
		Maria Patton	Teacher			1803		1880	76	
		Joseph Goodrich	Minister	1836	12	1794	1822	1852	57	7
		Martha Barnes				1801		1840	39	
		James Ely	Minister	1828	5	1798	1822	1890	91	3
		Louisa Everest				1793		1848	55	
		William Richards	Minister		24	1793	1822	1847	54	8
		Clarissa Lyman				1795		1861	66	

*Company   **Number of children

Co.*	Year	Missionary	Position	Left	Years	Born	Married	Died	Age	Ch.**
		Charles Stewart	Minister	1825	2	1795	1822	1870	75	3
		Harriet Tiffany				1798		1830	32	
		Betsey Stockton	Teacher	1825	2	1798		1865	67	
3	1828	Lorrin Andrews	Minister		40	1795	1827	1868	73	7
		Mary Ann Wilson	Teacher			1804		1879	75	
		Ephraim Clark	Minister	1864	36	1799	1827	1878	79	8
		Mary Kittredge				1803		1857	53	
		Jonathan Green	Minister		50	1796	1827	1878	81	4
		Theodotia Arnold				1792		1859	67	
		Asenath Spring				1820	1861	1894	73	2
		Peter Gulick	Minister		46	1796	1827	1877	81	8
		Fanny Thomas				1798		1883	85	
		Gerrit Judd	Phys.		14	1803	1827	1873	70	9
		Laura Fish				1804		1872	68	
		Maria Ogden	Teacher		40	1792		1874	82	
		Steven Shepard	Printer		3	1800	1827	1834	34	3
		Margaret Slow				1801		?		
4	1831	Dwight Baldwin	Phys.		46	1798	1830	1886	87	8
		Charlotte Fowler	Teacher			1805		1873	67	
		Sheldon Dibble	Minister	1837	8	1809	1830	1845	36	3
		Maria Tomlinson				1808		1837	28	
		Antoinette Tomlinson		1847		1809	1839	1897	88	3
		Andrew Johnstone	Asst. Supt.		28	1794	1830	1859	65	
		Rebecca Worth	Teacher			1792		1879	87	
		Reuben Tinker	Minister	1840	9	1799	1830	1854	55	7
		Mary Wood				1809		1895	85	
5	1832	William Alexander	Minister		52	1805	1831	1884	79	9
		Mary McKinney	Teacher			1810		1888	78	
		Richard Armstrong	Minister		16	1805	1831	1860	55	10
		Clarissa Chapman	Teacher			1805		1891	86	
		Alonzo Chapin	Phys.	1835	3	1805	1831	1876	71	1
		Mary Ann Tenney				1804		1885	81	
		John Emerson	Minister		35	1800	1831	1867	66	8
		Ursula Newell	Teacher			1806		1888	82	
		Cochran Forbes	Minister	1847	16	1805	1831	1880	75	5
		Rebecca Smith				1805		1878	72	

Co.*	Year	Missionary	Position	Left	Years	Born	Married	Died	Age	Ch.**
		Harvey Hitchcock	Minister		20	1800	1831	1855	55	4
		Rebecca Howard	Teacher			1808		1890	81	
		David Lyman	Minister		52	1803	1831	1884	81	8
		Sarah Joiner	Teacher			1805		1885	80	
		Lorenzo Lyons	Minister		54	1807	1831	1886	79	
		Betsey Curtis				1813		1837	24	2
		Lucia Smith	Teacher			1808	1838	1892	84	3
		Edmund Rogers	Printer		21	1807	1833	1853	46	
		Mary Ward	Teacher			1799		1834	35	
		Elizabeth Hitchcock	Teacher			1802	1836	1857	54	4
		Ephraim Spaulding	Minister	1836	4	1802	1831	1840	37	4
		Julia Brooks	Teacher			1810		1898	88	
6	1833	John Diell	Minister	1840	7	1808	1832	1841	32	4
		Caroline Platt				1807		1901	93	
		Lemuel Fuller	Printer	1833	1/2	1810		?		
		Benjamin Parker	Minister		43	1803	1832	1977	73	4
		Mary Barker				1805		1907	102	
		Lowell Smith	Minister		58	1802	1832	1891	88	5
		Abigail Tenney	Teacher			1809		1885	75	
7	1835	Titus Coan	Minister		47	1801	1834	1882	81	
		Fidelia Church	Teacher			1810		1872	62	
		Lydia Bingham	Teacher			1834	1873	1915	80	
		Lydia Brown	Teacher		30	1780		1865	85	
		Edwin Hall	Printer		14	1810	1834	1883	72	
		Sarah Williams				1812		1876	63	
		Mary Dame	Teacher			1848	1878	1908	59	
		Henry Diamond	Bookbinder		15	1808	1834	1895	86	
		Ann Maria Anner				1808		1893	85	
8	1837	Seth Andrews	Phys.	1848	11	1809	1836	1893	83	
		Parnelly Pierce				1807		1846	39	
		Edward Bailey	Teacher	1850	13	1814	1836	1903	89	
		Caroline Hubbard				1814		1894	79	
		Isaac Bliss	Minister	1841	4	1804	1832	1851	47	
		Emily Curtis	Teacher			1811		1866	54	

Co.*	Year	Missionary	Position	Left	Years	Born	Married	Died	Age	Ch.**
		Samuel Castle	Asst. Supt.		14	1808	1836	1894	85	
		Angeline Tenney	Teacher			1810		1841	30	1
		Mary Tenney				1819	1842	1907	87	10
		Daniel Conde	Minister	1856	19	1807	1836	1897	90	7
		Andelucia Lee				1810		1855	44	
		Amos Cooke	Asst. Supt.		14	1810	1836	1871	60	7
		Juliette Montague	Teacher			1812		1896	84	
		Mark Ives	Minister	1850	13	1808	1836	1885	77	4
		Mary Ann Brainerd				1810		1882	71	
		Edward Johnson	Teacher		30	1813	1836	1867	53	8
		Lois Hoyt	Teacher			1809		1891	82	
		Horton Knapp	Teacher		8	1813	1836	1845	32	
		Charlotte Close	Teacher			1813		1874	61	
		Edwin Locke	Teacher		6	1813	1836	1843	30	4
		Martha Rowell				1812		1842	29	
		Charles McDonald	Teacher		2	1812	1836	1839	26	2
		Harriet Halstead				1810		1901	90	
		Bethel Munn	Teacher	1841	4	1803	1836	1849	45	2
		Louisa Clark				1810		1841	31	
		Marcia Smith	Teacher	1852	12	1806		1896	89	
		Wm. VanDuzee	Teacher	1839	2	1811	1836	1883	72	
		Oral Hobart				1814		1891	77	
		Abner Wilcox	Teacher		32	1808	1836	1869	61	8
		Lucy Hart	Teacher			1814		1869	54	
9	1841	Elias Bond	Minister		55	1813	1840	1896	82	10
		Ellen Howell	Teacher			1817		1881	63	
		Daniel Dole	Minister		37	1808	1840	1878	69	2
		Emily Ballard	Teacher			1807		1844	36	
		Charlotte Knapp	Teacher			1813		1874	61	
		John Paris	Minister		51	1809	1840	1892	82	
		Mary Grant				1807		1847	39	2
		Mary Carpenter				1815	1851	1896	81	2
		William Rice	Teacher		13	1813	1840	1862	48	5
		Mary Hyde	Teacher			1816		1911	94	
10	1842	George Rowell	Minister		41	1815	1842	1884	69	7
		Malvina Chapin				1816		1901	85	

Co.*	Year	Missionary	Position	Left	Years	Born	Married	Died	Age	Ch.**
		James Smith	Phys.		45	1810	1842	1887	77	9
		Melicent Knapp	Teacher			1816		1891	74	
11	1844	Claudius Andrews	Minister		32	1817	1850	1877	59	7
		Anne Gilson	Teacher			1823		1862	38	
		Samantha Gilson	Teacher			1828	1863	1904	75	
		Timothy Hunt	Minister		4	1821	1843	1895	73	8
		Mary Hedges				1821		1861	40	
		John Pogue	Minister		33	1814	1848	1877	62	4
		Maria Whitney	Teacher			1820		1900	79	
		Eliphalet Whittlesey	Minister	1854	10	1816	1843	1889	73	
		Elizabeth Baldwin				1821	1843	?		
12	1848	Samuel Dwight	Minister		32	1815		1880	65	6
		Anna Mahoe				1839	1854	1879	40	
		Henry Kinney	Minister	1854	6	1816	1847	1854	37	3
		Maria Walsworth				1822		1858	35	

Independents

Co.*	Year	Missionary	Position	Left	Years	Born	Married	Died	Age	Ch.**
	1822	William Ellis	Minister	1824	1-1/2	1794	1815	1872	77	4
	1842	Asa Smith	Minister	1845	3	1809	1838	1886	76	
		Sarah White				1813		1855	41	
	1842	Samuel Damon	Minister		42	1815	1841	1885	70	5
		Julia Mills				1817		1890	72	
	1848	Townsend Taylor	Minister	1854	6	1818	1847	1883	64	6
		Persis Thurston	Teacher			1821		1906	84	
	1849	Charles Wetmore	Phys.		49	1820	1848	1898	78	5
		Lucy Taylor	Teacher			1819		1883	63	
	1852	Luther Gulick	Phys.	1870	18	1828	1851	1891	62	7
		Louisa Lewis		1830		1894	63			
	1853	Sereno Bishop	Minister		24	1827	1852	1909	82	5
		Cornelia Sessions	Teacher			1826		1920	94	
	1854	William Shipman	Minister		7	1824	1853	1861	37	3
		Jane Stobie	Teacher			1827		1904	76	
	1855	William Baldwin	Minister	1860	5	1821	1854	1902	81	3
		Mary Proctor				1822		1872	49	
	1857	Hiram Bingham II	Minister		51	1831	1856	1908	77	2
		Minerva Brewster				1834		1903	69	

Co.*	Year	Missionary	Position	Left	Years	Born	Married	Died	Age	Ch.**
	1857	Orramel Gulick	Minister		66	1830	1855	1923	93	
		Ann Eliza Clark	Teacher			1833		1938	105	
	1858	Anderson Forbes	Minister		30	1833	1858	1888	55	4
		Maria Chamberlain				1832		1909	76	
	1860	Henry Parker	Minister		67	1834		1927	93	
	1877	Charles Hyde	Minister		22	1832	1865	1899	67	2
		Mary Knight			1840			1917	77	
	1889	Emerson Oliver	Minister		14	1845	1896	1938	93	
		Eugenie Homer					1854	1940	86	
	1894	John Leadingham	Minister	1904	10	1853	1887	1935	81	
		Anna Rich					1857	1913	55	

SUMMARY OF ARRIVALS

Co.	Year	Ministers	Teachers Men	Phys.	Printers	Agents	Wn. [1]Teachers	Wives	Ch. [1]	Natives	Total
1	1820	2	3	1	1			7	5	4	23
2	1823	5		1		1	1	6		4	18
3	1828	4		1	1		4	6		4	20
4	1831	2		1		1		4			8
5	1832	8		1	1			9			19
6	1833	3			1			3		1	8
7	1835	1			2		2	3			8
8	1837	3	9	2		1	2	15			32
9	1841	3	1					4			8
10	1842	1		1				2			4
11	1844	4					1	2			7
12	1848	2						1			3
	Total	38	13	8	6	3	10	62	5	13	158
	Ind.	14		2				13	11		40
	TOTAL	52	13	10	6	3	10	75	16	13	198

Remained under ABCFM to death or to end of mission in 1863	33
Remained to death or to retirement	23

[1] Women teachers

[2] Children

APPENDIX C

SPECIAL SUBJECTS INDEX

APPENDIX D

MISSION CHURCHES IN HAWAII

1820, Apr. 16	First church service in Hawaii at Kailua
23	First church service in Honolulu
1821, Sep. 15	First Honolulu church dedicated, 54' x 21'
1823, Aug. 24	First Lahaina church dedicated
Dec. 10	First Kailua church dedicated, 60' x 30'
1824, Mar. 29	First Kaawaloa church dedicated
	Kaawaloa church burned
July 18	Second Honolulu church dedicated, 70' x 25'
1826, Sep. 27	Second Kailua church dedicated, 180' x 78'
1827, July —	Third Honolulu church dedicated, 86' x 30'
———	Third church destroyed by storm
1828, Sep. 14	Lahaina— first stone church in Hawaii, cornerstone laid, 104' x 50', with galleries
1829, July 3	Fourth Honolulu church dedicated, 190' x 63'
1830, Oct. 15	First Hilo church dedicated
1832, Mar. 4	First stone church, Lahaina, dedicated
1833, Nov. 24	Seamen's Bethel Chapel, Honolulu, dedicated
1835, Dec. 6	Kaluaaha Church near Pukoo, Molokai, dedicated, 90' x 42', stone, (still standing)
Dec. —	Second Kailua Church burned
1837, Feb. 4	Mokuaikaua Church at Kailua dedicated
1838, ——	Wananalua Church, Hana, Maui, founded
1839, Aug. 29	First Kaumakapili Church, Honolulu dedicated, 125' x 60', adobe — burned Jan. 20, 1900
1840, ———	Second church at Kaawaloa built, 120' x 57', stone
1841, Dec. —	First church at Waioli, Kauai
1842, June —	First framed church in Hilo dedicated
July 21	Fifth Honolulu church, Kawaiahao, opened, 144' x 78'
1846, Nov. —	First Kohala church completed
1849, Dec. 21	First Kohala church destroyed by storm
1855, Aug. 29	Imiola Church at Waimea, Hawaii, cornerstone laid
Oct. 11	Kalahikiola Church at Kohala dedicated
1857, ——	Imiola Church dedicated
1858, Feb. 20	Whirlwind rips off steeple and half of roof of stone church at Lahaina
1859, Mar. 31	Lahaina church rededicated
Apr. 8	Haili Church at Hilo dedicated

Compiled from Ethel M. Damon's *Early Hawaiian Churches & The Stone Church at Kawaiahao*, plus author's additions.

APPENDIX E

CHRONOLOGY

1778, Jan. 18	Captain James Cook sights Oahu
Jan. 20	Lands on Kauai
1779 Jan. 17	Captain James Cook at Kealakekua Bay
Feb. 14	Captain James Cook killed
1793 & 1794	Vancouver visits
1808	Obookiah leaves Hawaii on *Triumph*
1810	Obookiah meets Samuel Mills
1812	Kamehameha retires to Kailua
1815, Apr. 9	Obookiah made member of church at Torringford
1817, May	Foreign Mission School at Cornwall, Ct.
1818, Feb. 17	Obookiah dies at Cornwall
1819, May 8	Kamehameha dies at Kailua
Oct. 23	*Thaddeus* sails from Boston
1820, Apr. 4	*Thaddeus* arrives at Kailua
Apr. 12	*Thaddeus* departs Thurstons & Holmans at Kailua
Apr. 14	*Thaddeus* reaches Honolulu
July	Holmans leave for Lahaina
1821, July 30	Holmans Sail west to U. S.
1823, Apr. 27	2nd company arrives at Honolulu
May 31	Richards & Stewart start Lahaina station
July 18	Missionaries explore Hawaii Island
24	Whitney & Ruggleses start station at Waimea, Kauai
Sep. 3	Explorers arrive back at Kailua
Nov. 5	Thurstons back at Kailua
Dec. 10	First church at Kailua finished
1824 Jan.	Goodrich & Ruggles start Hilo station
———	Ely starts station at Kaawaloa
Dec. 22	Kapiolani at volcano, defies Pele at Kilauea Volcano
1826, Feb.	Start second church building at Kailua
Sep. 27	Church dedicated
1828, Feb. 21	Elizabeth Bishop dies
Mar. 9	First Hawaiians baptized at Kailua
Mar. 30	3rd company arrives at Honolulu
Dec. 1	Bishop marries Delia Stone
1830, Oct. 15	Hilo church dedicated
1831, ———	Bishop builds stone house in Kailua
June 7	4th company arrives at Honolulu
Sep.	Lorrin Andrews starts seminary at Lahainaluna
1832, Jan.	Baldwin starts station at Waimea, Hawaii
May 17	5th company arrives at Honolulu
July 16	Lymans at Hilo

	————	Lyons at Waimea, Hawaii
	————	Emerson starts Waialua, Oahu, station
	————	Green starts Wailuku station, Maui
	Nov.	Hitchcock starts Kaluaaha station, Molokai
1833,	May 1	6th company arrives at Honolulu
1834,	July	David Douglas killed in bull pit
	————	Peter Gulick starts Koloa, Kauai, station
	————	Alexander starts Waioli, Kauai, station
	————	Benjamin Parker starts Kaneohe, Oahu, station
	————	Lowell Smith starts Ewa, Oahu, station
1835,	June 6	7th company arrives at Honolulu
	Dec.	Second church at Kailua burned by arsonist
1836,	Jan. 1	Mokuaikaua Church cornerstone laid
	Sep.	Hilo Boys Boarding School opens
1837,	Jan. 31	Mokuaikaua Church completed
	Feb. 4	Mokuaikaua Church dedicated
	Apr. 9	8th company arrives at Honolulu
	May 14	Betsey Lyons dies in Honolulu
	Nov. 7	Hilo Bay tidal wave
1838,	July 14	Lyons marries Lucia Smith
1841,	————	Dole starts Punahou School
	May	Kapiolani dies
	May 21	9th company arrives at Honolulu
	June 26	Bond at Kohala
	Sep. 10	Paris at Waiohinu
1842,	Feb.	Ellen Bond opens school for girls
	June	First framed church at Hilo dedicated
	Sep. 12	Bond opens boarding school for boys
	21	10th company arrives at Honolulu
1843,	Jan.	Coan & Paris visit Mauna Loa eruption
1844,	July 15	11th company arrives at Honolulu
1846,	Sep. 29	Parnelly Andrews dies at Kailua
	Nov.	First church at Kohala completed
1847,	Feb. 18	Mary Grant Paris dies at Hilo
1848,	Feb. 16	12th company arrives at Honolulu
	Oct.	Measles epidemic on Hawaii
1849,	Dec, 21	Storm destroys Kohala church
1852		Paris at Kealakekua
1853		Smallpox epidemic
1855,	Aug. 29	Imiola Church cornerstone laid
	Oct. 11	Kalahikiola Church dedicated
1856,	Feb.	Mauna Loa eruption threatens Hilo
1857,	Nov. 14	Haili Church cornerstone laid
	————	Imiola Church dedicated
1859,	Apr. 8	Haili Church dedicated

1863, Feb. 14	Kohala Sugar Company organized
1868, Mar. 11	Asa Thurston dies at Honolulu
———	Destructive earthquakes on Hawaii
1869, Jan. 17	Foreign Church at Kohala dedicated
1872	First year of profit for Kohala Sugar Co.
Sep. 29	Fidelia Coan dies at Hilo
1874, Dec. 3	Kohala Girls School opens
1876, Oct. 13	Lucy Thurston dies at Honolulu
1879, July	Wetmore sets up first telephone on Hawaii
1881, May 12	Ellen Bond dies at Kohala
Aug.	Mauna Loa again threatens Hilo
1882, Dec. 1	Titus Coan dies at Hilo
1883, July 23	Lucy Wetmore drowns in tub
1884, Oct. 4	Lyman dies at Hilo
1885, Dec. 7	Sarah Lyman dies at Hilo
1886, Oct. 6	Lyons dies at Waimea
1892, Apr. 27	Lucia Lyons dies at Waimea
July 28	Paris dies at Kealakekua
1893, Feb. 17	Seth Andrews dies at Romeo, Mich.
1896, July 24	Bond dies at Kohala
Aug. 18	Mary Carpenter Paris dies at Kealakekua
1898, Feb. 8	Wetmore dies at Hilo

APPENDIX F

THOSE WELL-EDUCATED MISSIONARIES

Of the 84 missionaries, 63 had college or university education. Of the 52 ministers, 50 studied at theological seminaries, usually in addition to college.

Colleges		Theological Seminaries	
Amherst	8	Andover	14
Berkshire Medical	1	Auburn	12
Bowdoin	2	Bangor	4
Centre Col. (Ky.)	1	East Windsor	1
Cherry Valley Medical	1	Lane	2
Dickinson (Pa.)	1	New Haven	2
Dartmouth	3	Princeton	9
Hamilton	2	Union	6
Hanover (Ind.)	1		
Harvard	1	Total	50
Jefferson (Pa.)	1		
Marietta	1		
Marion (Mo.)	2		
Medical (Mo.)	2		
Middlebury (Vt.)	4		
Mission Inst. (Ill.)	1		
New York Physicians	2		
New York U.	2		
Oberlin (Ohio)	1		
Princeton	2		
Transylvania Medical (Pa.)	1		
Union	4		
University of Pa.	1		
University of Vt.	1		
Western Reserve Col. (Ohio)	1		
Williams	8		
Yale	8		
Total	63		

APPENDIX G

MISSIONARY YEARS OF SERVICE

Years		Total	Count
67	Henry Parker (Ind)*		
66	Orramel Gulick (Ind)	133	2
58	Lowell Smith (6)	58	
55	Elias Bond (9)	55	
54	Lorenzo Lyons (5)	54	
52	David Lyman (5)		
	William Alexander	104	
51	John Paris (9)		
	Hiram Bingham II (Ind)	102	
50	Jonathan Green (3)	50	423	8
49	Artemas Bishop (2)		
	Charles Wetmore (Ind)	98	
48	Edwin Hall (7)	48	
47	Asa Thurston (1)		
	Titus Coan (7)	94	
46	Peter Gulick (3)	46	
45	James Smith (10)	45	
43	Benjamin Parker (6)	43	
42	Samuel Damon (Ind)	42	
41	George Rowell (10)	41	
40	Lorrin Andrews (3)		
	Maria Ogden (3)	80	537	12
37	Daniel Dole (9)	37	
36	Ephraim Clark (3)	36	
35	John Emerson (5)	35	
33	John Pogue (11)	33	
32	Abner Wilcox (8)		
	Caludius Andrews (11)		
	Samuel Dwight (12)	96	
30	Lydia Brown (7)		
	Edward Johnson (8)		
	Anderson Forbes (Ind)	90	327	10

*Independent
( ) Company numbers

28	Andrew Johnstone (4)	28		
26	Levi Chamberlain (2)	26		
24	Samuel Whitney (10)			
	William Richards (2)			
	Sereno Bishop (Ind)	72		
22	Charles Hyde (Ind)	22		
21	Edmund Rogers (5)	21		
20	Hiram Bingham (1)			
	Harvey Hitchcock (5)	40	209	9
19	Daniel Conde (8)	19		
18	Luther Gulick (Ind)	18		
16	Richard Armstrong (5)			
	Cochran Forbes (5)	32		
15	Henry Dimond (7)			
	Marcia Smith (8)	30		
14	Sheldon Dibble (4)			
	Edwin Hall (7)			
	Gerrit Judd (3)			
	Samuel Castle (8)			
	Amos Cooke (8)			
	Oliver Emerson (Ind)	84		
13	Samuel Ruggles (1)			
	Edward Bailey (8)			
	Mark Ives (8)			
	William Rice (9)	52		
12	Joseph Goodrich (2)			
	Marcia Smith (8)	24		
11	Seth Andrews (8)	11		
10	Eliphalet Whittlesey (10)			
	John Leadingham (Ind)	20	290	21
			1919	62

The remaining 26, contributing from 2 to 9 years
each, totalled 112 more years

			112	26
			2031	88

APPENDIX H

MISSIONARY BIRTHPLACES BY TOWN, STATE, AND YEAR

CONNECTICUT
Branford
  1793 Samuel Whitney
  1805 Mary Barker (Parker)
Brookfield
  1793 Lucia Ruggles (Holman)
  1795 Samuel Ruggles
Cornwall
  1793 Louisa Everest (Ely)
Danbury
  1810 Amos Cooke
Durham
  1798 Dwight Baldwin
East Haddam
  1792 Theodotia Arnold (Green)
East Windsor
  1791 Nancy Wells (Ruggles)
  1795 Lorrin Andrews
Enfield
  1803 Sybil Chapin (Ely)
Fairfield
  1808 Henry Dimond
Goshen
  1808 Mark Ives
Greenwich
  1813 Charlotte Close (Knapp) (Dole)
      Horton Knapp
  1816 Melicent Knapp (Smith)
Harwinton
  1808 Abner Wilcox
Killingworth
  1801 Titus Coan
Lebanon
  1796 Jonathan Green
  1798 Fanny Thomas (Gulick)
  1820 Charles Wetmore
Lyme
  1791 Jemina Marvin (Blatchely)
  1798 James Ely
Madison (East Guilford)
  1787 Abraham Blatchely

Milford
  1812 Ruth Tweedy (Lafon)
New Hartford
  1803 David Lyman
New Haven
  1793 Thomas Holman
Northford
  1805 Charlotte Fowler (Baldwin)
Salisbury
  1816 Eliphalet Whittlesey
Southington
  1801 Martha Barnes (Goodrich)
Stamford
  1798 Harriet Tiffany (Stewart)
Torringford
  1817 Julia Mills (Damon)
Wethersfield
  1824 William Shipman
Woodbury
  1807 Parnelly Pierce (Andrews)

DELAWARE
Wilmington
  1810 Mary Ann McKinney (Alexander)

KENTUCKY
Paris
  1805 William Alexander
Washington
  1804 Mary Ann Wilson (Andrews)

MAINE
Falmouth
  1848 Mary Dame (Hall)
Hallowell
  1807 Emily Ballard (Dole)
  1813 Elias Bond
Milo
  1857 Anna Rich (Leadingham)

Portland
  1817 Ellen Howell (Bond)
Skowhegan (Bloomfield)
  1808 Daniel Dole

MASSACHUSETTS
Attleborough
  1810 Lemuel Fuller
Barre
  1809 Abigail Tenney (Smith)
Brimfield
  1820 Asenath Spring (Green)
  1840 Mary Knight (Hyde)
Brookfield
  1793 Lucia Ruggles (Holman)
Buckland
  1810 Julia Brook (Spaulding)
Chester
  1799 Reuben Tinker
  1809 Mary Wood (Tinker)
Colerain
  1807 Lorenzo Lyons
Fitchburg
  1795 Asa Thurston
Great Barrington
  1800 Harvey Hitchcook
  1802 Elizabeth Hitchcock (Rogers)
Heath
  1802 Lowell Smith
Holden
  1814 Edward Bailey
  1815 Samuel Damon
Hopkinton
  1786 Jerusha Burnap (Chamberlain)
Hudson (Marlborough)
  1795 Lucy Goodale (Thurston)
  1798 Elizabeth Edwards (Bishop)
Lunenburg
  1822 Mary Proctor (Baldwin)
Nantucket
  1792 Rebecca Worth (Johnstone)
New Bedford
  1812 Sophia Parker (Lafon)

Newburyport
  1804 Maryann Tenney (Chapin)
Newton
  1807 Edmund Rogers
Northampton
  1795 Clarissa Lyman (Richards)
  1815 Samuel Dwight
  1834 Minerva Brewster (Bingham)
Pittsfield
  1795 Mercy Partridge (Whitney)
  1819 Lucy Taylor (Wetmore)
Plainfield
  1793 William Richards
Reading
  1803 Benjamin Parker
Roxbury
  1854 Eugenie Homer (Emerson)
Russell
  1805 Clarissa Chapman (Armstrong)
South Amherst
  1826 Harriet Nutting (Smith)
Sunderland
  1812 Juliette Montague (Cooke)
Warren
  1804 Isaac Bliss
Westboro
  1782 Daniel Chamberlain
West Brookfield
  1813 Sarah White (Smith)
Westfield
  1792 Sybil Mosely (Bingham)
West Springfield
  1805 Alonzo Chapin

NEW HAMPSHIRE
Chester
  1800 John Emerson
Cornish
  1812 Martha Rowell (Locke)
  1815 George Rowell
Fitzwilliam
  1813 Edwin Locke

Greenfield
    1821 William Baldwin
Haverhill
    1799 Ephrain Clark
Hollis
    1813 Edward Johnson
Mount Vernon
    1803 Mary Kittredge (Clark)
Nelson
    1806 Ursula Newell (Emerson)
Newport
    1816 Malvina Chapin (Rowell)
Walpole
    1810 Edwin Hall
Warner
    1809 Lois Hoyt (Johnston)
Wilton
    1780 Lydia Brown

NEW JERSEY
Elizabeth
    1812 Sarah Williams (Hall)
Flemington
    1795 Charles Stewart
Frankfort
    1821 Elizabeth Baldwin (Whittlesey)
Freehold
    1796 Peter Gulick
Newark
    1821 Mary Hedges (Dwight)
Orange
    1803 Bethuel Munn
Princeton
    1798 Betsey Stockton
Springfield
    1805 Rebecca Smith (Forbes)

NEW YORK
Adams
    1826 Cornelia Sessions (Bishop)
Albany
    1807 Mary Grant (Paris)
Amenia
    1816 Henry Kinney
Bloomfield
    1800 Delia Stone (Bishop)
Burlington
    1806 Marcia Smith

Butternuts
    1808 Lucia Smith (Lyons)
Cairo
    1814 Lucy Hart (Wilcox)
Cazenovia
    1809 Samuel Castle
Champion
    1801 Margaret Slow (Shepard)
Charlton
    1807 Daniel Conde
Cherry Valley
    1808 John Diell
Cooperstown
    1820 Hannah Williams (Conde)
Elbridge
    1811 Emily Curtis (Bliss)
    1813 Betsey Curtis (Lyons)
Hartford
    1796 Maria Sartwell (Loomis)
    1811 William Van Duzee
Homer
    1814 Oral Hobart (Van Duzee)
Johnstown
    1800 Stephen Shepard
LaGrange
    1818 Townsend Taylor
Manlius
    1809 Antoinette Tomlinson (Dibble)
Middlebury
    1799 Mary Ward (Rogers)
New York
    1808 Ann Anner (Dimond)
    1810 Harriet Halstead (McDonald)
    1830 Louisa Lewis (Gulick)
    1832 Charles Hyde
Oswego
    1813 William Rice
Owasco
    1808 Rebecca Howard (Hitchcock)
Paris
    1803 Gerrit Judd
Pittsford
    1815 Amelia Dyke (Andrews)
Plainfield
    1804 Laura Fish (Judd)
    1819 Mary Tenney (Castle)
Plattsburg
    1807 Caroline Platt (Diell)

212

Pompey
   1795 Artemas Bishop
Riga
   1810 Fidelia Church (Coan)
Rochester
   1821 Timothy Hunt
Rushville
   1799 Elisha Loomis
Sandy Hill
   1834 Sarah Nash (Hunt)
Seneca Village
   1816 Mary Hyde (Rice)
Skaneateles
   1809 Sheldon Dibble
   1810 Louisa Clark (Munn)
Troy
   1808 Maria Tomlinson (Dibble)

OHIO
   Cleveland
      1822 Maria Walsworth (Kinney)
   Kinsman
      1817 Claudius Andrews

PENNSYLVANIA
   Easton
      1812 Charles McDonald
   Goshen
      1805 Cochran Forbes
   McEwensville
      1805 Richard Armstrong
   Philadelphia
      1792 Maria Ogden
   Salisbury
      1803 Maria Patton (Chamberlain)

VERMONT
   Bennington
      1789 Hiram Bingham
   Dover
      1792 Levi Chamberlain
   Jericho
      1810 Andelucia Lee (Conde)
   Ludlow
      1802 Ephraim Spaulding
   Norwich
      1812 Sarah Hall (Clark)

Putmey
   1809 Seth Andrews
Reading
   1823 Anne Gilson (Andrews)
Rutland
   1828 Samantha Gilson (Andrews)
Sudbury
   1810 Angeline Tenney (Castle)
Williamstown
   1809 Asa Snith

VIRGINIA
   Chesterfield County
      1801 Thomas Lafon
   Staunton
      1809 John Paris

TABULATION BY STATES

State	Men	Women	Total
Connecticut	18	16	34
Delaware		1	1
Kentucky	1	1	2
Maine	2	4	6
Massachusetts	15	24	39
New Hampshire	8	5	13
New Jersey	4	4	8
NewYork	15	26	41
Ohio	1		1
Pennsylvania	4	1	5
Vermont	5	5	10
Virginia	2		2
TOTAL	75	87	162

SELECT BIBLIOGRAPHY

Alexander, Mary Charlotte. *Dr. Baldwin of Lahaina*. Berkley: Stanford University Press, 1953
——, *William Patterson Alexander in Kentucky; Marquesas; Hawaii*. Honolulu: Privately printed, 1934.
Alexander, W. D., *A Brief History of the Hawaiian People*. New York: American Book, 1891
Anderson, Dr. Rufus, *The Hawaiian Islands: Their Progress and Conditions under Missionary Labors*. Boston: Congregational Publishing Board, 1864
——, *History of the Mission to the Sandwich Islands*. Boston: Gould and Lincoln, 1872
Barrere, D. B., *Kamehameha in Kona*. Honolulu: Bishop Museum, 1975
Barrot, Theodore-Adolphe, *Unless Haste Is Made*. Kailua: Press Pacifica, 1978
Bingham, Hiram, *A Residence of Twenty-One Years in the Sandwich Islands*. Hartford: Hezekiah Huntington, 1848; Rutland, Vt.: Tuttle, 1981
Bird, Isabella L, *Six Months in the Sandwich Islands*. University of Hawaii Press, 1966
Bishop, Sereno Edwards, *Reminiscences of Old Hawaii*. Honolulu: Hawaiian Gazette, 1916
Broeze, Frank J. A., translator, *A Merchant's Perspective: Captain Jacobus Boelen's Narrative of His Visit to Hawaii in 1828*. Honolulu: Hawai'i Historical Society, 1988
Campbell, Archibald, *A Voyage Around the World from 1806 to 1812*. Honolulu: University of Hawaii Press, 1967
Cheever, Henry T., *Life in the Sandwich Islands*. New York: A. S. Barnes, 1851
Coan, Titus, *Life in Hawaii*. New York: Anson D. F. Randolph & Co., 1882
Cumings, A. P., *The Missionary's Daughter: A Memoir of Lucy Goodale Thurston*. New York: American Tract Society, 1842
Damon, Ethel M., *Early Hawaiian Churches*. Honolulu: Privately printed, 2nd edition, 1924
——, *Father Bond of Kohala*. Honolulu: The Friend, 1927
——, *Samuel Chenery Damon*. Honolulu: The Hawaiian Mission Children's Society, 1966
——, *The Stone Church at Kawaiahao 1820-1944*. Honolulu: Honolulu Star-Bulletin Press, 1945
Daws, Gavan, *Shoals of Time*. Honolulu: University of Hawaii Press, 1974
Day, A. Grove, *History Makers of Hawaii*. Honolulu: Mutual Publishing, 1984.
Dibble, *A History of the Sandwich Islands*. Honolulu: Thos. G. Thrum, 1909
Doyle, Emma Lyons, *Makua Laiana*. Honolulu: Advertiser Publishing Co., 1953
Dwight, Edwin, *Memoirs of Henry Obookiah*. Kingsport, Tenn.: Kingsport Press, 1968
Ellis, William, *Journal of William Ellis*. Honolulu: Advertiser Publishing Co, 1963
Emerson, Oliver Pomeroy, *Pioneer Days in Hawaii*. Garden City, N. Y.: Doubleday Doran & Co., 1928
Eveleth, Ephraim, *History of the Sandwich Islands*. Philadelphia: American Sunday-School Union, 1831
Feher, Joseph, *Hawaii: A Pictorial History*. Honolulu: Bishop Museum Press, 1969
Frear, Walter F., *Anti-Missionary Criticism*. Honolulu: Advertiser Publishing Co., 1935
Gallagher, Charles F., *Hawaii and Its Gods: The Living Faiths of the Islands*, Honolulu: Weatherhill/

Kapa, 1975

Gast, Ross H., *Contentious Consul: A Biography of John Coffin Jones, First United States Consular Agent at Hawaii*. Los Angeles: Dawson's Book Shop, 1976

——, *Don Francisco de Paula Marin*. Honolulu: University of Hawaii Press, 1976

Greenwell, Jean, *Crisis in Kona*. Honolulu: *The Hawaiian Journal of History*, The Hawaiian Historical Society, 1987

Grimshaw, Patricia, *Paths of Duty: American Missionary Wives in Nineteenth-Century Hawaii*. Honolulu: University of Hawaii Press, 1989

Gulick, Rev, and Mrs. Orramel Hinckley, *The Pilgrims of Hawaii*. New York: Fleming H. Revell Co., 1918

Halford, Francis John, *9 Doctors and God*. Honolulu: University of Hawaii Press, 1954

Hawaiian Mission Children's Society, *"Hawaii" Fact and Fiction*, Honolulu, 1947

——, *Missionary Album*. Honolulu, 1969

Holman, Lucia Ruggles, *Journal*. Honolulu: Bishop Museum. Press, 1931.

Ii, John Papa, *Fragments of Hawaiian History*. Bishop Museum Press, 1963.

Jarves, James J., *History of the Hawaiian or Sandwich Islands*. Boston: Tappan & Dennet, 1843

Joesting, Edward, *Hawaii: An Uncommon History*. New York: W. W. Norton & Co., 1972

Judd, Gerrit P. IV, *A Hawaii Anthology*. New York: Macmillan, 1967

——, *Dr. Judd: Hawaii's Friend*. Honolulu: University of Hawaii Press, 1960

——, *Hawaii: An Informal History*. New York: Collier Books, 1961

Judd, Laura Fish, *Honolulu*. Honolulu: Honolulu Star-Bulletin Press, 1928

Kamakau, Samuel M., *Ruling Chiefs of Hawaii*. Honolulu: Kamehameha Schools Press, 1961

Kirkpatrick, Doris, *The City and the River*. Fitchburg, Mass.: Fitchburg Historical Society, 1980

Kuykendall, Ralph S., *The Hawaiian Kingdom, 1778-1854*. Honolulu: University of Hawaii Press, 1980

Lee, W, Storrs, *The Islands*. New York: Holt, Rinehart and Winston, 1966

Loomis, Albertine, *Grapes of Canaan: Hawaii 1820*. Honolulu: Hawaiian Mission Children's Society, 1972

——, *To all People*. Kingsport, Tenn.: Kingsport Press, 1970

Loomis, Elisha, *Copy of the Journal of E. Loomis*. Honolulu: University of Hawaii, 1937

Lyman, Chester S., *Around the Horn to the Sandwich Islands and California 1845-1850*. New Haven: Yale University Press, 1924

Lyman, Henry M., *Hawaiian Yesterdays: Chapters from a Boy's Life in the Islands in the Early Days*. Chicago: A. C. McClurg & Co., 1906

Malo, David, *Hawaiian Antiquities*. Honolulu: Bishop Museum Press, 1980

Martin, Margaret Greer, *The Lymans of Hilo*. Lyman House Memorial Museum, 1979

Miller, Char, *Fathers and Sons: The Bingham Family and the American Mission*. Philadelphia: Temple University Press, 1982

Mulholland, John F., *Hawaii's Religions*. Rutland, Vt.: Charles E. Tuttle, 1971

Musick, John R., *Hawaii: Our New Possessions*. New York: Funk & Wagnalls Co., 1897

Nordhoff, Charles, *Northern California, Oregon and the Sandwich Islands*. Berkley, Calif.: Ten Speed Press, 1974

O'Brien, Frederick, *White Shadows in the South Seas*. Garden City, N. Y.: Garden City Publishing Co., 1919

Olmsted, Francis Allyn, *Incidents of a Whaling Voyage: To Which Are Added Observations on the Scenery, Manners and Customs, and Missionary Stations of the Sandwich and Society Islands*. New York: Bell Publishing Co.

Paris, John Davis, *Fragments of a Real Missionary Life*. Honolulu, 1926

Pogue, John F., *Moolelo of Ancient Hawaii*. Honolulu: Topgallant Publishing Co., 1978

Porteus, Stanley D., *Calabashes and Kings*. Rutland, Vt.: Charles E. Tuttle, 1970

Restarick, Henry Bond, *Hawaii 1778-1920 from the Viewpoint of a Bishop*. Honolulu: Paradise of the Pacific, 1924

Richards, Mary A., *The Hawaiian Chiefs' Children's School: Amos Starr Cooke and Juliette Montague Cooke*. Tokyo: Charles E. Tuttle Co., 1970

Schneider, Herbert W., *The Puritan Mind*. Ann Arbor, Mich.: University of Michigan Press, 1958

Schoofs, Robert, *Pioneers of the Faith*. Honolulu: Sturgin Printing Co., 1978

Smith, Bradford, *Yankees in Paradise*. New York: J. B. Lippincott Co., 1956

Smith, Lucius E., *Heroes and Martyrs of the Modern Missionary Enterprise*. Providence: O. W. Potter, 1856

Steegmuller, Francis, *The Two Lives of James Jackson Jarves*. New Haven: Yale University Press, 1951

Stewart, C. S., *Journal of a Residence in the Sandwich Islands, During the Years 1823, 1824, and 1825*, Honolulu: University of Hawaii Press, 1970

Thurston, Lucy G., *Life and Times*. Ann Arbor, Mich.: S. C. Andrews, 1882; Honolulu: The Friend, 1934

Whipple, A. B. C.., *Yankee Whalers in the South Seas*. Garden City, N. Y.: Doubleday & Co., 1954

Wilcox, Abner and Lucy, *Letters from the Life Of Abner and Lucy Wilcox, 1836-1869*. Honolulu: Honolulu Star-Bulletin Press, 1950

Wright, Louis B., and Fry, Mary Isabel, *Puritans in the South Seas*. New York: Henry Holt & Co., 1936

Index